WHY THE AMERICAN CENTURY?

WHY THE
AMERICAN CENTURY

OLIVIER
ZUNZ

the university of chicago press
chicago & london

OLIVIER ZUNZ is professor of history at the University of Virginia. He has held visiting appointments at the École des Hautes Études en Sciences Sociales and the Collège de France. He is the author of *The Changing Face of Inequality: Urbanization, Industrial Development, and Immigrants in Detroit, 1880–1920* and *Making America Corporate, 1870–1920*, both published by the University of Chicago Press.

The University of Chicago Press, Chicago 60637
The University of Chicago Press, Ltd., London
© 1998 by The University of Chicago
All rights reserved. Published 1998
07 06 05 04 03 02 01 00 99 98   1 2 3 4 5

ISBN: 0-226-99461-9 (cloth)

Library of Congress Cataloging-in-Publication Data

Zunz, Olivier.
    Why the American century? / Olivier Zunz.
        p.   cm.
    Includes bibliographical references and index.
    ISBN 0-226-99461-9 (cloth : alk. paper)
    1. Social change—United States—History—20th century. 2. Social history—20th century. 3. Great powers. 4. United States—History—20th century. 5. United States—Foreign relations—20th century. 6. United States—Civilization—20th century. I. Title.
HN57.Z83 1998
306′.0973—dc21   98-18972
                                                                          CIP

♾ The paper used in this publication meets the minimum requirements of the American National Standard for Information Sciences—Permanence of Paper for Printed Library Materials, ANSI Z39.48-1992.

To the memory of

Bernard Ostier (1931–1958) and Patrick Zunz (1943–1993),

heroes of my childhood

CONTENTS

PREFACE

"The New Colossus"

Self government and internal development have been the dominant notes of our first century; administration and the development of other lands will be the dominant notes of our second century. SENATOR ALBERT BEVERIDGE, 1900[1]

Henry Luce, the publisher of *Life,* struck a responsive chord by entitling a February 17, 1941, editorial "The American Century." Writing nine and a half months before Pearl Harbor to persuade his fellow Americans to join the war, Luce argued that American civilization was critical to the fight against dictatorship. Bred to a belief in manifest destiny by missionary parents in China, Luce articulated America's potential for global leadership as a "creative opportunity" for his countrymen to secure their domestic achievements by exporting "democratic principles throughout the world." Reflecting on the changes in science and industry that had marked the first half of the century, he challenged Americans to recognize that their own welfare was dependent on the world's freedom and to rise "spiritually and practically" to their status as citizens of the world's "most powerful and vital nation." However tempting it may have been previously to remain aloof, Americans could no longer afford their splendid isolation.[2]

I am borrowing the title of this preface from Emma Lazarus's famous sonnet, chosen as an inscription for the pedestal of the Statue of Liberty in 1886.

In the preceding decades, American elites had struggled to articulate a vision for the United States as a distinctive national community with a historical mission consistent with the endowments and constraints presented to it by history. These Americans had entered the twentieth century with two large but unfinished projects. The first was the creation of an industrial economy on a continental scale. That undertaking required inventing technologies for exploiting the nation's natural resources, building a huge industrial plant, relocating millions of workers, investing in research, and devising organizational strategies to improve the ways Americans produced national and individual wealth. The project was controversial, generating much anxiety about loss of individuality. While optimistic "modernizers" like time management expert Frederick Winslow Taylor confidently asserted in 1911 that "in the past, the man has been first; in the future, the system must be first," other Americans were not as sanguine about surrendering their individuality to the demands of a system of mass production and distribution.[3] Alarmed that his contemporaries increasingly interacted "largely with great impersonal concerns," Woodrow Wilson called in 1913 for a "New Freedom" to save individualism.[4] Wilson's fear that drastic change was afoot would be echoed abroad. André Siegfried conveyed the same anxieties in *America Comes of Age* (1927), writing that Americans were creating "an entirely new conception of production and life."[5]

The second project Americans pursued as the century dawned was that of expanding the scope of their democratic institutions. For even at the end of the nineteenth century, just one hundred years ago, democracy had yet to become a truly mass phenomenon. Only white males benefited fully from the democratic principles promoting individual freedom and self-government that had been written into the Constitution. Much remained to be done to include all Americans, especially women and minorities, in the polity. Despite a radical program of Reconstruction, the freedmen had been effectively disfranchised and segregation affirmed as the law in much of the land.

Americans would disagree over the conduct of these two projects and their likely outcomes. In his first and most important book, *The Promise of American Life* (1909), Herbert Croly, one of the founding editors of the Progressive magazine *The New Republic*, offered a positive resolution.[6] Instead of believing that economic reorganization precluded the realization of eighteenth-century ideals, Croly suggested that the organizational revolution would make possible a new Declaration of Independence. Croly was optimistic that America's newfound means of generating abundance would have a beneficial effect on the moral tenor of the times and believed that "by virtue of the more comfortable and less trammeled lives which Americans were enabled to lead, they would constitute a better society and would become in general a worthier set of men."[7] When Luce revived the idea of the "American Promise" some forty years later, many of the changes Croly had foreseen had come to pass and had moved the United States to a place of prominence on the international scene. This ascendancy had not been merely the result of Europe's breakdown—German defeat in the Great War, French exhaustion, and British industrial decline.[8] Rather, as Luce and other commentators understood, America's rise to prominence rested on an array of original achievements in science and industry and on a concurrent and deliberate reorganization of society.

BUILDING AND EXPORTING AN AMERICAN MODEL

By the end of the second world conflict, various elites had positioned America for hegemony in a global mass society. With new organizational techniques and principles of social order, they believed they had salvaged their own mass society from potential chaos. Their ideas and programs, which derived their specific qualities from the American experience, are the topic of this book. My purpose is to uncover how the "American century" was formed, not to narrate again the implementation of the "Pax Americana," whether from a commercial or military perspective.[9] I am therefore sharply differentiating the ideological construction—the "American century"—that would justify, in Americans' eyes, their intervention into the world from its actual execution—the "Pax Americana." By separating the often conflated concepts of the "American century" and the "Pax Americana," I show how one could eventually support the other. For Americans had in effect constructed the necessary ideology of an "American century" before imposing it on a world recovering from the Second World War.

My first task is to understand the ways big business, government, and the expanding sector of higher education built a partnership in the late nineteenth century and early twentieth to engineer and manage a new America. A newly created institutional matrix of business corporations, research universities and institutes, government agencies, and foundations allowed producers, brokers, and users of knowledge to interact fully for the first time and develop together an array of cognitive strategies. The partnership among them was firmly in place by the 1920s and would gain strength throughout the century (chap. 1). This institutional matrix was the prerequisite for the "American century," for it is the reorganization of knowledge, not merely the power of capital accumulation, that gave Americans the means both to generate prosperity at home and expand their presence into the world. The new institutional arrangements facilitated the buildup of a large military-industrial complex during World War I, the creation of a technology-based consumer economy, and an enormous expansion of consumption.

Social scientists worked from various points in the matrix to promote social engineering and policy-oriented research. With a newfound belief in social intelligence, they developed techniques of behavioral research that provided the raw data to organize mass society, and they turned statistical methods into ways of thinking about people. Although Vice President Henry Wallace still talked about the "common man" in the 1940s, he no longer had in mind the citizen of the Jacksonian era but the abstract "average" middle-class American that arose from hundreds of surveys and studies fashioned by social scientists during the interwar years (chaps. 2 and 3).

As its size increased and its standard of living improved, the middle class became the hallmark of the "American century." In the "America-as-model" paradigm, the middle class, not the working class, is the revolutionary ideal. Promoting its values became the American alternative to Marxism. With middle-class expansion as national project, American policymakers saw full participation in the mass market not only as a democratic right but as an effective way of blurring the old nineteenth-century divide between blue- and white-collar workers and giving credibility to a market model theoretically capable of deradicalizing class. That model would become a central tenet of the postwar economic order under American leadership. In exploring its creation, I focus on the mass consumption policies that corporate executives, labor leaders, and government officials devised in the interwar years to turn the market to the service of the social contract (chaps. 4 and 5).[10]

Market solutions geared toward middle-class inclusiveness, however, had keenly felt limitations. Designed to respond best to the needs of an abstract average American, they bypassed individual or group aspirations that did not fit a reductionist formula. At the same time, a large assimilative center, drawing on so many components, threatened to homogenize all citizens and to foster a normative conformity.[11] These circumstances prompted some American intellectuals to promote a pluralist ideology of respect for difference early in the century in the name of democratic inclusiveness. Alexis de Tocqueville, who had understood the significance of community life for the nineteenth-century decentralized society, had seen *voluntarism* as minimizing the conflict between individual and society. Twentieth-century Americans found in *plural-*

ism a solution—albeit one with serious weaknesses—for the new bureaucratic mass society.

Critical to the adoption of pluralism was the diversity of American churches. I therefore explore the ways in which the religious establishment in the twentieth century enlarged its boundaries to become the common ground on which Protestant, Jewish, and Catholic Americans could maintain—often by a process of mutual avoidance—distinctive identities, outlooks, and politics in a mass society (chap. 6). Churches, however, did not do much better than business, educational, and governmental institutions in ending discrimination. Ultimately, pluralism became a loose social contract among middle-class Americans that failed to extend the privileges of membership to those who could not approximate the average. As a result, those Americans who had to fight especially hard for their rights, African Americans, women, and workers, have, since the first Reconstruction, increasingly invested their search for individual realization into strategies of collective action where mutual commitments overshadow personal pursuits (chap. 7).

Those middle-class, mainstream Americans who defined the contours of this knowledge-driven, market-oriented, pluralistic model heeded Luce's advice. They sought to secure their prosperity by exporting their principles. As events showed, they grossly underestimated the difficulty of carrying out such a project. I therefore conclude this book with the history of the postwar reconstruction of Japan, for Japan became arguably almost a laboratory for duplicating America abroad (chap. 8). The unique circumstances of the seven-year American occupation, where Americans alone made all the important decisions, make Japan as pure a case as I could ever hope to find of revealing how Americans understood the model they had constructed at home in the interwar years and exposing its internal contradictions. In Japan, I am looking at the ways in which the "American century" was reconceived during the implementation of the "Pax Americana."

WHO ARE THE "AMERICANS" IN THIS BOOK?

The "American century" has its chroniclers and actors among a loosely structured elite. Some were public figures, but all were conscious of the challenges at home and beyond and believed in progress and the need to keep modern mass society democratic. Although a diverse cast of characters, these belonged to a growing group of influential Americans who, since the 1870s, had been looking for a "via media" between *laissez-faire* and the dangers of socialism.

They felt both were inadequate for an industrializing nation: *laissez-faire* not capable of responding to the challenges of a new political economy; socialism too drastic a departure from American traditions of individualism and entre-preneurship.[12] Early in the twentieth century, people with such predispositions called themselves Progressives. It is the troika of *The New Republic*—Croly, Walter Weyl, and Walter Lippmann—who, in 1916, appropriated the word liberal from more conservative quarters in order to disassociate themselves from Theodore Roosevelt's Progressives and to support Wilson's international engagements.[13]

Liberals spoke often in contradictory voices. Too dissimilar to be a cohesive "power elite" in C. Wright Mills's sense, they constituted rather an early incar-nation of the best and the brightest and were among the first navigators of the institutional matrix.[14] They were the graduates of an expanding network of educational institutions and were drawn to the connection among science, management, and policy. They believed simultaneously in the experts' ability to generate wealth, in the need for social engineering, and in the possibilities of individual improvement. Because they had faith in Americans' commitment to the democratization of wealth, they "tolerated," in Dorothy Ross's judg-ment, "a high degree of inequality and class immobility, as well as a high rate of human failure, in the interest of long-term moral and productive gain that they saw accruing from the capitalist market."[15] They worked in politics, gov-ernment, business, science, the professions, higher education, philanthropy, journalism, social work, or moved among several of these fields. They pos-sessed a self-assurance that today's experts have largely lost, and they articu-lated the ideals and practices we associate with the "American century."

Historians writing in the 1950s and early 1960s conceived of the liberals' project as truly representative of the larger national ideology. This is why Ar-thur M. Schlesinger, Jr., called their America the "vital center" and liberalism "an expression of the total national experience." Exploring the ways in which liberals contributed to the so-called mid-century consensus, Schlesinger de-fined "liberalism in America" as "a party of social progress rather than of intel-lectual doctrine, committed to ends rather than to methods." At about the same time, Louis Hartz saw the "American liberal tradition" as the key to American exceptionalism, and Henry Steele Commager made pragmatism the official philosophy of liberal America.[16]

These leading interpreters of the 1950s tended to dismiss the emerging criticism of pragmatism as a purposeless ideology, and they viewed in Ameri-can elites' willingness to make strategic alliances a sign of national consensus. No doubt, Americans in opposing camps struck bargains. Schlesinger argued that the 1952 election was the epitome of the American "consensus" because it marked the permanent acceptance by "the Republican party, as the party of conservatism," of "the changes wrought in the American scene by a generation of liberal reform."[17] But such partnerships masked distinct visions.

These interpretive schemes exploded in the late sixties when the deficiencies of the liberal consensus became all too clear to members of my generation. Giving voice to all who had been kept at the periphery of the liberal establishment, we promoted alternative visions of American democracy. In our renderings as well as in real life, immigrants, blacks, and other minorities rejected assimilation, women put an end to the "fraternal social contract,"[18] agrarian populists and working-class radicals spoke as if they had not missed their historic meeting of the Gilded Age, and fundamentalists and creationists claimed they might have saved the country from tolerance.[19] Recognizing the agency of neglected actors was essential, and it remains a matter of equity.[20] Systematically focusing our attention on discriminated-against Americans, however, led us to deny the existence of a central American model and promote instead as many models as could be claimed. Affirming the impossibility of speaking in America's name has become our dominant interpretation of the past in the last thirty years. Have we not gone too far?

In this book, I reinstate the center not as a fixed place we can all visit comfortably but as a lost idea we need to reconstruct to understand our century. How a nation's image is embedded in its history remains, in Clifford Geertz's opinion, "one of the deeper mysteries of the human sciences."[21] We can begin to solve the riddle for our time by probing the ways in which distinct members of the liberal elites conceived of their task, responded to pressures from the people they kept at the periphery, and claimed compromises as American solutions for the democratic world to follow. Their thoughts and actions combined into a single national project because of their often unpredicted convergence. Inconsistency was the rule; the ultimate coherence of a liberal project the gift of history.

At the same time that I am hoping to reconcile interpreters of the American past with the notion of the center, I am not attempting to impose a new homogenizing vision. I am searching instead for constructive animating principles. Hence my explorations into the power of a certain type of knowledge organization, into economic policymaking as the basis of a social contract of abundance, into the ideology of pluralism. I see a new center as an open platform where we can debate ideas and programs that benefit the greatest number of people and perhaps recover some of the vigor of the liberals' project even though we may have exhausted many of its solutions. As we find ourselves again in the midst of self-doubt, the early twentieth-century spirit of uncertainty is more important for our times than the mechanical certainties of the mid-twentieth century.

Reflecting on the 1989 collapse of the Soviet Union that conceded final victory to the Americans, French historian François Furet pointed to the fact that the former Soviet superpower may have been a formidable political and military force but never a civilization. The proof is that it could vanish without leaving any substantial legacy behind it.[22] My premise in describing the "American century" that helped shape the "Pax Americana" is to show exactly the opposite. The United States became a superpower precisely *because* of its civilization.

This important point, however, was quickly forgotten. When the United States reached its maximum influence in the post–World War II era, Cold War politics prompted many observers to neglect the question of why Americans had shaped the institutions of mass society in the way they did prior to America's world domination. Critics no longer pointed to the "promise of American life" but to Americans' unfair advantage in providing a large part of the world with both the goods for reconstruction and the money to buy those goods, as well as to the hypocrisy inherent in indiscriminately claiming moral superiority in their global containment of communism. Furthermore, the intended American control seemed to many to be based on a dubious theory of modernization as a way to generate abundance while the theory's links with democracy were left conveniently vague.

Although modernization lacked the universalizing power to inspire the world that many Americans seemed to attribute to it, it was a genuine reflection of the ways in which Americans had discovered their own strength. In attempting to construct a new world order, Americans were making the connection Luce had articulated between life at home and internationalism. Americans had traditionally believed they were better than others. Now they had the opportunity not just to claim their superiority to the rest of the world but to take on the much more difficult task of global leadership.

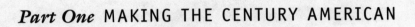

Part One MAKING THE CENTURY AMERICAN

CHAPTER ONE

PRODUCERS, BROKERS, AND USERS

OF KNOWLEDGE

Observations constitute the history of physics; systems its fable.

MONTESQUIEU[1]

The "American century" was founded on Americans' increasingly sophisticated ability to turn knowledge of the physical world into market and military
advantages, thus challenging Europeans' economic, scientific, and technological leadership. Starting in the 1870s, Americans created a vast institutional
matrix of inquiry to promote this endeavor. Ambitious research universities
like Johns Hopkins University (1876) and the University of Chicago (1892),
funded with large donations from wealthy businessmen and directed by leg-
endary academic entrepreneurs, were only the more visible points in a network
of new establishments that came to include federally and state-funded land-
grant colleges and agricultural stations, specialized institutes of technology,
large and small corporate laboratories, and private and public foundations.
This institutional matrix of inquiry gained in strength throughout the first
half of the twentieth century as Americans explored new markets and mobilized the nation's resources for two world wars. As a knowledge organization,
the matrix enabled investigators from separate fields of inquiry and institutions
to come together and collaborate.

The American matrix possessed a critical advantage. It was flexible, allowing
industrialists, managers, scientists, engineers, self-taught inventors, and other
entrepreneurs to move among institutions that in Europe, as we will see, remained aloof and independent. Although their interaction was not free of
conflict, it energized them. Operating within this matrix allowed Americans
to integrate science into the daily economic life of the nation. It also gave
them the assurance that they had the resources and the know-how to improve
quality of life at home and elsewhere. Encouraged by success, Americans
would eventually promote this system as a model for others to follow.

THE INSTITUTIONAL MATRIX IN COMPARATIVE PERSPECTIVE

The singularity of the American system appeared clearly to the Directors of
Industrial Research, who traveled together to investigate the relationship between industry and science in Europe on the eve of World War II. Chartered
in 1923 at the suggestion of Robert M. Yerkes of the Laboratories of Comparative Psychobiology at Yale and chairman of the Research Information Service
of the National Research Council (NRC), the Directors of Industrial Research
initially comprised executives of the GM Research Corporation, AT&T, the
Mellon Institute, Western Electric, the Engineering Foundation, Du Pont,
GE, and a few other large corporate laboratories.

From its inception, the Directors of Industrial Research was a loosely structured association, a fraternity of research directors that chose new members

on the basis of interests and personality rather than power or corporate status. A commitment to expanding the intellectual boundaries of corporate America was more important in securing entry than their title as head of an industrial laboratory.

Frank Jewett, research director for the Bell system, was a typical member. Jewett had earned a Ph.D. in physics under Albert Michelson at the University of Chicago, taught at MIT, had been AT&T's chief engineer, and would go on to serve on the National Defense Research Committee during World War II. He once described the directors as "an informal limited membership club made up of elected members who were congenial to one another."

Once a month, members met at the University Club or at the Century Club in New York for lunch. They discussed research policies, planned lobbying campaigns (for instance, to create a Scientific Research Division within the National Bureau of Standards), and listened to speakers chosen from among the ranks of prominent academic researchers, policymakers, or distinguished foreign visitors.[2]

It was with this spirit of enlightened inquiry that the Directors of Industrial Research organized a trip to Europe in 1937 to compare the cooperation between industrial and academic researchers in the United States with those of Great Britain, France, and Germany. Their findings revealed striking differences in tradition and approach. In England they noted that the "brilliant scientists" they had met, whether at Cavendish Laboratory or at the National Physical Laboratory operated in isolation from their industrial counterparts. Although scientists developed "additional university research centers in the industrial cities of Great Britain," they did not find "opportunities in industry comparable to those in America." That observation, corroborated by many contemporaries, supports the common diagnosis that British industrialists' late and weak investment in scientific research aggravated that country's economic decline. As the history of Britain's first industrial revolution amply demonstrates, British industrialists had once been technologically innovative without much help from scientists, but the complexity of twentieth-century science called for a partnership with academic researchers that had not been forthcoming. At the time of the directors' visit, British engineering education remained scientifically unsophisticated, and the government's weak antitrust policy, which allowed companies to expand by mergers rather than meeting new market challenges through research, only widened the gap between industry and science.[3]

The situation in France was no better. There, the directors found the Léon Blum government trying to promote a new idea: industrial and academic cooperation. They were told, however, that "the task was difficult because French industrial laboratories were most secretive." In many instances, industrial management "resented the efforts of government officials," while "distinguished men of science in France do not seem to have much interest in the industrial application of their work."

In Germany the circumstances were altogether different. Although the directors realized that the "forced emigration of eminent Jewish scientists" was "a serious loss to the future science and industrial plans of Germany," they were impressed by the state's determination to run Germany's industrial machine and to use science to replace "lacking natural products in every major field of industry." German research, they noted, was "characterized by its fundamental and basic quality" and fueled by a constant flow of young scientists into industry with at least a doctorate in hand.

The Germans had supported industrial research in the nineteenth century not by forcing it on reluctant universities but by creating independent technical schools. The strong institutional separation Germans imposed early on between the universities for scientific knowledge and the colleges of technology for industry was, in Thomas Kuhn's view, a key to their early success in both theoretical and applied fields, a feat rarely achieved.[4] With dramatic advances in organic chemistry in the late nineteenth century, these German institutional boundaries were increasingly blurred, at least in that field, as large chemical firms came to rely on advanced scientific research conducted at universities for innovation. Among them, Bayer, which later became part of the giant I. G. Farben, built a model in-house research and development laboratory, staffed it with scientists who held doctorates, and channeled funds to professors and graduate students. As the members of the American fact-finding mission knew, the Germans were their most serious competitors.

The arrangement at home, however, was quite distinct from any they had found in Europe. There was neither the separation between industry and academic research that characterized France and England nor the well-coordinated efforts fostered by the exceptionally strong interventionist policy of the German state on the eve of World War II. Although more than 10,000 American students had studied in Germany in the nineteenth century and the scientists among them had been deeply impressed by German laboratory culture, Americans had devised their own more fluid style of interaction between science and industry that would prove very effective.[5] Once created, the American matrix flourished. Cooperation in the United States evolved over the years as a voluntary, contractual, often unpredictable but powerful relationship among researchers both inside and outside universities, across a wide array of institutions. The peculiarity of the American system was that no single institution in the matrix could really succeed without some significant interactions with the others, and innovators could lead from any point in the matrix. Consequently, Americans unleashed an unprecedented level of creative energy among partners who were producers, brokers, and users of knowledge.

UNIVERSITIES, INDUSTRIAL LABORATORIES, AND AGRICULTURAL STATIONS

The United States was uniquely positioned to take advantage of the meeting between science and industry during the second half of the nineteenth century. The encounter followed, in Thomas Kuhn's words, "the maturation of organic chemistry, current electricity, and thermodynamics during the generations from 1840 to 1870." The advent of industrial science "transformed communication, the generation and distribution of power (twice), the materials both of industry and of everyday life, and also both medicine and warfare."[6] Whether scientists nearly always led the way, as Kuhn argues, or technological inventors pushed the envelope, as Thomas Hughes insists, remains a point of contention.[7] The convergence of these two streams, however, was especially visible in those fields of the natural sciences that were critical in transforming the economy—chemistry, biology as it applied to agricultural research, and specialized branches of engineering, such as electrical engineering, which depended heavily upon physics and chemistry. Until then, scientists had been primarily searching for the laws of nature; tinkerers and industry for new products and markets. The division of labor became irrelevant when finding new markets became increasingly dependent on understanding the laws of nature. While the tinkerer and the scientist had heretofore coexisted and often pursued similar ends using their separate methods, the institutional and technological changes of the late nineteenth century made their mutual avoidance more and more difficult. Tinkerers, who could no longer ignore scientific discourse (what Claude Lévi-Strauss called the "non-meaning" of science), had to compromise with science and continue under a larger cognitive scheme.[8]

Prior to this encounter, the American academic establishment had remained undeveloped. It was not, as is often said, that the natural philosophy taught in colleges governed by religious denominations before the Civil War was not up to levels of European abstraction. It was rather that Americans were notably behind in organizing and disseminating the practical knowledge that did exist. At a time when France and Germany had created formal engi-neering schools, there were few degree programs in engineering in the United States. Although some civil and mechanical engineers received training at West Point and the Naval Academy, and Yale and Rensselaer recognized some "possibilities of curriculum specialization" as early as the 1820s, higher educa-tion looked irrelevant to most professional callings until the 1870s. The num-ber of lawyers and doctors who had college degrees actually declined in the 1870s.[9]

Industrial innovation remained isolated from the larger world of knowl-edge. Although tinkerers such as clockmakers and manufacturers of firearms, who had to pay dearly for scarce labor and capital in a new nation, had invested early on in labor-saving machinery and interchangeable parts to produce large quantities of technologically complex products, their efforts did not generate a sustained dialogue with scientists. Only in a few learned societies did crafts-men and scientific communities exchange ideas.[10] That restraint, however, would change radically and rapidly in the postbellum decades. From then on, evidence of the interactions between promoters of pure research and of practical technology accumulated, whether we look at the creation of the academic scientific network or at the larger American environment for re-search.

A late-blooming society has significant advantages beyond merely benefit-ing from lessons learned by societies that mature earlier.[11] Being late in build-ing both a large industrial plant and a large academic establishment gave Americans the opportunity to integrate industrial expansion with new scien-tific ventures in innovative ways. Harvard president Charles Eliot captured the emergence of this new climate for learning when he suggested, in 1869, that Americans were well positioned to create an original knowledge synthesis of their own:

A university, in any worthy sense of the term, must grow *from seed*. It cannot be transplanted from England or Germany in full leaf and bear-ing. It cannot be run up, like a cotton-mill, in six months, to meet a quick demand. Neither can it be created by an energetic use of the in-spired editorial, the advertising circular, and the frequent telegram. Numbers do not constitute it, and no money can make it before its time. . . . When the American university appears, it will not be a copy of foreign institutions, or a hot-bed plant, but the slow and natural outgrowth of American social and political habits, and an expression of the average aims and ambitions of the better educated classes.[12]

The conceptual relationship between science and industry that emerged in the late nineteenth century was determinant in the expansion of both the American academic establishment and industrial production. As a result of it, not only could American educators tap the enormous resources generated by the country's recent accumulation of industrial wealth, they could write an agenda for American higher education that reflected the very needs of an industrial nation. Despite the resistance of a few independently wealthy intellectual elitists like Alexander Agassiz who condemned both government and corporate support for research, new institutions emerged and combined to create our modern academic landscape.[13] Expanding simultaneously the industrial and academic establishments would prove a great boost to America's economic ascent.

American universities responded to the Gilded Age project of creating a corporate network spanning a continent by training the mechanical and electrical engineers who would run the new railroads and large factories and by creating specialized science departments. The number of undergraduates rose from 52,300 in 1870 to 237,600 in 1900, and the number of graduate students in doctoral programs from fewer than 50 to about 6,000. The new American university also fostered the broader professionalization of academic knowledge. The 245 national professional associations founded in the United States between 1870 and 1900 attest to the diminishing intellectual authority of generalists as well as to the emerging tensions among interdependent specialties and the development of multiple loyalties among professors, scientists, and engineers. Late nineteenth-century professional leaders gained recognition no longer only for individual achievements but as mentors of large numbers of like-minded individuals.[14]

While universities were growing and expanding their influence, industrial firms maintaining research laboratories were also transforming the old ways of doing things. The current wisdom among business historians is that only a few business organizations, after the precursors—the ever-enterprising Thomas Edison and the Pennsylvania Railroad—could engage in *Wissenschaftliche Massenarbeit* (scientific teamwork) on the German model. American corporate managers, however, were increasingly turning to research as a way of overcoming the restrictions of U.S. antitrust policy. If the firms would not be allowed to expand by acquiring other firms, they would expand by introducing new products and creating new markets. The laboratory that General Electric established in 1900 brought to America the type of research institution pioneered by the German chemical and pharmaceutical industry. Du Pont opened one two years later. AT&T, which had begun investing in R&D in the 1880s, opened its own laboratory in 1907. These large in-house corporate laboratories drew on university-trained researchers for their staff.[15]

Industrial laboratories were created everywhere. What historians who emphasize the biggest and most advanced firms or the most important inventors have missed is the diversity of the research effort underway. The scope of innovation extended far beyond the handful of dominant corporate laboratories and the invention factories of such well-known independent entrepreneurs as Orville Wright and Glenn Curtiss in aviation, Charles Steinmetz in electricity, Reginald Fessenden and Lee de Forest in wireless communication, among others, whose tribulations with corporations, universities, and the military have been well rendered.[16]

In 1921, the National Research Council listed 526 industrial laboratories. Upon closer examination, the NRC files reveal that at least 819 laboratories were actually in operation at the time, of which 102 had opened *before* 1900. They were created by mining companies, petroleum firms, food product and chemical companies, railroads, makers of machinery and agricultural products, and so on. Alfred D. Flinn, who compiled the first list of industrial labs for NRC, suggested at first a distinction between scientific and industrial research, categorizing scientific research as tending toward the discovery of new truths for the sake of increasing human knowledge and industrial research as applying scientific facts to the service of mankind. But he quickly added that in practice, it was difficult to separate the two. Most research may have been tinkering, but tinkering often gave birth to more formal research and continued alongside it within a larger cognitive scheme.[17]

Many a research laboratory that "evolved from the dingy corner allotted to a plant chemist" drew strength from the growing research networks of trade journals, professional associations, and technical and scientific schools. In chemistry, industrialists needed a wide variety of expertise. Although Andrew Carnegie was delighted with the learned German doctor who tested steel at the Carnegie Works, the doctor's understanding of the principles of chemistry remained basic.[18] That situation changed in the United States as it had in Germany. In the German manufactures of dyes, laboratory workers moved back and forth between the traditional tricks of the trade and unraveling the frontiers of organic chemistry. In their newly created industrial laboratories, American chemists also learned how to manufacture a variety of dyes and other products by recombining the same basic elements, thus realizing "economies of scope" that would lead both to product diversification and to new scientific formulations.[19]

As the new century came on, the large corporations, driven by the need to remain competitive, increasingly viewed access to the academic network as critical to the training of their employees and ultimate success. As their operations grew larger and more capital-intensive, corporate managers became loath to entrust their fortunes to the hands of uncredentialed tinkerers when more systematic and, perhaps, more sure routes to innovation were at hand. Creating, managing, and devising strategies and policies for the acquisition of knowledge and for research became a major challenge for corporate development departments. Deciding what role the laboratories should play in diversification, how much should be invested in research, how invention should be rewarded, scientists recruited, and relationships with research universities maintained became key strategic decisions.[20] The scientists who moved to industry would now "tinker" within a body of theory. The influx of academically trained scientists into corporate laboratories tended to enlarge the scope of the research practiced there. At the same time, corporate laboratories played an increasingly significant role in basic research, for basic research was both a precondition and a by-product of their activity.

Not only chemistry but communication involved much abstract science, for the physics of the transmission of electric impulses had to be understood before the telegraph could become functional. As Joel Mokyr argues, the most fully scientific/inductive approach to technology in the late nineteenth century culminated in the invention of the telephone. The work of Alexander Graham Bell and others, which combined theory with artifacts and craft knowledge, signals the beginning of a new trend in the development of technology where inventors would incorporate scientific advances, often based on research conducted at universities, in their practical applications.[21]

It was not a matter of corporations simply adopting the theoretical outlook of academic science. Corporations never really moved away from pushing for practical experiments that could lead to quick marketable results. But they simultaneously embraced a new commitment to the scientific pursuits conducted by universities. Universities, for their part, were responsive to corporate needs and accepted their funds. Several science departments met corporate demands because they trained their students in practical problems especially well. At AT&T, Frank Jewett hired newly minted Ph.D.s trained in molecular physics at the University of Chicago for their laboratory skills in handling electron discharge devices that were important in the making of electron tubes. Willis Whitney, head of the R&D lab at GE and a German Ph.D., hired physical chemists from MIT because of their special knowledge of light bulb filaments. Whitney's best recruit was Irving Langmuir, trained both at Columbia and Göttingen, who would win a Nobel Prize in chemistry in 1932 for his work on incandescent filaments. In his biographer's judgment, "to Langmuir, as well as to other veterans of the laboratory, understanding the principles of the physical world and making improvements to technology were part of the same venture."[22]

It was naturally tempting for corporations to hire the best minds away from the universities, but that was no simple proposition. Despite a formal commitment to a fundamental research program and a major financial outlay, it was never easy for Du Pont to hire famous chemists away from a prestigious academic chair. The company was often turned down. Du Pont addressed this problem by hiring newly minted Ph.D.s. By the 1920s, most of the scientists who worked in R&D at Du Pont and elsewhere had Ph.D.s. Several had received training in the German academic institutions that had been partial models for American research universities. Many were initially recruited from the new American research universities, especially Johns Hopkins and Chicago. After that the network widened rapidly. In the 1920s, Du Pont supplemented its in-house expertise through a wide program of academic consulting, through fellowships to support academic research, and, especially, by recruiting many young Ph.D.s from the University of Illinois Chemistry Department. Du Pont also maintained ties with other corporate laboratories. By the 1920s the high level of training required for R&D personnel in a growing number of firms signaled the consolidation of a large, integrated corporate-scientific complex populated with experts who knew how to address both theoretical and practical issues.[23]

In addition to private and public research universities and corporate-sponsored industrial laboratories, the federal government funded agricultural stations, which formed the third major node in the new matrix of inquiry (the military would later become the fourth). The creation of agricultural stations is an important, yet poorly understood, moment in the rise of the regulatory state. Connecticut launched the first agricultural experiment station in 1875. By 1887 the Hatch Act guaranteed federal funding to all state experimental stations and channeled the funds through land-grant colleges to give them a new life, for by all accounts the land-grant colleges were unsuccessful in keeping the best students on the farm. Many of them failed to register even a decent proportion of their students in agricultural courses; in Minnesota, out of 293 students, only one reportedly studied agriculture at the time of the congressional debate on the Hatch Act.

Dependent on rural votes, Congress had already created scientific bureaus within the Department of Agriculture, but it extended its investment with agricultural stations, which helped revitalize the land-grant colleges. The

Grangers feared that if federal funds for experimental stations were channeled through colleges they could not control rather than through state legislatures they hoped to control, the practical concerns of the farmers would be secondary to those of the scientists. But the Grangers lost, and experimental stations were modeled as research facilities. The creation of the agricultural stations was a massive effort. By 1903 there were already sixty federally funded experimental stations in operation in the country, employing a large number of personnel, many with doctorates. Land grant colleges added to these some mining experiment stations and some engineering stations (five by 1910) needed locally. They also boosted their curriculum in statistics to respond to the agricultural stations' demand.[24]

In her study of hybrid corn, Deborah Fitzgerald captures the mix of people and interests in the agricultural stations characteristic of the emerging matrix of inquiry and the ways in which the new research facilities remained attuned to the farmers' concerns, despite the Grangers' fears. She shows the juxtaposition of "the practical breeder" or the agricultural tinkerer, who, "often without the benefit of a scientific education, attempted to improve corn yield by means of selection and varietal crossing," and the botanist or biologist, "generally affiliated with an agricultural college" and using corn as a "scientific device to study the general laws of inheritance." The distinction, however, was one of emphasis. Although biologists' "long-term interest was scientific rather than agricultural," they could not work in an insulated setting. If their research culminated in the development of hybrid corn, it is because they were dwelling in a "peculiar juncture of pure and applied science, an *institutional juncture*."[25]

PURSUING A CAREER WITHIN THE INSTITUTIONAL MATRIX OF INQUIRY

In the span of thirty years, then, from the 1870s to the early 1900s, the country was dotted by expanding academic institutions, industrial laboratories that influenced the work of the universities and recruited their graduates, and experimental stations that provided a bridge between farming and agricultural science.[26] These institutions soon formed an institutional matrix of unprecedented proportions without parallel in Europe. Not that every point in the matrix was equal. Its very existence and the diversity of its components are what counted in fostering interaction among investigators and promoting cross-fertilization among separate communities of inquiry. Dominant cognitive strategies emerged in the United States from this stimulating interdependence, marked especially by a frequent exchange of personnel, among private and public institutions.

American investigators who were increasingly relying on their connections in the institutional matrix established a new and powerful relationship between science, industry, and agriculture which, in turn, deeply affected their understanding of themselves and their vision of the wider world.[27] The concrete process by which a wide array of institutions came together to create the American research establishment can be traced in the career of many of the participants. How much of a common purpose did they share? What brought them together? What led them to commit their energies to separate institutions and to build linkages among them?

The graduates from the Sheffield Scientific School at Yale who moved back and forth along the matrix of inquiry testify to the matrix's pervasiveness. The school opened its doors in 1846. Sponsored by such giants of the new research ethos as Daniel Coit Gilman, who would become the first president of Johns Hopkins University in 1876, it was devoted to the scientific study of nature. Although pioneer chemist Benjamin Silliman was active at Yale as late as 1845, there were no facilities for systematic laboratory courses in analytical chemistry prior to the school's foundation.[28]

But by the 1870s, graduates of the Sheffield School were already moving among the various nodes of the enlarged scientific community. Thus Charles Dudley, a Sheffield graduate who received one of the thirteen Ph.D.s awarded in the United States in 1874, became the chief chemist of the Pennsylvania Railroad (the largest in America) in 1875 when it opened its Testing Department, one of the first industrial chemical laboratories devoted to metallurgy and the first in the railroad industry. From Altoona, Pennsylvania, Dudley soon acquired a worldwide reputation. He published the results of his studies of steel testing in numerous scientific publications, as Pennsylvania Railroad standards became industry standards. Dudley was rewarded with the presidency of the American Chemical Society.[29]

The Connecticut Agricultural Station opened its doors the same year as the Pennsylvania Railroad Testing Department and also attracted graduates of the Sheffield School. One of them, Horace Wells, started out in agricultural chemistry at the Connecticut station, but Dudley persuaded him to move over to private industry and work for the Pennsylvania Railroad as an assistant chemist in 1877. After a stint in Altoona, Wells moved on to the Colorado mining district, where he worked for the research laboratory of a mining business, before returning to Yale as a junior faculty member in the early 1880s.

As a new professor, he went to Munich to broaden his knowledge of analytical methods and returned home to a chair in analytical chemistry.[30]

What we see illustrated by Dudley's and Wells's experience are the conditions that Eliot believed would foster the American university and an example of how these circumstances shaped the lives of those participating in higher education and industrial research. Similar examples can be found among other young scientists within such expanding fields as petroleum research, electricity, communications, photography, and so on. Producing a stream of new goods in the United States transformed not only the economic market but created the knowledge market. The American conditions of frequent exchange within the growing matrix of inquiry helped foster the transformation of some classical colleges into scientific universities, the expansion of agricultural schools, and the wholesale creation of new research institutions. Engineering now embraced shop culture, science, and professionalization.[31] One can certainly think of such interactions among university, government, and corporate science as corrupting American academic life. An alternative is to think of Charles Eliot's "seed" as germinating into a knowledge organization capable of sustaining America's powerful rise in the twentieth century.

OTHER INSTITUTIONS JOIN THE MATRIX

The new institutional matrix of knowledge would continue to grow throughout the next century to include the American military, as we can see in following Elmer Sperry's career. Sperry is a striking example of a self-taught American inventor who tapped the matrix at different points early in his life before becoming instrumental in building an industrial and scientific partnership with the military. The more successful he becomes, the more enmeshed he is in the matrix's diversification.

Sperry first made his mark in the newly developing field of electrical engineering, arguably the sector whose spectacular growth influenced every other economic sector in the late nineteenth century. In the single class he took at Cornell in the late 1870s, the young Sperry built a modified dynamo and soon was recognized as one of America's electrical pioneers when he launched his own company. With the merger of Thomson-Houston and Edison into GE in 1892, however, Sperry could no longer compete with the emerging giant in the field and moved on to streetcars and then to the automobile, working on batteries and electrochemistry. It was only in 1907 that he began applying his abundant skills to the problems of airplane and ship stabilization. This is how he became, as Thomas Hughes has shown, "the father of modern feed-back controls," or cybernetics.[32] His new activities inevitably led him to work with the military.

In 1910 Sperry organized the gyroscope company that was to become the "brainmill" for the military mobilizing for World War I. And by June 1914, Sperry's son, Lawrence, could be seen flying near Paris, raising his hands in the open cockpit of the Curtiss plane he was piloting to demonstrate that he had turned the controls over to the automatic gyrostabilizer while young and daring French mechanic Emile Cachin walked out on the wing of the stabilized plane. With the plane steady, it would become for the first time possible to target specific sites for bombing.[33]

At the outbreak of World War I, Sperry was asked to sit on the Naval Advisory Board, where he joined other leaders in industrial research and became one of the architects of the first industrial-military complex. In the 1920s, Sperry maintained an active set of relations with research universities for the purpose of improving his technologies: Harvard, Columbia, the University of Chicago, and the California Institute of Technology, all different types of institutions, ranging from traditional colleges that had grown into research universities, to a research university, to a specialized, high-caliber engineering school.

As head of the Sperry Gyroscope Company, Sperry conducted extensive measurement research with physics Nobel prize winner Albert Michelson at Chicago. Among his associates and friends was Robert A. Millikan, another Nobel laureate, who had led with astronomer George Ellery Hale the American physicists' war effort on the development of sound-detection for submarine warfare and other military devices. Sperry wrote in 1921 to Millikan at the Ryerson Physical Laboratory of the University of Chicago how pleased he had been to see the Harvard faculty and graduate students so keenly interested in the "extreme case of wheels" he had to show. Millikan, who had just moved west to the Norman Bridge Laboratory of Physics at CalTech, responded by luring Sperry to talk to his group of young engineers: "We have here about 435 thoroughbreds," as he described them, "among whom there are already 21 graduate students in physics and chemistry." As when at the University of Chicago, Millikan was looking for jobs for his graduates.[34]

The mobilization for World War I reinforced the matrix in yet two other ways. The first one was to systematize the means that newly created philanthropic foundations could use to channel funds to scientific and technological ventures. During the war, not only did the National Research Council induce corporations to fund basic research at universities across the country, but it also tapped foundations. Although these philanthropic institutions had charted a lofty course in the hope that neither politics nor profits would shape the direction of intellectual growth, they had no easy access to the range of talent they wanted to promote. It was only when the NRC, upon its creation, organized a centralized committee structure capable of interacting with a diffuse national research establishment that foundations relied on it to establish durable links with the scientific community. Well-known scientists attracted the funds initially, but the number of beneficiaries grew rapidly as investigators used these funds to build laboratories and support graduate students. Foundations were thus liberated from Carnegie's search for the undiscovered "exceptional man." At the same time, their infusion of funding helped train a generation of scientists.[35]

It was also at NRC that scientists and inventors reinforced their ties with the military.[36] World War I was therefore a major turning point in bringing the military, at least temporarily, to the status of full participant in the matrix of inquiry. The kind of reluctant attitude that had led the War Department initially to rebuff the Wright brothers disappeared. The Navy welcomed Sperry's innovations. It was also the Navy that lent its organizational structure and financial resources to give Americans the edge in wireless communications. In this instance, promoters of commercial radio followed the military lead. Among them, David Sarnoff, a Russian immigrant and one of many self-taught engineers who dabbled in wireless communication when radio was still exclusively oriented toward the Navy market, had the vision of a receiver in each American home. Sarnoff managed to move up the corporate hierarchy in the 1920s, to negotiate the Radio Corporation of America's independence from its Navy and corporate sponsors and eventually to build an impressive radio empire connecting science, business, and the military.[37] It was a dress rehearsal for the military-industrial complex of our own times when prosecuting war and expanding the consumer society have become part of the same scientific and technological venture.

A WAR OF WORDS: NEW WAYS OF BEING PRACTICAL

The constant exchange among scientists, professors, inventors, businessmen, managers, patent lawyers, and representatives of the government and the military—all of whom belonged to overlapping communities of inquiry within the institutional matrix—had become routine for problem solving by the beginning of the century. From different locations in the matrix, elite and non-elite producers, brokers, and users of knowledge met and interacted to formulate theories and design products. Different groups pushed for their own agendas and cognitive strategies but none could succeed at high levels of productivity without the others. As the NRC reported, the various investigators located at different points in the matrix often played interchangeable roles: "sometimes it was the college professor of science, pure or applied, sometimes it was the inventor or the professional engineer, and sometimes it was the manufacturing industry that took the initiative, conceived the new idea, or made the discovery, and sought the assistance of the other in realizing it in practice."[38]

Such unprecedented levels of cognitive interdependence at the same time stood in the way of special agendas. It was clear that businessmen wanted new products and generals demanded weapons, but professors increasingly reorganized scientific language into a set of axiomatized propositions that denied the traditional, intuitive connection between research and exposition. This led to a war of words among participants in inquiry.

The war of words had at least one famous precedent. For all his penetrating brilliance, Alexis de Tocqueville stipulated some of its most confusing terms when he claimed the American practice of trial and error as part of an antitheoretical bent in the nation's "character," borrowing the latter concept from Montesquieu to describe the mutual influences of the environment, institutions, and social organization on a people's habits. Tocqueville, however, had failed to appreciate the scientific liveliness of American learned societies, which he did not visit during his journey, and he had overlooked the achievements of the American savants of his days, men like geologist Alexander Dallas Bache, zoologist Louis Agassiz, or physicist Joseph Henry who, as if they had wanted to prove him right, had chosen for their group the Neapolitan name Lazzaroni for "beggar" or "idle."[39]

Three quarters of a century later, some of the participants in the new matrix of inquiry were still tempted to explain their practicality by pointing to timeless American traits rather than to the specific factors and circumstances that shaped their lives as investigators. Stressing the practical resonated well with the view many had of themselves and of their fellow workers. Sperry revealed as much when he wrote to his old friend David Eugene Smith, a specialist in the history of mathematics and the chairman of the Mathematics Department at Columbia: "I am a great worshiper of old Archimedes, but never had so much use for his contemporary, Euclid. . . . There is no evidence whatever that [Euclid] ever drew [a circle]. On the other hand, Archimedes spent a large part of his life in sitting down and saying, 'Let's see if we cannot determine what the area of a circle really is.' . . . Did you hear that a contemporary

German historian has called Archimedes the 'Yankee of Antiquity'? I have voted to have a leather medal awarded to this German."[40] American investigators wanted to believe that their way of being practical helped them be more open than others to the unexpected.

More significant than these claims of practicality as the product of American character was the real difference that working within the new matrix of inquiry made in investigators' lives. The institutional matrix, once established, defined new possibilities for all who interacted within it. The exchange of personnel grew more frequent, the number of Ph.D.s greater, the information channels more established, the products more varied, and the science more sophisticated. In other words, Americans built modern institutions of knowledge that transformed what it meant to be practical.

The philosophers and public figures who addressed these organizational and epistemological issues were read avidly in all kinds of places. With the institutional matrix—and related systems, machinery, and networks—growing in size and significance, it would become tempting for contemporary observers to use the matrix as a proxy for American technological prowess. Blending organization and outcomes, commentators found metaphors that applied both to investigators and their larger environment.

Some intellectuals focused on the shift away from nineteenth-century unity of thought. Thus Henry Adams captured early in the twentieth century the essence of this large intellectual transformation when he observed that the ordered universe that philosophy and science had heretofore embraced was being dismantled. He realized that the time was gone when natural philosophers pursued scientific inquiry to find, in a cleric's words, "God's truth in God's facts."[41] Adams accurately, if reluctantly, understood the sequence that led from "abstract truth," that "absolute" or "innate conviction" of the nineteenth century, to truth as a "convenience" or even a mere "medium of exchange." Adams was tormented by the opposing pulls of "the force of the Virgin," which attracted him, and the "occult dynamism" of the dynamo, and torn between the unity of truth and the indeterminacy of the new physics. He summed it up forcefully in his autobiographical *Education:* "The child born in 1900 would . . . be born into a new world which would not be a unity but a multiple."[42] Adams described in these terms the intellectual crisis that would break out sporadically in the late nineteenth and early twentieth centuries. For intellectual historians, our modern cognitive strategies are rooted in this crisis, that is, the collapse of the "unity of truth," "the separation of morality and knowledge," and the replacement of unitary systems of thought, in the face of uncertainty, with provisional knowledge.[43]

Other contemporaries connected the paradigmatic shift more directly with the institutional transformation that occurred at the same time. They attempted to locate the intersection between the emerging practice of inquiry developed by producers, brokers, and users of knowledge, and the multiple intellectual viewpoints Adams referred to. Thus the author of a study of engineering education published in 1918 by the Carnegie Foundation for the Advancement of Teaching turned to philosopher John Dewey in addition to scientific management expert Frederick Winslow Taylor for guidance. The study had been completed in 1916, the year when the federal government, in its drive to mobilize scientific resources for national service, formally recognized the engineering profession in the NRC.[44] Dewey's text, on which the author relied, was *How We Think* (1910), with its quest for "that attitude of mind, that habit of thought, which we call scientific." Dewey's loose definition of science worked well within the new matrix of knowledge: science was "a method of thinking"; it was "thinking so far as thought has become conscious of its proper ends and of the equipment indispensable for success in their pursuit." Dewey clearly stated science's goals: "the transformation of natural powers into expert, tested powers."[45] Dewey's conception of science epitomizes the period, but one could also point to a number of lesser figures who argued along the same lines.[46] Theory, for the engineers-turned-scientists and the pragmatist philosophers alike, was primarily a way to coordinate and extend practices or inquiries, only occasionally to generate them.[47]

Dewey's ideas also help us to understand a critical moment in the history of the United States. They are revealing in part because he formulated them between the post-Darwinian world and the Einstein controversy of the 1920s. Horace Kallen captured the significance of that period and of Dewey's contribution when, stressing the lack of unitary thought as Adams had before him, he wrote that "the findings of Darwinian science . . . provided a new ground for translating freedom and reason from abstract universals into concrete workings in the specific experiences of living men. Understood in the light of Darwinian theory, scientific discovery is less the uncovering of an *a priori* order everywhere the same, waiting from eternity to be found out, and more invention by man of diverse devices, material, linguistic, symbolic, with which to accomplish the most specific, the simplest, the most economical, the most convenient and elegant solution of the problems his experience presents him with."[48]

By linking discovery to action and insisting that "inquiry was an activity open to the rank and file membership of an educated democratic society," to borrow David Hollinger's apt phrase, Dewey and others described not the ordinary "busybody," as heralded by the popularizers of his ideas and also by neo-Tocquevilleans, but instead a new American specifically engaged in the task of inquiry in a large institutional matrix.[49] That American was often a combination of a scientist and a tinkerer who did not make a clear distinction between theory and practice. "Are technologists not thinkers as well as doers?" asked Charles Beard in his preface to *Toward Civilization,* a 1930 volume in which he turned to Elmer Sperry, wireless communication inventor Lee de Forest, and electrical engineer Michael Pupin, among others, to reflect on the connection between science and technology in America. In a previous companion volume, *Whither Mankind,* also edited by Beard, Dewey underscored how the "application of natural science in industry and commerce" had transformed American lives.[50]

The doers' ideas of themselves and the world they helped fashion were, however, increasingly challenged by scientific formulations moving away from a common sense apprehension of the world. No matter how successful the doers were, a hierarchical distinction between theory and practice would become critical to the twentieth-century discourse on inquiry. Today's readers of Sinclair Lewis's novel *Arrowsmith* are struck by the scientific reductionism, that is, the attempt to concentrate on a small numbers of axioms, that came to the fore so quickly in the 1920s. Lewis captured a new ideal type who was moving to center stage. As we know, the model for Gottlieb, Martin Arrowsmith's mentor and the archetype of the scientist, was the biologist Jacques Loeb, of the Rockefeller Institute, whose influential experiments on the chemistry of living matter and artificial parthenogenesis eventually persuaded him that living processes could be reduced to the laws of physics and chemistry.

Philip Pauly, Loeb's biographer, is careful to distinguish between two distinct periods in the biologist's career. He locates first "the engineering ideal" that animated Jacques Loeb in his years of experimental work at the University of Chicago. That first Loeb, who would not motivate Sinclair Lewis, had provided John Dewey with a live model for the experimental scientist. It is a second Loeb, who had turned away from those concepts Dewey codified and moved instead toward increasingly mechanistic views, who inspired Lewis.[51] Loeb, like Einstein, became driven by only one goal, that of narrowing down his universe to the smallest possible number of laws. Influential branches of science in the twentieth century became reductionist in the sense of searching for the simplest set of axioms to explain phenomena. That Jacques Loeb worked at the Rockefeller Institute—an independent institution not associated with any university, government agency, or corporation, and protected by a new kind of philanthropy—shows that the institutional matrix had come of age. Although the matrix continued to foster interaction and pragmatism, it had grown large enough for some of its components to become temporarily insulated. At least some scientists who wanted to free themselves from the burden of practical applications could do so.[52]

Producers, brokers, and users of knowledge fought loudly over the scientific concepts that modern society was embracing, that inspired Walter Lippmann's search for mastery as well as Dewey's promotion of democratic communities of inquiry. Although the separation between inquiry and application certainly did not happen "at one stroke" as some historians of physics have argued, "physical theory" became significantly "removed" from experience.[53] The new physics especially, divorcing science from our common sense perception of experience, reinforced a trend that had started earlier with the axiomatization of mathematics.

John Dewey, who had understood the significance of the institutional matrix for American civilization better than anybody else, but who was also entangled in the war of words, sought to demonstrate the persisting congruence of his pragmatism (or "instrumentalism") with the theories of relativity of the 1920s. He responded to the challenge by endorsing the second scientific revolution. The new physics' principle of indeterminacy, he argued, only reinforced the pragmatists' rejection of fixed laws.[54] But Dewey got caught between "engineering" and scientific formulations that overlapped with one another without really blending.

In the end, Dewey failed to realize his real purpose, which was to end the old confusion between science as the uncovering of relationships and science as mirror of the real world. By the late 1930s, he was attacked from many camps. Bertrand Russell, instead of heeding William James's advice to preserve his "relations with concrete realities," quipped that Dewey could not discern the difference between a scientist and a bricklayer.[55] Russell's attack was aimed at Dewey's most essential proposition, the latter's resolve not to confuse the process of inquiry with the search for truth. Most important, Russell argued that Dewey's views were best understood "in harmony with the age of industrialism" and that it was no surprise that "his strongest appeal should be to Americans."[56]

Nobody, however, could escape worldly tensions altogether, for more abstract science led only to more applications. Ernest Lawrence funded his cyclotron at Berkeley with promises to the Rockefeller Foundation not of final theory but of new X-ray technology and neutron cancer therapy. Highly abstruse polymer chemistry led to the development of nylon. Jacques Loeb's most lasting influence would be on modern biotechnology and the invention of the oral contraceptive.[57] The list goes on and on. When John Dewey wrote *How We Think* in 1910, Americans were well on the way to creating a mass-consumption economy. Their institutional matrix of inquiry, whose birth I have described, would only continue to expand under the pressures of market and military imperatives and provide the framework for new investigations, largely undisturbed by the vocal fights among participants in inquiry.

CHAPTER TWO

DEFINING TOOLS OF SOCIAL

INTELLIGENCE

Original thinking springs up on its own; its history is its only
tolerable form of exegesis; its fate its only form of criticism.
MICHEL FOUCAULT[1]

The idea of the "American Century" entailed more than developing products, controlling markets, and wielding power; it had a missionary component. Speaking of his compatriots' "manifest duty" to come to the world's rescue, Henry Luce envisioned a new kind of "Good Samaritan" who would become a "*skillful* servant of mankind" by exporting his expert knowledge. Although Luce was oblivious to the disparity between creed and conduct that limited the scope of reform at home, he conveyed a widespread American belief in the link between expertise and progress.[2]

American social scientists' and reformers' faith in their resulting ability to improve society had been influenced by two large movements that had flourished on American soil in the late nineteenth and early twentieth centuries. The Protestant home mission movement, which climaxed with the Social Gospel, had infused a sense of urgency in the prosecution of social investigation and boosted the social sciences. At the same time, large philanthropic foundations pushed American social scientists to come up with tangible solutions to the problems of the day.

Specialists in the history of the social sciences have tended to downplay the large influence of religion on the fledgling specialized disciplines while focusing instead on their scientific ethos and their European antecedents. They have illuminated the tensions that emerged between generalists and specialists who formed communities "of full-time practitioners" and narrated the social scientists' investment in "quantification as a route to positive knowledge," topics to which I return in the next chapter.[3] Their interpretations have been especially effective in tracing the ways in which twentieth-century social scientists became service intellectuals who mobilized the important public resource of technical knowledge but progressively divorced themselves from a larger world of ethics.[4] While historians have exposed a real conflict between objectivity and advocacy in the formative years, my purpose is to show that late nineteenth- and early twentieth-century practitioners in the overlapping fields of economics, political economy, political science, sociology, and social work were intent on overcoming this conflict. Social scientists nearly always kept sight of large political and moral goals, for they felt the continuous reinfusion of Christian concerns in their professional lives as they moved within the institutional matrix of sponsoring universities, professional associations, churches, corporations, state and local governments, foundations, labor unions, and others. This exchange, however, provoked the simple recognition that their research, no matter how inspired by Christian principles, would be effective only if they could translate it into practice. They had to find ways of turning understanding into acting, or, to use their own words,

social intelligence into policy. In the end, the missionary impulse behind the
American century was channeled into a belief that problems could be solved.

A SPIRITUAL CRISIS

The social scientists' commitment to social progress emerged in no small part
from the crisis Protestant churches faced when confronting an industrial society. These churches unleashed scores of young men and women eager to demonstrate that they were good Christians by doing good work. They investigated social conditions to help the masses of immigrants cope with cyclical
unemployment and cultural adjustments. Many among the self-appointed social missionaries of the Gilded Age were middle-class Protestants, often sons
and daughters of ministers, who proselytized among Catholic and Jewish immigrants. Small groups of liberal Jews and Catholics also formulated their
own versions of the Social Gospel.[5] These late nineteenth-century participants
on the front lines of home missions, settlement houses, and other outposts of
the charity organization movement preached assimilation. They increasingly
turned to the conceptual tools and investigative methods the fledgling social
sciences proposed as a way to improve their effectiveness in alleviating poverty.
Conversely, social scientists embraced this missionary movement and gave it
direction.[6]

Laymen and clerics alike joined forces in the missionary endeavor. When
economists Richard Ely, Simon Patten, Edwin Seligman, and others formed
the inherently activist American Economics Association in 1885 to combat
the *laissez-faire* school championed by Yale Professor William Graham Sumner, they were joined by thirty-three ministers. Together, they attempted to
unite the "efforts of church, state, and science" to shore up or replace communal institutions that could no longer keep up with the numbers of individuals
needing assistance.[7]

Among the leading evangelical advocates of harnessing the emerging social
science to Christian ends was Baptist minister Walter Rauschenbusch.
Rauschenbusch, whose immigrant father had converted from German Lutheran to Baptist minister, was pastor of a working-class German Baptist parish
in Hell's Kitchen on New York City's west side. He argued that the evolution
of modern sociology and political economy, along with the new historical
understanding of society, equipped men like himself with conceptual tools to
improve the material existence of others and eventually make Christian ideals
real. As he put it, political economy, which "in the past has misled us" had
left "its sinful *laissez-faire* ways" and was finally "preparing to serve the Lord

and human brotherhood." Rauschenbusch, who taught history at the Rochester Theological Seminary, embraced the social sciences. In contrast to Josiah Strong or Dwight Moody who clung to individualism, Rauschenbusch championed the understanding of community.[8]

Walter Rauschenbusch's academic counterpart was Richard Ely, who joined the Johns Hopkins University faculty in 1880, four years after the new research school opened its doors. Ely had begun his studies of municipal problems in Berlin. Along with other German-influenced economists of his time, he rejected classical political economic thinking and emphasized instead the historical and humanitarian dimensions of political economy in concrete social investigations and proposals to use state and local taxation in Maryland and Baltimore for social purposes. As a leader of the Social Gospel, he viewed social science as a way to "love thy neighbor" and to bring about "human happiness." It was in the "duty to love and serve our fellows" that Ely found "the most convincing proof of the divinity of Christ." His *Social Aspects of Christianity and Other Essays* (1889) became a standard text for Protestant social reformers and also penetrated the reform Catholic milieu.[9] Ely had corresponded with John Bascom, president of the University of Wisconsin and initiator of the "Wisconsin Idea" of cooperation between the experts of the university and the administration of the state. When Bascom's successor offered Ely a position, he joined the Wisconsin faculty in 1892 as director of the School of Economics, Politics, and History, and later recruited his former student, John R. Commons, to pursue the effort of turning academic social science to the service of the state.[10]

Like his mentor, who was only eight years older, Commons saw his academic work as an extension of his personal religious impulse. He even thought of his commitment to political economy as a tribute to his mother's desire that he become a minister. When at Hopkins, he followed Ely's suggestion to work for building and loan associations in Baltimore and to join the local Charity Organization Society as a caseworker. Emulating his teacher, Commons wrote sociological and economic books for ministers. His *Social Reform and the Church* (1894), prefaced by Ely, illustrates the close connection among Christianity, fact-finding, sociology, and social legislation needed to bring the rich and the poor together in brotherly harmony. In addition, Commons urged ministers to study taxation, municipal monopolies, and civil service in the hope of raising their ability to fight poverty.

The professors' reformist zeal would sometimes clash with the university trustees' conservatism. In 1894, the year President Cleveland sent federal troops to end the violent Pullman strike, Ely was accused in the *Nation* of

using his academic chair to foment labor unrest. Although his colleagues ral-
lied around him, and Ely was ultimately vindicated, the affair left him with
deep scars. In 1899, it was Commons's turn to be singled out when his commitment to social issues was perceived as too radical. He was asked to leave
the University of Syracuse for having taken a pro-labor stance at a public rally.
Insisting that he was merely following his conscience, Commons later noted
in his memoirs that "it was not religion, it was capitalism that governed colleges." After five years of journalism and social and economic investigative
work, Commons joined the Wisconsin faculty in 1904. His move to Madison
gave him the opportunity to reconcile his academic work and his evangelical
impulse. In his own words, he was "born again." It is under Commons's
guidance that the Wisconsin Idea initiated by Bascom of putting academic
experts to the service of policymaking came to fruition. Ironically, achieving
this goal exemplified the shift from evangelically motivated social science to
policy-oriented social science by mid-century.[11]

Commons's "new birth" thrust him, in his own words, into a "conflict"
that would last for the rest of his career. In Madison, the state capitol was
"only a mile apart" from the university. It was easy for Commons to go back
and forth between the two as he worked out connections among "instruction,
research, extension, economics, class conflict, and politics." Commons wrote
civil service and public utility legislation for Governor La Follette and consulted for the state industrial commission. He also pushed ahead his landmark
historical studies of labor as a way to fight for the acceptance of collective
bargaining by skilled workers.[12]

Working with the labor movement was not easy. Although reformers from
academia like Ely and Commons were sympathetic to labor, they had too
inclusive a vision of political economy to collaborate effectively with, or receive
much support from, labor unions, for AFL leaders stuck close to bread-and-
butter issues in part because they knew that conservative courts would strike
down broader reform agreements on the basis of the employers' claim of the
sacrosanct freedom of contract. Distrust rather than cooperation therefore
marked the relationship between the American Association for Labor Legislation, where Ely, Commons, and many others reformers devoted much work,
and the AFL, which deliberately stood aloof from a large reform agenda. While
labor unions focused on bargaining for wages, reformers who could afford to
maintain a broader perspective on collective action and labor-management
relations, tended to cooperate instead with the employer-dominated National
Civic Federation to promote the regulatory state.[13]

By the time the Wisconsin Workman Compensation Act—the crowning achievement of Commons's program—was passed in 1932, the Wisconsin Idea had evolved from its evangelical beginnings into a full-blown program for a social science aimed at improving governance and social conditions. With the State Federation of Labor finally lending its support to the bill, a half-dozen years before the national American Federation of Labor would join in such efforts, the Wisconsin Idea emerged as a model of cooperation among social scientists, state policymakers, and labor leaders. The continuity with the Social Gospel was clear in the identity of those who worked for the passage of the act and who labored to carry it out. These included Paul Raushenbush, the son of Walter Rauschenbusch (he dropped the *c*'s) and a Wisconsin graduate student who was one of the so-called Friday Niters who gathered for dinner with Commons every week's end, as well as his wife Elizabeth, the daughter of Justice Louis Brandeis and also Commons's student. When Wisconsin enacted the pioneer unemployment compensation legislation, the young Raushenbush became director of the Unemployment Compensation Department of the Wisconsin Industrial Commission. Raushenbush put into practice the ideal his father had championed, but gone was the explicit linkage with Christianity. Instead a creative synthesis had emerged between social knowledge and social action.[14]

THE NEW PHILANTHROPY

The second force that shaped the reformers' efforts were the philanthropic foundations established by wealthy industrialists. The meeting of the social investigators' evangelical fervor with affluence led to a paradoxical situation. Numerous emerging social scientists who were religiously motivated, sympathetic to the labor movement's confrontation with capital, and dedicated to building the regulatory state found themselves turning to the wealthy moguls' new philanthropy for support. Other potential funding sources were slow to materialize. Only a handful of progressive states like Massachusetts and Wisconsin were building a strong tradition of labor and social investigation.[15]

The meeting of large foundations and academic researchers transformed the nature of philanthropy—departing from the traditional emphasis on local welfare and embracing science as an instrument of progress. So long as the economic system remained localized so did efforts to cope with social problems. According to Merle Curti, who surveyed the giving practices of 4,047 millionaires up to 1892, virtually all philanthropy, including that of the very rich, was still "directed toward the local community." In the highly localized process of almsgiving, the biggest donors asserted their control over community institutions of health care and education. Relief to the poor, sick, and aged took about a third of the millionaires' largesse, religious organizations a quarter, civic improvements about a tenth. Contributions to education, that is, to local liberal arts colleges, technical and vocational education, public libraries, and the adult education movement, rivaled health and welfare by accounting for about a third of the money given away. Wealthy donors, however, were satisfied with almsgiving and aid to local institutions and showed little interest in using their wealth to attack large problems or move beyond their immediate surroundings. As a result, they gave virtually nothing directly "to further research in either the social or natural sciences."[16]

With the rise of corporations, the scale of giving changed in a way that would alter the tools Americans used to maintain a stable social order. Many of the new generation of corporate leaders were keenly aware of the fragile balance among individual profit, self-fulfillment, and social justice. They saw that the new economic system that generated their wealth was also the source of heretofore unknown problems. They recognized that conditions were ripe for a new kind of philanthropy. Turning vast fortunes over to nonprofit foundations was a way for capitalists simultaneously to redistribute wealth, generate new knowledge, and control social problems in the hope of insuring the survival of their economic system for years to come. By launching new inquiries, the large not-for-profit foundation became therefore a logical complement to the previous generation's creation of the graduate school.[17] Furthermore, the very rich shared many of the religious beliefs of the professors and the reformers who conducted social investigations. Despite much talk about income tax as the incentive for their largesse, wealthy donors still had little to worry about taxation in the early twentieth century. Instead, they feared God. Carnegie was alarmed at the idea of dying rich. At the University of Chicago, John D. Rockefeller retreated into president William Rainey Harper's office to kneel and pray.[18]

But Carnegie's and Rockefeller's efforts were not always welcome. In 1892, the *Saint Louis Post-Dispatch* echoed the deeply felt resentments of local workers against Carnegie's beneficence. The newspaper argued that "ten thousand 'Carnegie Public Libraries' would not compensate the country for the direct and indirect evils resulting from the Homestead Lockout."[19] Such feelings of indignation would linger for years to come. Rockefeller's efforts were also mired in controversy about "tainted money" that reached a climax just before World War I. In the span of a few months, Congress turned down Rockefeller's proposal for a public foundation that advisor Frederick Gates had touted; the Walsh industrial commission denounced his labor relations tactics; the press accused him of covering up his unfair employment practices with bogus investigations. Congress even ordered the Department of Agriculture to discontinue funding from the Rockefeller General Education Board for the farm visitation program that had been so effective in the South under reformer Seaman Knapp's guidance. Such incidents led the Rockefeller charities to concentrate their investments in science and medicine and stay away for a time from social science.[20]

Idealism, nonetheless, marked these early efforts. When Andrew Carnegie established the Carnegie Endowment for International Peace in 1910 on the occasion of his seventy-fifth birthday, the industrialist and philanthropist seemed confident that he had allocated sufficient money to suppress war in rather short order! Once his primary goal was accomplished, the revenue from the $10 million gift would be used to eradicate, as the endowment charter specified, "the next most degrading evil or evils, the suppression of which would most advance the progress, elevation and happiness of man."[21] However naïve Carnegie's belief in the possibility of permanently establishing peace may sound, his confidence was symptomatic of the widespread belief in the salutary effect of large-scale philanthropy and of a systematic approach on a previously unimagined scale. The amassing of capital had already produced radical changes in American life when employed by the corporations that controlled it. It seemed only logical that the superrich, by reinvesting their fortunes for the public good, could infuse an extraordinary new level of vitality in the attack on society's ills by creating new structures for managing and administering this effort.

The transformation in American philanthropy gave a powerful stimulus to the fledgling social sciences. Poverty was only the most visible of the problems that it could help address. Other dysfunctions—local governmental inefficiencies and corruption, illiteracy, threats to public health, impediments to social mobility—all threatened to slow the growth that had led the United States to industrial dominance in a matter of decades. As Ely remembers it in his memoirs, despite growing pains, social scientists of his generation "were building up departments . . . schools and institutions (such as the National Consumers League, the Child Labor Committee, and the American Association for Labor Legislation) to make scientific work easier" for the next generation.[22] The generation was buoyed by the availability of new resources, optimism in their problem-solving ability, and faith in progress. No problem looked insurmountable. To guarantee a continuing partnership among money, expertise, and policy, investigators were successful in persuading donors to give them maximum flexibility and independence. They insured that foundations' charters remain vague so that trustees could adjust their programs to changing needs. The Russell Sage Foundation was dedicated "to the improvement of social and living conditions"; the Rockefeller Foundation "to promote the well-being of mankind."[23] As a result, American foundations became an important link that was missing in Europe among academic theory, sweeping and expensive investigations stimulated by this theory, and the process of governance based on the resulting findings.

By contrast, social scientists in much of Europe remained circumscribed by traditional academic boundaries. In Germany, Max Weber, who had pushed for social and economic reforms from within the *Verein für Sozialpolitik,* abandoned his lifelong efforts, discouraged as he was by the undisputed dominance of ill-informed bureaucrats in German affairs. In France, the tension between policymaking and social science remained unresolved; there was never any real overlap, for instance, between the politicians and reformers of the *Musée social* who fed the colonizing rhetoric of the Third Republic, and the more rarefied theoretical work around Emile Durkheim's *L'année sociologique.*[24]

THE SURVEY MOVEMENT, THE SEARCH FOR SOCIAL KNOWLEDGE, AND THE MEANING OF KNOWING

One of the first tasks facing newly endowed social scientists was to compile basic facts about society so that they could order them and present them in ways that others could act upon. The new philanthropic impulse thus found its best expression in funding the survey movement, an ambitious attempt to gather as much information as humanly possible on social problems.

The study of working-class social problems began in the 1870s with experts in social statistics like Carroll D. Wright conducting some of the first investigations. Officials at the Census Bureau followed suit. So did leading reformers. Robert DeForest, a lawyer who presided over the New York City Charity Organization Society, coauthored with architect and tenement-house reformer Laurence Veiller one of the most powerful investigations into housing of the Progressive Era.[25] It was DeForest who advised Margaret Olivia Sage and drafted her foundation's charter in 1907. Following such precedents, the Russell Sage Foundation, the most important among the agencies of the new philanthropy in the Progressive Era, pushed the idea of social investigation to a new level of technical excellence and imbued it with a new blend of science and conscience. Mrs. Sage, who established her foundation when already in her seventies, took great delight in doing good works in her late husband's name. A speculator in railroad securities, Russell Sage, partially by resisting all philanthropic endeavors, had made his wife the richest woman in America. Armed with his money, Mrs. Sage engaged in a posthumous family feud with her deceased husband for the purpose of improving social conditions.

The ethos of social science, which marked the creation of the Russell Sage Foundation, fueled much speculation in the press by social workers and professors. In the words of W. Frank Persons of the New York City Charity Organization Society, "the deepest significance of the Russell Sage Foundation lies in its bold purpose: not to attempt to bestow belated social justice—or charity—upon the individual about to be crushed by the pressure of his needs, but to discover why he has reached or even approached that end." Lee Frankel, of the United Hebrew Charities and soon of Metropolitan Life, was also impressed by the new emphasis on research and the opportunity for "calm, dispassionate and earnest inquiries into the causes of our social evils." Reformer Jacob Riis, famous for his lantern slide lectures delivered in New York City Sunday schools, remarked that even the best-trained and most intelligent philanthropists could not find the answers by themselves. Professors also lent their support. E. R. A. Seligman, from Columbia, who divided his time between economic science, public administration, work in social settlement, and the Society for Ethical Culture, saw the foundation as "a scientific laboratory of social experimentation" that "contain[s] within itself the germs of social reconstruction." Richard Ely, in turn, underscored that the time had come "to pass over from general exhortation to the careful scientific study of specific problems."[26]

Surveys were instruments of progress. Although leaders of the survey movement refrained from explicit references to their religious impulses, they borrowed from the Protestant Charity Organization Society its case study approach and casework method. The method of investigation remained partly linked to traditional philanthropy. It was designed for the understanding and improvement of local conditions. Paul Kellogg, who directed the landmark Pittsburgh survey of industrial life funded by Russell Sage in 1906, emphasized this point when addressing the Academy of Political Science in 1912. In his speech, Kellogg underscored the characteristics of the social survey: an exercise that concerned the conditions of human life in a given place. The survey looked at the circumstances of common people and rendered them in "graphic portrayal" in the service of advocacy and governmental reform. By putting the facts in front of the community, the survey became "a distinctive and powerful implement of democracy"—the result of both a civic and a scientific commitment. To Kellogg, the survey was a way to combat the corruption of political machines that had staffed local offices with people who lacked "civic pride." He advised his audience to rely on civic-minded officials in each town like the commissioner of public health, the superintendent of schools, the local judge, engineers, and other volunteers. The expert sanitarian and the average mother could join forces in, for instance, a campaign to clean up stables and insure the distribution of quality milk. As experts and citizens collaborated, the survey appealed to the "aroused social conscience" of the progressive generation by blending the efficiency movement with the impulse toward greater democracy.[27]

Kellogg was ecstatic when U.S. Steel stockholders began asking about working and living conditions as a result of the Pittsburgh survey. He got what he wanted: capitalists paying attention and realizing that addressing social conditions was important to both their conscience and their own well being. After the initial work of the Pittsburgh Survey, foundations like Russell Sage produced streams of surveys that investigated all aspects of working-class life in many places. Like a social history of the present, these surveys produced powerful images with their graphic, block-by-block maps of tuberculosis cases and charity recipients. By 1913, the Russell Sage Foundation library and its department of surveys and exhibits counted about 140 surveys in both rural and urban areas, covering such topics as neighborhood recreation, public health, delinquency, housing conditions, municipal administration, and school reform in all sections of the United States.

Russell Sage encouraged studies targeted at specific problems that were being considered for regulatory action. Thus, Mary Van Kleeck began her employment at the foundation by investigating women's work in the needle trades to assist in the regulatory process and the implementation of protective legislation. Another probe was launched to support the writing of legislation putting an immediate end to the predatory practices of loan sharks. Much of the new work was at the frontier of social science inquiry, especially in the education and child-helping divisions, where investigators relied on the latest psychological techniques, but also in demography (the measurement of infant mortality), criminal sociology, and other fields.[28] Hence the Russell Sage Foundation institutionalized both the "spiritual dynamics of social work" and a scientific program for performing it. Hastings H. Hart, the first director of the child-helping department, made the point well in a 1915 commencement address. Social science, Hart insisted, is becoming the "greatest of the sciences" with applications "not only to the immediate relief of suffering but to the development of individuals and families, and to practical efforts for the removal of the causes and the extirpation of pauperism, vice, and crime."[29]

Meanwhile, the Carnegie Corporation and the Rockefellers bankrolled other vast efforts of data collection. In 1920 they financed together Wesley Mitchell's National Bureau of Economic Research for the study of business cycles. They also funded such coordinating institutions as Charles Merriam's Social Science Research Council (SSRC) in 1923. The Brookings Institution, which combined the Institute for Government Research (est. 1916) and the Institute for Economics (est. 1922), was also set up in 1927 to collect objective economic data. There was a broad consensus in American intellectual circles on the eventual beneficial outcome of accumulating the facts of economy and society.[30] To the new experts, the ability to know and coordinate made solutions inevitable.

PRECEPTS OF SOCIAL INTELLIGENCE

Knowing, however, is not the same as understanding, nor, as we have come to learn, does it necessarily lead to problem solving. As early researchers found out, attempts to put social knowledge to the service of governance proved less than satisfying even when the best minds were called to collaborate. The large goal of creating a permanent and systematic relationship between the acquisition of knowledge and policymaking was therefore targeted in the 1920s by a new generation of investigators. Experts engaged in building this enlarged social science groped for new operating concepts to guide their efforts. They sought to develop social intelligence, a theoretical proposition that was, in Rockefeller Foundation official Edmund Day's words "a positive and vigorous" effort for "the understanding and control of social institutions and social processes in the solution of pressing social problems." Pursuing "social intelligence," that is, a successful synthesis of theory and action, would become the alternative that American twentieth-century social scientists offered to the nineteenth-century Americans' commitment to the idea of community.

Distinct from previous efforts of tackling social problems, social intelligence was neither uplift, as in the Charity Organization Society, nor efficiency, as in the halls of the American Society of Mechanical Engineers. It went beyond the descriptive limitations of the survey movement's scientific reporting to imply a grasp of cause and effect. "Social technology," a phrase sometimes used instead of "social intelligence," made it clear that the new knowledge would be used to fix things up. "Effective planning" would, then, "take the place of the existing aimlessness."[31]

It was under Beardsley Ruml's leadership that the Laura Spelman Rockefeller Memorial became the most instrumental of all the new agencies in supporting social science and pushing for a new understanding of the complexities of society through social intelligence. When James Angell left the Carnegie Corporation for the presidency of Yale, his young assistant Ruml went to work for the Rockefeller charities. Ruml had trained in psychology at the University of Chicago and worked on psychological testing during World War I. In 1918, he transformed the Laura Spelman Rockefeller Memorial, a modest social work program geared exclusively toward almsgiving, into a major social science agency, successfully guiding the Rockefeller charities into what had heretofore been for them the mined terrain of society.

Ruml led the memorial to invest the bulk of its resources in universities themselves in order to enlarge the pool of experts within the institutional matrix who could create fields of research that would be useful in building the theoretical foundations of social intelligence. To succeed, Ruml had to create a new "habit of mind" among researchers to attain first social intelligence and, then, "the betterment of the social order." He looked to fill a "basic need" in the field of "social welfare": the production of a body of "substantiated and widely accepted generalizations as to human capacities and motives and as to the behavior of human beings as individuals and in groups."

Ruml argued that the social sciences were still young—the first psychological laboratory for instance had been established in Leipzig only fifty years before—and a great deal of groundwork was yet to be done; the correlation coefficient had been invented only forty years before, and the measurement of "general intelligence" and other human traits only within the century.[32] Accordingly, the Laura Spelman Rockefeller Memorial funded more than $58,000,000 in research between 1922 and 1928. In the ten months between October 1926 and July 1927, the Memorial spent over $7 million, of which $5.2 was for social science at universities. Of the rest $743,000 went primarily to agencies of social work, $895,000 for child welfare, $224,500 for race relations, $54,000 for governmental agencies, and another quarter million dollars on miscellaneous local projects of the YMCA, YWCA, and various city and state organizations.[33]

Ruml also noted that the number of investigators for the work was small. The bulk of social science research was conducted at Chicago, Columbia, Harvard, Pennsylvania, Wisconsin, followed by California and Michigan, and then by Cornell, Hopkins, Illinois, Minnesota, Northwestern, Princeton, Stanford, and Yale. In 1922, these 15 schools had together 221 faculty members in economics, sociology, and political science, but a combined enrollment of only 137 Ph.D. candidates. Ruml realized that it was important to increase the number of able people in the social sciences if the promise of social intelligence was to be realized.

In favoring universities, Ruml wanted to entice professors and graduate students together to formulate new theories for a usable social science. He saw in universities stable organizations comprising a wide range of professional opinion with "scholarly and scientific standards of work." What was needed, he felt, was to permanently link university studies to the real world of observable "concrete social phenomena." This is why major beneficiaries of the new philanthropy were University of Chicago sociologists Robert Park, Ernest Burgess, and Albion Small, who took the city as their laboratory, as well as the anthropological investigations of Franz Boas at Columbia University, the studies of migration sponsored by Robert Yerkes of the National Research Council, and Howard Odum's investigation of life in the New South conducted at the University of North Carolina.[34]

By the time the Laura Spelman Rockefeller Memorial became a part of the Social Science Division at the Rockefeller Foundation in 1929, Ruml had become the dean of social sciences at Chicago.[35] Economist Edmund Day, who succeeded him after years at the Harvard Business School, tried to improve on his predecessor's definition of social intelligence. Whereas Ruml had emphasized basic knowledge, Day borrowed the paradigm of community decline from the French and German founding fathers of sociology. He saw social intelligence as an American alternative to their declension models, whether Emile Durkheim's shift from mechanic to organic solidarity or Ferdinand Tönnies's switch from Gemeinschaft to Gesellschaft. Social intelligence offered Americans hope against such descent. For Durkheim, modern industrial society was afflicted by a new sense of organic solidarity that took place outside the bonds of traditional community. Day, who partly adopted this position, went on to describe to an attentive audience of college graduates "the afflictions of modern competitive society" that could lead to anomie but affirmed his foundation's commitment to finding solutions. It was that conviction that had led philanthropists to move beyond the limited world of community to society at large. If social problems were to be cured at all, Day concluded, they would require "a high order of technical skill and social intelligence."[36] Day therefore posited that "social intelligence," which connotes both "understanding and mastery in dealing with the problems that confront society," would restore the grasp of a world no longer intelligible either through individualism or the bonds of communal solidarity.

THE SYNTHESIS OF SCIENCE AND CONSCIENCE

As social scientists grew in influence, the controversy over the place of the human sciences in social affairs only widened and with it the debate over motivation and purpose. To be sure, many social scientists promoted a limited if more rigorous view of their work by advocating a kind of social science sanitized by the methods of natural science. Often foundation officials added their authority to this safe view of the business of improving society. Taking the natural sciences as a possible model for the social sciences, Rockefeller Foundation officials noted that "whatever the forms under which genuine social intelligence is finally achieved, a more complete knowledge of social forms and social processes is bound to be indispensable. Science has penetrated far into the ways of the world of nature; it still stands on the frontier of the world of man. Objective, realistic, far-sighted studies of social phenomena are essential if the insights are to be gained which social planning requires."[37] But even the big money providers were skeptical that objectivity could be maintained or was even desirable. Witness Beardsley Ruml as he dedicated the Social Science Research Building at the University of Chicago. Although Ruml praised social science investigators' impartiality and their attempts to "eliminate judgments of value and as far as possible the presence of any ethical bias," he also pointed to the limitations of measurement for the study of "irrational factors."[38]

No matter how hard some twentieth-century investigators pushed the language and methods of natural science, the social sciences remained normative. Loyal to their religious heritage and moral goals, social scientists pursued not a technocratic and dispassionate social science but one intent on bringing about social improvement. They echoed John Dewey's fear of the standardization of the individual and responded to his call for the development of new "tools of social inquiry" to understand and manage new social and institutional mechanisms that would give an informed and increasingly educated citizenry the means of empowerment.[39]

The social intelligence movement in the 1920s added a new dimension to the evolution of social science. At Chicago, Hopkins, Columbia, and elsewhere in the late nineteenth century, social scientists had been instrumental in developing sociology, economics, and political science that had rendered the gentlemen and amateurs of the previous generation who met in the American Social Science Association irrelevant. The new professionals, however, never abandoned their commitment to better society. Although they had succeeded in creating institutions where full-time practitioners exercised their talents from within a community of peers, they were still committed to a program of moral and social improvement, and they continued to view their work as part of an evangelical mission. At Chicago, sociologist Albion Small designed courses such as "The Sociology of the New Testament" to introduce Divinity School students to the social sciences. Of the 190 doctorates in the social sciences granted by the University of Chicago Graduate School between 1893 and 1927, 25 were in "practical theology." The Divinity School, in turn, granted five doctorates in sociology during the same period.[40]

The influential voices of the 1920s, although no longer directly associated with the Social Gospel, were pursuing social intelligence and moral reform simultaneously. Thus Robert Park, who moved to the University of Chicago late in his life, did formulate an ecological theory of the city replete with biological references to population cycles and natural areas. His new commitment to a science of society, however, never shadowed his dedication to social reform. Park remained a crusader. As a journalist, he had explored the inner recesses of the city of Detroit. As Booker T. Washington's secretary, he had traveled the South to promote racial justice.[41] As a professor, he carried these predilections into the new sociology.

Charles Beard perhaps best articulated the relationship between scientific inquiry and moral purpose. Like Walter Lippmann, Beard had been involved in British socialist circles in his student years, an attachment that he would keep all his life. Beard had resigned his Columbia professorship during World War I in defense of academic freedom. He had enough literary talent to make a living writing American history, but he had always enough time to become involved in the most technical aspects of urban reform. Beard may have been the most consistent spokesman for social intelligence as social scientists of the 1920s understood it.

Beard's program was to promote ethical goals through scientific means. He insisted that "historic morals and common sense" would no longer do in a new age of systems and experts, where government had become "an economic and technical business on a large scale."[42] But he also claimed that the social sciences were above all "ethical sciences" and launched a sustained attack on the movement to make them neutral and objective. In an argument reminiscent of that Kellogg had made on behalf of the survey movement, Beard viewed science as absolutely necessary for informing democratic practice. Municipal research, Beard wrote, depended on "applying the methods of natural science to the study of government and administration, not by putting on sackcloth and ashes or by waiting in the streets for political messiahs." Because of Beard's work at the Rockefeller-funded Bureau of Municipal Research, Count Gotō, Tokyo's mayor, wasted no time seeking Beard's advice to help rebuild Tokyo after the disastrous 1923 earthquake. Beard took the job with the intent of replacing propaganda with "the spirit of free and objective inquiry which is the strength of all-conquering natural science." "Facts, facts, and still more facts, verified and tested" will help us lay a "firm foundation for sound judgment and wise action," Beard wrote of his Japanese experiment.[43]

The same belief in the emancipating power of science led Beard to support a World Bureau of Municipal Research to be sponsored by the League of Nations. There he argued that "if democracy is to reach its maximum efficiency and the forces of intelligence and humanity are to triumph over the drift of things," then administrative officials needed to have "the results of the world's experience" at their command, no matter where they lived. To that end, Beard also endorsed a proposal for intermunicipal cooperation made by Cuba at the Fifth Assembly of the League of Nations in September 1924. Such cooperation between the city governments of different nations would raise the general level of administrative efficiency. Keenly aware of the need to unite "power and responsibility," Beard never lost sight of his democratic goals. Social intelligence would not be enslaved to a science that would maintain the status quo.[44] Instead science provided the means to implement those social improvements that were needed as a precondition of democracy.

As prominent a member of the political science establishment as Charles Merriam, a founder of SSRC *and* a Chicago alderman, stood closer to Beard's views than either he or Beard was willing to admit at the time.[45] So did former Presbyterian minister Robert Lynd, who had made a mark as a Progressive muckraker by denouncing Rockefeller's mistreatment of workers in Midwestern oil fields. The bureaucratization of philanthropy, however, changed Lynd's career when he accepted an assignment from Rockefeller's Institute of Social and Religious Research to investigate the oil fields. Lynd later served as the first secretary of the Rockefeller-funded SSRC.[46] Armed with the concept of social intelligence, philanthropists and academicians alike proceeded to define priorities for both expanding knowledge and improving social conditions. Theirs was a normative social intelligence that occupied much energy, talent, and money in the 1920s and beyond.

FROM SOCIAL INTELLIGENCE TO POLICYMAKING

The institutional matrix for the social sciences was well established by the 1920s. Within it, investigators shared a missionary spirit and a commitment to use science to foster democracy. The social survey reached new heights with such important works as W. I. Thomas and Florian Znaniecki's *Polish Peasant in America* (1918–1920) and Robert and Helen Lynd's *Middletown* (1929). At Russell Sage, the bulk of the foundation's resources were now devoted to a vast *Regional Plan* for New York—the twentieth-century's single most important effort to put social intelligence techniques to the service of planning.[47] By decade's end, the social sciences had received an extraordinary boost from the funding coming from the new foundations. Taken together the foundations and research institutes primarily in New York but also in Washington had influence well beyond what they directly funded. They actually formed new cultural foci for processing ideas, projects, and money as well as bringing together investigators from different institutions. Their staff had a say in the conceptualization and support of much of what counted in social science, both basic and applied, in universities, professional associations, and government agencies. And they increased their influence by moving among these different institutions.

With success, however, entered a new type of investigator, increasingly referred to as "the service intellectual." Philosopher John Dewey had predicted his coming as a product of the new American environment for the social sciences. Dewey believed that the mutual distrust between intellectuals and other professionals, "a carry-over from the class societies of the Old World," was being increasingly discarded in America. As Dewey saw it, American social scientists "could promote both intellectual and social progress" in the larger institutional matrix by putting their knowledge to "work for the reform of society," without "a surrender of the business of thought, for the sake of getting busy at some so-called practical matter."[48] Theoretically, the service intellectual could take social intelligence beyond the level of planning to action without compromising ideals. Practically, the search for immediate solutions set severe limits on larger scientific or moral goals.

Improving government became one of the first priorities of the service intellectual. Foundation officials and scholars alike expressed the urgency of applying knowledge to this task. "The quality of governmental services [must] be raised to a higher level just as rapidly as is humanly possible," declared Rockefeller Foundation officials. With the best minds, from Charles Merriam to Charles Beard, promoting the marriage of science and government and working closely with the agents of the new philanthropy to make it happen, a new kind of knowledge penetrated American policymaking institutions and led to specific kinds of action. To implement such a program, the foundations helped make expertise available to local governments, to federal agencies, and to the White House.

In attacking the problems of governance, the social sciences became subject to the forces of politics. Conversely, social intelligence began to infuse the core of politics as the pyramid of expertise that was being established across the nation at all levels of government culminated in Herbert Hoover's efforts to give social scientists a central role in his "associative" state. Rockefeller, Carnegie, and Russell Sage Foundation officials contributed to Hoover-sponsored committees from his days as commerce secretary to the presidency.[49]

Social scientists acknowledged that the transition from knowledge acquisition to policy formulation was difficult primarily because all the information needed to make policy was hard to come by, and they were not ready. Presenting *Recent Social Trends*, a series of reports undertaken in the late twenties at Hoover's behest, investigators explained that American life had become everywhere more integrated and interdependent, although not always smoothly or completely. They suggested that more information and a better understanding of social complexity would eventually produce a more harmonious society.[50] Scholars on the committee were struggling to master the complexities of social knowledge and at the same time to formulate policy initiatives.

The Great Depression years did much to give urgency to the agenda of policymakers. They could hardly wait until all the facts were in. As Edmund Day, of the Rockefeller Foundation, put it, the "costs of demoralization, broken health, disorganized families, neglected children, lowered living standards, permanent insecurity, impaired morale, as well as financial distress" were calling for urgent solutions.[51] Capitalism's own survival was at stake. Accordingly, social scientists attempted to provide a scientific base for partnership among government, business, and labor.[52] Meanwhile Rockefeller Foundation officials continued to stress that social intelligence would help discard well-entrenched but outdated views about individualism.

Investigators responded to the pressure by moving away from broadly defined social inquiries toward research designed specifically to serve policy. But policymakers brought to the table a priori conclusions they wanted social science to support. Some, like Hoover, clung to the idea of building cooperative associations that preserved voluntarism. Others, like planner Rexford Tugwell, were prepared to discard older notions of private property. Still others would rather allow interest groups to influence public policy as would be done in New Deal agricultural planning.[53] The time had come for social scientists nationwide to transcend these conflicting views, to follow the Wisconsin example and focus on the specific tasks of creating unemployment reserves, old age pensions, accident and sickness insurance, slum clearance, low-cost housing, and the like. Social scientists responded with prescriptions that balanced their continuous search for a science of society with a new ethics of mediation among politicians, bureaucrats, and the public. By the late thirties, 2,500 social scientists were employed in federal agencies.[54] And according to the authors of the FDR-sponsored reports on agricultural policy, the president himself had "broadened the function of the expert in modern society, who must not only discover truth, but also guide, plan, and program."[55]

The Great Depression led social scientists to focus extensively on the meaning of prosperity, which many had come to take for granted in the 1920s. The task of restoring and maintaining a political economy of abundance became a defining feature of an American social science. Early in the century, economist Simon Patten had emerged from the Social Gospel to conceptualize abundance as an attribute of the American century. As Patten had explained it in his *The Social Basis of Religion* (1911), economic scarcity produced both the old economic thinking and the old individualist Christianity, with its emphasis on sin, sorrow, and suffering. Modern industrial society instead required cooperation to distribute the social surplus and eliminate poverty.[56] From his chair at the University of Pennsylvania, Patten's ideas had their greatest influence on a diverse body of students who pursued careers in social and government work. They ranged from Edward T. Devine, who was appointed general secretary of the New York City Charity Organization Society in 1896, to Frances Perkins, who was a social worker before becoming industrial commissioner of the State of New York and labor secretary from 1932 to 1945, to Rexford Tugwell, who became FDR's assistant secretary of agriculture, director of the Resettlement Administration, and governor of Puerto Rico.[57] Given these antecedents, it is clear that the service intellectual was also the product of the early social science emphasis on the Social Gospel as much as the increasing technical sophistication of the new social sciences.

Thus was written into American social science the spirit of Protestant reform. Social science at the service of policymaking, however, was a retreat from the broad promise of social intelligence. In the aftermath of the Great Depression, the fate of the social sciences became increasingly tied to the decision-making process. Research was devoted to creating "a body of principle to guide action." Armed with the concept of social intelligence, social scientists had held the promise of bringing about a new conception of society. By concentrating on formulating policy for the governing of the parts, social scientists ran the risk of losing sight of the whole and leaving the status of the individual as well as of the various social groups uncertain. They could no longer afford a large and detailed strategy of intelligence. Under the banner of policy, the social sciences became more relevant but only to the governing process. It was perhaps unavoidable but the price to pay was dear. Serving policy meant abandoning the full array of possibilities embedded in social intelligence.

CHAPTER THREE

INVENTING THE AVERAGE AMERICAN

The rights of the whole can be no more than
the sum of the rights of individuals.
THOMAS JEFFERSON[1]

In a trend to develop a theoretically neutral field of applied statistics that paralleled the search for social intelligence, the United States became the land of human engineering. With an agenda that was slanted toward the moment and toward generating easily communicable results, the influence of applied statistics on a range of social sciences, first among them psychology, turned out to be critical. Human engineers created guidelines for selecting personnel, organizing hierarchies, selling goods, and winning elections. If only psychologists could get at the psyche of not just individuals but groups, starting with factory workers and continuing on to large masses of employees and consumers, they could improve the effectiveness of both private and public organizations.

So vigorous were America's human engineers in giving concrete form to an abstract vision of individuals and community that the concepts and methods they put forth came to define mass society. It is largely their theory of an average American and the techniques of measurement they invented to define such a hypothetical human being that accounts for our understanding of modern society as "mass." Constructing a democratic mass society, however, was no easy proposition, involving as it did a significant departure from ideals of individualism, voluntary associations, and localism inherited from the nineteenth century.

INDIVIDUALS AS STATISTICS

The intellectual impulse to order the mental universe of Americans statistically came initially from Europe. Since the eighteenth century, much European social science had as one of its goals quantifying human behavior. From England, Jeremy Bentham's formulas for "felicific calculus," which aimed at maximizing pleasure and minimizing pain had been, in Horace Kallen's words, "the first powerful philosophy of human nature expressive of the growing importance of counting and accounting which came with the industrial revolution."[2] Among other pioneers of modern social statistics, Belgian savant Adolphe Quetelet, a disciple of the French philosopher Condorcet, promoted the statistical study of human behavior. By collecting large numbers of observations for the fitting of normal curves, he conceptualized and coined the term *l'homme moyen*.

Quetelet's founding efforts were followed by the brilliant work in England of both Sir Francis Galton, Charles Darwin's first cousin and the father of eugenics, and his disciple Karl Pearson. The two perfected the study of statistical distributions, regressions (reversions as they were then called), and correlations. They invented and promoted the methodology of modern statistical science.[3] That Galton was motivated by his lifelong effort to prove racial differences scientifically and, in his words, "check the birth rate of the unfit," long before such efforts were finally discredited by the Nazis' crimes, should not take away his achievement in bringing modern statistics to bear on social analysis.

The new ideas about statistical distribution crossed the Atlantic quickly where they were to flourish in ways unfathomable in Europe. However influential they may have been in elite circles, European pioneers of social engineering rarely moved beyond the rarefied world of learned societies. Their *homme moyen* presented a challenge only to the elite "reasonable man" as a reference point in the "search for mechanical rules of rational belief and actions."[4] American social scientists, however, translated statistical knowledge into methods of managing social aggregates from within the new institutions of mass society.

From Cambridge, Massachusetts, Harvard psychologist and philosophy professor William James expressed his dismay as early as 1893 at the thought that individuality was being reduced to a series of quantifiable traits defined in reference to a statistical system. James described the conflict between two versions of the individual. The older one was based on the concept of the whole person capable of full interaction with others. The new one, however, was a product of non-introspective, behavioral analysis. In a measured universe, individuals became statistics, points in a normal distribution massing around, or deviating from, a population mean. James sensed early on that real and tangible human beings were being replaced by an abstract and impalpable average person. It would be only a matter of time for that abstract average character to be perceived as typical and become the norm. As James put it, "an unlearned carpenter of my acquaintance once said in my hearing: 'there is very little difference between one man and another; but what little difference there is, is very important.' "[5] James understood that twentieth-century individualism, should it survive the crisis he was diagnosing, would be only a faint image of its predecessors.

He was right. American human engineers replaced the common man close to Abraham Lincoln's heart with the theoretical average man. What was at stake was nothing less than social control on a grand scale. Early in the twentieth century, social control did not carry today's essentially negative connotation of devising "mechanisms of imposed compliance."[6] It was not necessarily viewed as antidemocratic or antithetical to free choice. The term reflected instead a faith in the ability to regulate individuals for the improvement of society or, as sociologist Edward Ross would have phrased it, to create "harmony," however naïve that notion may seem in retrospect.[7] Blind to the danger of mismeasure (or self-serving measure), most social scientists were optimistic. By the early 1890s, John Dewey had sharpened his vision of a new social science that would allow the individual to "really participate, as an organ and member, in the life of the whole organism."[8] Herbert Croly exemplified the new attitude in the first sentence of *The Promise of American Life* (1909) by pointing to the nationalism of the "average" American.

Among statistically oriented social scientists, psychologists took the lead. With the United States entering the First World War, several succeeded in convincing the Army to let them sift and sort a large number of recruits. American psychologists, who had heretofore applied their skills only to individual cases or selected groups of school children or office personnel, saw in the nation at war not only their opportunity to improve the functioning of the Army and that of society but also of legitimizing their profession. The problem that they tackled for the Army was the measurement of intelligence. There was nothing obvious about what such an abstract term meant, how to measure it, or how to distinguish a quantity called "intelligence" from aptitude or achievement. By 1917, the idea of intelligence testing had been analyzed for some thirty-five years by major theorists in England, France, and Germany as well as the United States. The idea underwent drastic revisions in the short span of a generation, beginning with Francis Galton's opening in 1882 of a laboratory in London to conduct physical and mental measurements. Because he thought that there should be a correlation between dexterity and intelligence, Galton focused, with Pearson's assistance, on sensory acuity and reaction time tests.[9] It was, however, the American James McKeen Cattell who first used the term "mental tests." Presenting a series of sensory motor, reaction time, mental imagery tests given individually, Cattell accepted Galton's idea that idiots were physically slow and clumsy in their movements.[10] But as various subsequent tests in schools showed no significant correlation between his measurements and students' achievements or teachers' assessments, support for the enterprise waned.

A French psychologist, Alfred Binet, reoriented the field decisively. Binet and his assistant Victor Henri, who wanted to help disabled children, focused on measuring abstract reasoning abilities that separate intelligent from unintelligent children: memory, mental imagery, imagination, attention, comprehension, suggestibility, and moral sentiments. By 1905, some of Binet's results correlated well with both students' performance and evaluations. Binet also arranged problems in order of difficulty to get a general idea of mental development. In 1908, Binet and medical doctor Théodore Simon published a new, expanded test, where they grouped problems according to the age at which they were commonly solved. It was Binet and Simon who first used the term "mental age," and they made initial attempts, in addition to separating out subnormal children, to devise methods for ranking normal children.[11] A great many American psychologists returned to work on intelligence testing following Binet's new lead. Among them was Henry H. Goddard, who held a Ph.D. from Clark University and became director of the research laboratory of the Vineland Training School (New Jersey) for "feeble-minded" children in 1906.[12] By 1910, Goddard published an American version of Binet's 1908 test and tested public school children while proselytizing for intelligence testing in front of educational associations, social workers, and medical men. Goddard's efforts renewed American interest in testing.

Psychologists advanced their own careers by serving many bureaucratic interests. Enthusiasm for mental tests spread as psychologists offered competing and reputedly more accurate revisions of testing and scoring. In addition to tracking school children, they began advising companies on the hiring and assignment of workers at various levels and devising mental tests geared to specific occupations. German-American Harvard professor Hugo Münsterberg developed techniques in 1912 to identify the most reliable conductors for the Boston elevated railway company and the most effective traveling salesmen for the American Tobacco Co.[13] Meanwhile the number of universities offering training in testing increased. Walter V. Bingham, who earned his Ph.D. in psychology from Chicago in 1908 and taught at Columbia and Dartmouth, organized the first specialized division of applied psychology at the Carnegie Institute of Technology in 1915 and a Bureau of Salesmanship Research a year later. The professional networks of the expanded institutional matrix offered possibilities for recruiting and joint projects. Thus Walter Dill Scott, who, like Cattell, had earned his doctorate at Leipzig under Wilhelm Wundt and had borrowed much from Binet, left Northwestern University, where he was teaching advertising, to join Bingham in Pittsburgh. Scott also collaborated with Columbia educational psychologist Edward Thorndike on testing employees of Metropolitan Life in 1916. That year Thorndike was consulted by the Civil Service Commission about vocational testing.[14]

All this work and activity culminated in the "intelligence quotient" or IQ ratio, proposed by German psychologist William Stern in 1912 but improved by Lewis Terman, another graduate from Clark who had completed a dissertation on gifted children. Stern divided a quantity called "Intelligenzalter," a term his translator, G. M. Whipple, rendered as "mental age," by the "chronological age." Terman, then on the faculty at Stanford University, proposed to multiply this ratio by 100 to remove fractions and call it IQ. In 1916, Terman published the Stanford Revision of the Binet-Simon test that became standard in the United States, a compromise between Galton's insistence on quantification and Binet's attention to individual characteristics, and presented a well-organized series of instructions for administering and scoring tests.[15] It was also Terman's accomplishment, in *The Measurement of Intelligence* (1916), to increase the sensitivity of the Binet test so that it no longer just separated the subnormal from the normal. Terman's contribution was the quantification of a composite variable called intelligence across the whole range of the population, and the introduction of a single quality of "intelligence."

The stage was thus set by the time of the U.S. entry into the war for psychologists to make their influence felt in managing society. Mass mobilization gave them the opportunity to sell their newly discovered skills to the Army, which itself was searching for ways to absorb its hundreds of thousands of new recruits. Nonetheless, it was still quite a coup for the shy Robert Yerkes to persuade the Adjutant General's Office to create a psychology division under the Surgeon General. Yerkes, a disciple of Münsterberg and a respected animal psychologist who would teach at Minnesota and Yale after being denied tenure at Harvard, was president of the American Psychological Association at the time the United States entered the war. He used the personal backing of NRC's founder, astrophysicist George Ellery Hale, to promote the psychologists' project. Yerkes displayed enough persuasive skill to convince the War Department to use intelligence testing to place recruits in appropriate jobs. He also secured the collaboration of his initially unwilling colleagues, Scott and Bingham, who were establishing a distinct Committee on Classification of Personnel in the Army.[16] Once in place, he persuaded numerous reluctant officers to relinquish some of their prerogatives to a group of unknown psychologists to give the program a chance to succeed.

The Army testers' real innovation was the development, not of testing itself, but of mass testing. Their agenda was very different from their European counterparts. In France, Binet, Simon, and a handful of other psychologists had worked with small groups of children. The Binet-Simon test took a long time, required one-on-one testing, and had clear therapeutic implications. American applied psychologists, however, were not attempting to isolate handicapped individuals to treat them but to manage large social aggregates. The Army program, no matter its flaws, was the first experiment in the social science management of mass society.

The program brought together most of the luminaries in the field. Holding the rank of major, Yerkes was director of the Division of Psychological Testing. Clarence Yoakum, who had received his Ph.D. in animal psychology from Chicago in 1908, served as Yerkes's chief assistant and rose also to the rank of major. So did Lewis Terman. Among the commissioned psychologists, Scott would be awarded the Distinguished Service Medal as director of the Army's Committee on Classification of Personnel. There were also many civilian consultants from other areas of the institutional matrix. Bingham, from Carnegie Tech, contributed to the development of the tests. So did Thorndike, from Columbia, both as a civilian consultant for the Army and a member of the NRC's original 1917 committee.[17] Even though they were often short of staff, nowhere else was such an experiment in ordering a large human universe attempted. The one hundred and fifteen officers who were commissioned in the Sanitary Corps psychological service managed, with the help of several hundred enlisted men trained in the school for military psychology, to test 1,726,966 Army recruits.

Given the experimental quality of intelligence testing and the need to develop, administer, and interpret tests quickly, psychologists themselves had a hard time knowing exactly what they were doing. One of the first problems that psychologists needed to solve was a logistical one: how to test large numbers of recruits efficiently so that they could all be assigned an intelligence ranking. Once they made the decision to test all recruits, the psychologists realized that a group test should optimally last less than twenty minutes but no more than an hour in total elapsed time.[18] They created three tests. The "A" test, a preliminary examination developed by Thorndike and administered to 139,843 recruits, proved quite reliable for identifying men of average intelligence but less reliable for men at either end of the spectrum. The psychologists then developed two new tests to improve on their initial results and to identify incompetent, psychotic, and incorrigible men as well as to select men talented for special tasks. Terman and Yoakum produced the second test, dubbed the "Alpha," for all literate recruits, with exercises in reading, grammar, and arithmetic ability as well as quizzes in analogies and general knowledge. It would be administered to 1,149,596 recruits. The third test, the "Beta," consisting of construction puzzles, was designed for illiterates or non-English speakers and given to 483,469 men.[19]

Theoretically, the results should have correlated positively with officers' evaluations of enlisted men and also with the Stanford-Binet intelligence scores. But the speed with which psychologists constructed the tests, especially the "Beta," produced skepticism about the outcome. With such unrefined measurements, as Yerkes himself concluded, "only large crude differences" could be recognized as "significant." Nobody, however, expected the shocking and spurious result that the average mental age of draftees was only 13. That a full 47 percent of white draftees and 87 percent of blacks were considered "morons," a term coined by Goddard, was at first a national embarrassment and ultimately led to the tests being dropped.[20] It also made it hard to decide what to salvage from the enterprise.

The psychologists abandoned the initial goals of carefully matching specific intelligence levels with opportunities. Instead psychologists found themselves increasingly working on ways to group recruits into cohorts of average, above-average, and below-average intelligence and correlating these groups with rank. In a symptomatic move, they presented distributions and averages in each Army rank. Thus emerged the average commissioned officer (with the rank of major and under), the average sergeant, the average corporal, and the average private.[21] By creating the average soldier simultaneously in both the singular and the plural, they promoted not just the idea of a great social average but of diverse averages depending on categories and ways of dividing up a given human universe. It would be only a matter of time before social scientists in other institutions would follow suit. This turn of events, also initially unpredicted, is of great significance, for it would eventually lead to the widespread computation of stratified and weighted averages in managing employees or selecting students. Another surprising but lasting outcome is that American psychologists gave credibility to the abstract idea of average intelligence without ever really saying what it was.

Ultimately, the balancing of intelligence within regiments was the only significant contribution of the testing program and, according to General Order No. 74 of August 1918, the only one the Army recognized. There was some appeal in the idea of forming regiments with a statistically normal distribution of intelligence. The psychologists emphasized the "great center of intelligence spectrum." They recognized that "certain branches [of the service] might require a relatively normal distribution of mental ability, with the majority of cases massing about the average and a gradual dropping off in either direction" while others might require "a bimodal distribution."[22]

Despite all the limitations of the Army experiment, the experience gave psychologists influence and visibility. As a result, intelligence testing resurfaced in all sorts of industrial, office, and school environments in the 1920s. Critics were quick to voice loud concerns about what had actually been measured during the war. Walter Lippmann, who believed in the possibilities of testing the American population, attacked the psychologists in a widely publicized debate on the subject published in *The New Republic* during 1922–23. He argued that they certainly could not prove that they were measuring intelligence. He raised a host of unanswered questions: How reliable were the figures? Were the recruits representative of the entire American adult male population? Did the tests reveal hereditary patterns of intelligence? What was the role of the environment? And he rightly asserted that "if the tester could make good his claim" of matching intelligence and performance, "he would soon occupy a position of power which no intellectual has held since the collapse of theocracy."[23]

In response, Terman argued at length that whatever "intelligence" was, it was unevenly distributed across society. Everyone, he insisted, had different amounts of the same thing. A genius had quantitatively more intelligence than a moron. He admitted that native intelligence could be an elusive concept but went on, like Yerkes in circular fashion, to equate intelligence with "the sort of ability that is measured by these examinations."[24] Terman and Yerkes believed in a single line of intelligence along which all individuals could be plotted and then assigned socially useful tasks and educational tracks. Their method proved resistant to criticism because they could point to the statistical evidence of a normal distribution constructed from quantifiable observations and massing about the average.

Another reason for the acceptance of Terman's and Yerkes's approach is that it seemed to support the prejudices of the age. Millions of Americans were sympathetic in the 1920s to the resurgent Ku Klux Klan and "100 percent Americanism." They saw in the Army experiment plenty of ammunition to support sterilization of the unfit, immigration restriction, and a quota system. Carl Brigham, who had served under Yerkes before joining the Princeton faculty, spared no effort in blaming the decline of American intelligence on "racial admixture" in his *Study of American Intelligence* (1923). Prefaced by Yerkes, it was published during the debates on the immigration restriction act of 1924. As Steven J. Gould has forcefully shown in *The Mismeasure of Man,* American psychologists gave scientific backing to the superiority of white, Anglo-Saxon, middle-class culture, blind as they were to the pluralistic process of cultural adaptations and creations.[25] The war emergency, and its demand for uncompromising loyalty, had only reinforced that trend.

The statistical practices of intelligence testers were resisted by numerous commentators besides Lippmann. A number of Americans found it hard to leave behind a civic culture based on individualism and resisted the organizational constraints and new systems of social control that they perceived were limiting individualism. Harking back to an older America, they reified nineteenth-century ideals of self-realization. When Charles Lindbergh crossed the Atlantic at the height of the prosperity brought about by the corporate reorganization of the country, the animating principle that American journalists saw in the *Spirit of St. Louis* was that of old-fashioned individualism. Lindbergh was heralded in the press as the "lineal descendant" of Daniel Boone and Davy Crockett.[26] This nostalgic allegiance to the spirit of individualism was widespread even among the supporters of the new social sciences. As staunch an advocate of the engineering spirit as Herbert Hoover worried that "a man in the mass does not think but only feels" (1922).[27] Even John Dewey seemed to risk losing his optimism. Dissatisfied by the turn social science was taking, in *The Public and Its Problems* (1927) he called for the wholesale development of new "tools of social inquiry" to manage new institutional mechanisms for production, consumption, learning, and leisure. Soon after, he conceded defeat in *Individualism Old and New* (1930) by admitting that "quantification, mechanization and standardization" had "invaded mind and character, and subdued the soul to their own dye."[28]

Indeed, the tide seemed to turn against those who longed for nineteenth-century individualism. In 1927, the year Lindbergh landed at Le Bourget, political scientist André Siegfried expressed his French contempt for what he considered the abuse of psychology for the purpose of human engineering, which he saw as a characteristically American phenomenon. He pointed to the fascination that American eugenicists had with intelligence testing as long as it justified their sterilization campaign. Siegfried also reflected sententiously on the Americans' "love of the automatic." Mistaking the experts' claims of control for actual hold on their subjects and ignoring the enormous occupational and geographic mobility of large segments of the American people, the French professor believed that the results of the intelligence tests were "mechanically inscribed on each personal record, and ever after they pursue the unfortunate victim like a police record that can never be effaced. This test decides whether a boy is capable of becoming an artist, a book-keeper, or only a messenger, and whether he is likely to be advanced in the future or permanently kept in an inferior position." To this American reductionism, Siegfried opposed the French "spirit of finesse," a distinction he may have borrowed from Pascal's famous contrast between the spirit of finesse and that of geometry.[29] But had Siegfried not been romanticizing the French system, he might have appreciated the hard reality that managing a mass society must begin by taking its measure, even if that measure is rough.

The most direct effect of this large controversy was not the renunciation of testing but a retreat from measuring something as complex as intelligence and a reemphasis on evaluating individual predisposition for specific tasks, one of the initial goals of the Army experiment. Walter Dill Scott had argued all along that tests should measure only a variety of "common sense" traits that would render one fit or unfit for a certain job, without necessarily relating these specific vocational abilities to a general IQ. Psychologists finally imposed their methods when they advanced their tools as capable of countering the power of the monied elite in controlling access to the best institutions of higher education. If conducted with appropriate professional standards, their tests would help single out promising people who would not otherwise have found access to these universities.[30]

Another characteristic of the psychologists' program that escaped most critics with the exception of Horace Kallen was the fact that intelligence testers never "in any way" appealed to "introspection."[31] This last observation is of critical importance in understanding the management of mass society. Psychologists made inroads by advancing methods applicable to groups within society precisely because they neither wished nor were able, with the tools they used, to penetrate any individual in depth. Kallen might have added that psychologists were constructing a norm that was deceptively simple. Their theoretical average American became central to the functioning of society while simultaneously remaining a mystery. As the "average American" became more accepted, Americans wanted to act more like the average but they also struggled to measure the distance separating them from such a fictitious character.

BEHAVIORISM

The experience of Army psychologists during the First World War overlapped other efforts in psychology. Having a method for measuring "intelligence" was only one element of a much vaster social program of applied psychology. Altering the market required empirical knowledge of all society, an effort that preoccupied a growing corps of behavioral psychologists, economists, and sociologists. They found a terrain fertile for experimentation in the rise of middle-class Americans who, if they did not initially conform to the ideal average that the social scientists were creating, slowly adjusted to the idea of mass society.

Because behaviorism led the way in attempting to manipulate desires and control instincts, it stands as a complement to the statistical tools of social control. Darwinism had made the study of animal behavior a respectable scholarly pursuit, and behaviorists began with laboratory experiments on animals. Most psychologists who had worked in testing for the Army had received some training in animal psychology. Laboratory experiments, however, were not enough to fulfill the psychologists' ambitions. Just as the mental testers had moved to the Army, schools, factories, and offices, the behaviorists were not satisfied with their growing influence on social science disciplines. With the encouragement of business, they turned to consumers and the mass media. They devised selling campaigns guided both by manipulative strategies of their own devising and their analysis of data on potential buyers.

The most important figure in twentieth-century applied psychology, behaviorist John B. Watson, had trained with biologist Jacques Loeb at Chicago and, as a close friend of Robert Yerkes, had also worked in the Army testing program.[32] Psychology, he wrote in 1917, establishes "laws or principles for the control of human action so that it can aid organized society in its endeavors to prevent failures in adjustments."[33] Psychology was to Watson a way to predict which stimuli or, when complex factors were involved, which "situations" would provoke the responses needed to make "adjustments." Because the results, analyzed scientifically, "should fit any cultural age," Watson and his followers rejected outright any form of culturally bound introspection. Subjective terms like "sensation," "perception," "memory," "consciousness," "imagery," "feeling," and "thought" were purged from their vocabulary. Only stimulus and response remained.[34] In this scientific program for behaviorism, Watson insisted, there was little room for "the setting of social standards" and none at all for that of moral standards. He would have the opportunity to apply his theory to himself as his distinguished academic career came to an abrupt end when forced out of Johns Hopkins University in 1920 for an extramarital affair. Watson measured his heart beat to assess the intensity of his love for the young undergraduate who was to become his second wife.[35]

As Watson formulated his behaviorist program for a nonintrospective applied psychology, a group of his colleagues created the *Journal of Applied Psychology* in 1917. Although G. Stanley Hall, the founder of the American Psychological Association, assumed its editorship, he was already too old to take an active part in the program.[36] Hall surrounded himself with younger colleagues, and the journal brought intelligence testers and behaviorists together. The journal became a leading organ for the increasing number of specialists in intelligence testing, personnel issues, market research, and opinion polling spread across the institutional matrix and published such familiar personalities as Walter Bingham, Walter Dill Scott, Carl Seashore, and Edward Thorndike, all of whom had been prominent in the Army program. As the first issue announced, the journal was devoted to the application of psychology to vocational activities, especially problems of business, to the problems of mental diagnosis and choice of a career, and to the psychology of everyday activities. Therapy of individuals was explicitly excluded from a field devoted to the management of social aggregates. Typical articles analyzed such topics as consumer responses to advertising, the predictive value of general intelligence tests in the selection of clerks, or the influence of type form on reading speed. Other professional organs created at about the same time were the *Journal of Educational Psychology* and the *Journal of Personnel Research*. On the editorial boards of these journals, psychologists like Lewis Terman, Walter Bingham, Clarence Yoakum, and L. L. Thurstone would interact with other members of the institutional matrix like Alfred Flinn of the Engineering Foundation, Wesley Mitchell of the National Bureau of Economic Research, Joseph H. Willits of the Wharton School of Commerce and Finance, and Mary Van Kleeck from the Russell Sage Foundation.[37] Applied, nonintrosective psychology, then, excluded therapy, avoided social standards, did not address moral norms, but focused on the statistical study of measurable facts and traits and the manipulation of aggregates. Behaviorists and other applied psychologists limited themselves to predicting responses to given stimuli. What was, then, the importance of a science with these specific goals as it became widely applied to many sectors of American society? How far could the experiment go?

When fired from Hopkins, Watson made his services available to the large J. Walter Thompson advertising company. His advertising career gives us part of the answer. It was under Watson's partly symbolic guidance that the business of advertising claimed that it could become the business of scientifically exploiting "the bedrock human drives of love, fear, and rage"—applicable to all human beings—for the control of desires and purchasing habits.[38] Once hired by J. Walter Thompson, Watson's job became to find ways to make desires fit products. Some of Watson's advertising campaigns became at least on the surface textbook cases of manipulative strategies. Watson used images that prompted fear, rage, or love to stimulate emotional reactions favorable to the products he wanted to sell in competitive fields where there was little difference in usefulness or reliability among many products. Thus to sell Pebesco toothpaste, Watson's ads played on women's fear of being unattractive; they suggested to women that it was acceptable to smoke to enhance their sex appeal but only if they used Pebesco toothpaste to counter smoker's breath. With the success of the Pebesco and many similar campaigns, it seemed clear that desires could indeed be manipulated. But despite the behaviorist claims, the tools for mass manipulation remained crude. "Psychology as the Behaviorist Views It" never was the kind of new *Origin of Species* that Watson claimed for it. The possibility of manipulating the entire public may have been tempting but the results were unpredictable.

A safer and certainly more lucrative strategy in a mass market was to find something like an average, or the lowest common denominator, or the most attractive proposition to the largest number of people; in other words, to make individual behavior, modes of interaction, and group identification converge and make the world, to use Watson's own formulation, "a simpler place to adjust to." Since American consumers were becoming increasingly middle class, behaviorist campaigns were intentionally adapted to the growth of the middle class. Witness the famous campaign that Watson helped launch for Johnson & Johnson baby powder in 1924, a class-conscious campaign designed to appeal to "young, white, upwardly mobile middle-class" Americans and the millions who wanted to be like them.[39] Preliminary marketing surveys indicated that the total market for baby powder was 70 percent of American homes, primarily middle-class homes including those of modest means. Of these, already 50 percent bought Johnson & Johnson. To expand market share, Watson targeted this middle-class market. He then proceeded by playing again on the fear of young mothers not doing the right thing. He stressed the purity of the product. He told the young mothers not to listen to their grandmothers but to experts who had scientifically determined the product's health benefits. Manipulation, however, yielded to the search for the most likely customer. The potential buyers drove the campaign as much as the advertisers.

Middle-class identity was critical in the baby powder campaign. Because baby powder is best used sparingly, doctors and hospitals warned mostly uneducated mothers of possible irritation to the infant's skin and recommended they use vaseline or mineral oil. As one of the investigators in Watson's team at J. Walter Thompson put it, it would prove difficult to convince "lower class" mothers to buy the product when middle-class physicians told them to use oil instead. In designing the campaign, Watson consequently instructed field workers to bypass such questionable markets as slum districts and black neighborhoods. Investigations in the South confirmed that it was best to skip "negro homes" even though this meant losing about one million of an estimated ten million children under four years of age. Corporate America would not recognize African Americans as potential consumers in the mass market until the late 1940s. It was also clear to advertising field workers that many ethnic neighborhoods were poor bets. A Philadelphia dealer they investigated, located "on the edge of Chinatown," sold "practically no baby powder." Yet, some immigrants were real prospects. Cleveland dealers reported that Italians frequently asked for Johnson's Baby Powder "calling it Red Cross." So did better paid working-class families. As a dealer from South Bend, in the region of the Studebaker factories, reported, "Men buy shaving talc, women bath powder," so he could sell baby powder when appropriately packaged.

The ad campaign was therefore targeted at middle-class mothers, primarily the readers of *Woman's Home Companion, Ladies' Home Journal, Pictorial Review, American, Good Housekeeping,* and the *Delineator.* As many as 25,000 mothers had paid a surcharge when subscribing to *Good Housekeeping* in 1924 to receive monthly pamphlets issued by its baby department. Altogether 150,000 mothers had been enrolled by that journal's baby department. In other words, regardless of Watson's special skills as a behaviorist to manipulate desires and instincts, his campaign drew strength primarily from pitching the product to already well-understood middle-class inclinations. The advertisers worked with an image of an average housewife thoroughly familiar with one of the twenty-eight editions of Dr. L. Emmett Holt's manual, *The Care and Feeding of Children.* That book was, according to J. Walter Thompson's marketing studies, "a catechism for mothers and nurses of children, the Bible, one might say, by which millions of American children have been reared."[40] If Johnson & Johnson could sell at the lower end of the market, it was because workers and immigrants wanted to emulate the white middle class, perhaps even to gain middle-class status through emulation. The safest selling strategy was therefore to find the most likely consumer in a middle-class home and appeal to his or her taste. By targeting the most promising group of buyers, the marketing manipulator was also a follower.

Watson promoted the behaviorist views that one could determine customers' responses by appealing to universal instincts such as fear. In practice, the campaigns he helped design were based rather on the tacit recognition that such instincts were shaped by group mores, specifically those of an expanding American middle class and those who aspired to membership. Watson's work is better understood as an attempt to find the convergence between universal responses to stimuli and class/culture-bound adaptations to economic and social change. Ultimately, behaviorism as practiced in the advertising industry became a prisoner of the fictional average customer it had endorsed.[41] If behaviorism could make significant inroads in American culture, it was not because American behaviorists could manipulate everybody, as they claimed, but because they "neither wanted to nor could handle complex problems of cognitive processes" and quickly reached the limits on manipulation set by their self-imposed methodology.[42]

MEASURING PUBLIC OPINION

While sales executives and advertisers attempted to manage the market to suit the average American's aspirations, so did politicians and news organizations. They all came to rely on public opinion polls pioneered by market researchers for finding out what their customers wanted. In contrast to the surveys of the Progressive Era, the new surveys were based on statistical probability. In the process of developing unbiased, statistical ways of determining public opinion on specific issues, American human engineers refined and further publicized the concept of the average American.

The meaning of the term *public opinion* has been a matter of discussion since the seventeenth century. In contrast to intelligence quotients or indices of consumer tastes, the discussion of the concept preceded attempts to measure its effects on society. Public opinion was a concept central to the Enlightenment's project of making "public use of one's reason" to free "the great unthinking masses," to turn to Kant's classic formulation. Yet the debate over the respective roles of feeling and reason in determining opinion that marked the Enlightenment would carry well into the twentieth-century mass society.[43] Some clung to a traditional understanding of public opinion as the outcome of party politics as did Lord Bryce in *American Commonwealth* (1889).[44] Others worked on the ways mass opinion could be whipped up as the Creel Committee had shown so well with its propaganda efforts of the First World War. As Edward Bernays, a nephew of Sigmund Freud who had served on the committee, put it in his 1923 *Crystallizing Public Opinion,* mass opinion was malleable. The real issue was how to transform any given view into the majority opinion, in other words, creating "new authorities" by articulating a "mass opinion" against old beliefs.[45] Walter Lippmann, who characterized his own career as that of an opinion maker, rejected this coercive model in *Public Opinion* (1922) and *The Phantom Public* (1925). Lippmann's position drew inspiration from the ideal of the Enlightenment. Education, he believed, was more important in shaping opinion than manipulation. The real problem was therefore to find the true experts and scientists who could properly inform the public of the issues at stake.[46]

The debate on how to mold public opinion, however, would soon be left behind in the United States by the growing practice of polling consumers for their own opinions. As applied psychologists, pollsters sought again to find an average consumer/citizen, or, in George Gallup's words, "the average opinion of mankind." As the practice grew, public opinion became mostly those parts of a group's beliefs that could be collated and reported in percentages, that is, the definition the *Public Opinion Quarterly* reported in its first issue in 1937. Public opinion became "any collection of individual opinions."[47] Producing and selling products became not just a matter of understanding a consumer's psychological drives but knowing his or her buying habits. What could be simpler than asking people what they liked or thought using the available statistical techniques?

The main actors in the birth of polling had trained in applied psychology and were conversant with intelligence testing and behaviorism. George Gallup, who would later found the American Institute of Public Opinion, followed by the National Opinion Research Center, had studied psychology at Iowa, a department chaired by Carl Seashore, a psychologist best known for his tests of musical ability. Gallup's 1925 thesis for the master of arts was about personnel testing, "A Study in the Selection of Salespeople for Killian's Department Store, Cedar Rapids, Iowa." He then moved on to explore public-opinion polling in his 1928 psychology dissertation, also at the University of Iowa, which proposed "An Objective Method for Determining Reader Interest in the Content of a Newspaper."[48] From 1928 to 1931, Gallup was a professor, first at Drake University and then at Northwestern, teaching journalism and advertising and doing polls for various news organizations. In 1932 he was hired by the advertising agency Young & Rubicam to head their polling division and shortly afterwards opened his own polling group.

Among other pioneers, Elmo Roper, started out as a jeweler in Iowa before developing an interest in market research. He had received some education in philosophy at the University in Edinburgh immediately after World War I but did not have a college degree. In the early 1930s, Roper teamed up with his friend Richardson Wood, who had worked for J. Walter Thompson, the firm that employed John Watson. The two partners learned many marketing techniques from the firm's former director of research, Paul Cherington, who was now professor of marketing at the Harvard Business School. At the beginning of 1933, the firm of Cherington, Roper and Wood was created, with Cherington as senior partner. The firm originally specialized in market surveys and moved on to public opinion polling in 1934 with the backing of *Fortune* magazine. A third big pollster was market researcher Archibald Crossley.[49]

Using a new method of sampling—statistically representative surveys instead of the traditional unscientific, so-called straw polls without controls for reliability—to get a more accurate picture of what the public thought on certain issues, the *Fortune* surveys probed responses to such political initiatives as Huey Long's Share-the-Wealth programs and interviewed respondents about the respective fairness of taxes and utility rates; they focused on ideological issues such as antisemitism or birth control, on such matters of taste as modern architecture, and on consumer preferences among competing brands of automobiles and cigarettes. The samples were designed for "plumbing the public mind" by accurately rendering in microcosm the entire country and, in the end, giving a representative picture of the majority.

The strategy worked. George Gallup, who was now in business for himself, made a lasting impression by accurately predicting FDR's 1936 reelection while the *Literary Digest,* relying on a traditional straw poll of an unrepresentative sample of wealthier Americans, had confidently but erroneously predicted Republican Alfred Landon as the winner. George Gallup claimed more for his refined sampling tools than simply predicting specific elections. They would generate a more direct and representative form of democracy by communicating genuine public opinion to the nation's leaders. In George Gallup and Saul Forbes Rae's words, "in the democratic community, the attitudes of the mass of the people determine policy." The strength of the new sampling techniques was to recognize the American public as "a mosaic whose complex pattern of individuals is clustered together in a variety of social groups and associations." In effect, Gallup's average man was a super voter or super citizen.[50]

Here finally was a tool for dealing with the very diversity of the American social and cultural fabric. Identifying the interplay among various strata of the population led to a more sophisticated conception of the average. Gallup and Rae in taking "the pulse of democracy" realized that an average exists only as a composite of the majority opinion of several groups when their responses are weighted and balanced against each other. Because "people who live differently think differently," all the strata must be carefully considered, separately and jointly, and the average accordingly weighted before reaching a conclusion. This was Gallup and Rae's way to insure that "the democratic way of life rests firmly...on the actual experience of the mass of its citizens."[51]

Simply stated, majority rule would truly reflect majority opinion when average and majority meet. Thus academically trained applied psychologists teamed up with businessmen to expand the work already done on the measurement of intelligence and that of instincts to determine public opinion. Although increasingly sophisticated in the application of probability theory in the design of representative samples of consumers and voters, pollsters were not interested in diversity as an end in itself; rather they gave the notion of the average an added aura of credibility.

HUMAN ENGINEERING ON TRIAL

It would not take long for market-oriented, nonintrospective psychology to become a feature of western capitalism. And as applied psychologists made their presence and influence felt increasingly in the Army, in business firms, in the nation's universities, colleges, and high schools, in hospitals, in politics, in newspapers—just about everywhere—they were widely attacked as pernicious and manipulative. The fears of the Progressive generation, reiterated in the twenties, found new voices in the 1940s. Witness the reaction of German philosopher Theodor Adorno. Adorno, best known for his sociological studies of music and his book *The Authoritarian Personality* (1950), first encountered American-style research when he fled Nazi Germany in the years before World War II. Adorno's reaction is significant, not just because it is a view from European high culture, like that of French professor Siegfried, but because Adorno was part of a small group of influential German-born philosophers, including Hannah Arendt and Herbert Marcuse, all members of the so-called Frankfurt School, who drew a parallel between the methods of managing American mass culture, including consumer persuasion, and the propaganda of the Nazi Germany they had left behind, despite the widely different economic and social contexts that nurtured them.

Adorno called both the American "culture industry" and fascist propaganda "psychoanalysis in reverse," that is, the abolition of an individual's psyche "through the perception of dependence instead of the realization of potential freedom" and "through expropriation of the unconscious by social control instead of making the subjects conscious of their unconscious."[52] Although the American psychologists who perfected the human engineering of mass society did everything they could to be informed about Americans' opinions and desires, they were similarly involved, so went the charge, in an exercise in simplification of psychological wants and attempts to break down individuality. Adorno described the Nazis as demagogues who could guess correctly the cravings of those susceptible to their propaganda because they "resembled them psychologically." Hannah Arendt, however, correctly added that the Nazis had learned much from both American gangster organizations *and* the American advertising industry. We know also that Hitler and Goebbels had read French philosopher Gustave Le Bon's classic 1895 study *The Crowd* and were cognizant about crowd behavior.[53]

Mistaking the average man for the gregarious man, Adorno was unwilling to recognize the American human engineers as serious intellectuals. His first encounter with American culture as a refugee scholar initially reinforced his prejudices. Hired by Paul Lazarsfeld at the Office of Radio Research at Princeton University in 1940, Adorno was to work on a Rockefeller Foundation–funded project designed to assess public responses to the radio broadcasting of specific musical programs. The German scholar had been transported to a totally alien world. He could readily see that the study for which he was paid "was concerned with the collection of data, which were supposed to benefit the planning department in the field of the mass media." But Adorno could not recognize the connections between the data collected and the alleged purpose of the study. He rejected outright what his American colleagues saw as an obvious proposition: that whatever people responded when asked questions by survey researchers or when filling out questionnaires was important and to be taken seriously. Adorno instead challenged, in his own words, "what was axiomatic according to the prevalent rules of social research, namely to proceed from the subjects' reactions as if they were a primary and final source of sociological knowledge." Such a procedure seemed to him to be "thoroughly superficial and misguided." Steeped in György Lukács's concept of reification, Adorno believed that the measurements would be void of significance without determining "how far comprehensive social structures, and even society as a whole came to play" in influencing respondents' choices.[54] Before joining Princeton, Adorno had already argued that the radio listener was converted, along "his line of least resistance," into the "acquiescent purchaser." He believed that in mass culture "the reactions of the listener" had "no relation to the playing of the music."[55] The job at Princeton would give him a chance to confirm his theory, at least to himself. Thus Adorno recalled, "when I was confronted with the demand to 'measure culture,' I reflected that culture might be precisely that condition that excludes a mentality capable of measuring it."

American human engineering was not, like German fascism, psychoanalysis in reverse. For instead of appropriating the people's unconscious, American human engineers largely ignored it. Because human engineering bypassed the individual's unique identity, it has been quite common to contrast behaviorism with psychoanalysis. John Watson himself suggested the contrast. Horace Kallen also pointed to it when describing behaviorism in the *Encyclopedia of the Social Sciences*.[56] To fill the void, psychoanalysis would return the individual to the real discovery of him or herself in a mass society. By contrast, even when playing on the unconscious dimensions of hate and fear, the behaviorists' manipulative tactics remained superficial.

To find out what attracted Americans, social scientists were, as Adorno noted, intensely interested in people's responses to questionnaires as a proxy for what people thought. They endowed each respondent with at least a modest sense of individual agency or will to act by answering questions. In other words, American social scientists were involved in a reification more specifically of their own, that of the universal American, responsible for his or her action. They were further reinforced in their belief in Americans as free citizens capable of making independent choices by Americans' easy acceptance and participation in the surveys. As a result the American context was one where the "manipulator" had to provide the "manipulated" what he or she wanted.

To be sure, human engineers working for the market were fully aware that the business firms and other organizations who commissioned their services used the collected information to their advantage to the maximum extent feasible. Consumer manipulation was their agenda. But even when successful in persuading large numbers of consumers to buy the class of products they helped market, applied social scientists were not in a position directly to enhance or reduce Americans' universe by much. No matter the grand illusion of their own making, they were neither able to improve the contours of human lives as much as they claimed nor doomed to a reductive and repressive program of human manipulation. This is why inventing the average American was not the same as creating, in Herbert Marcuse's words, a "unidimensional" person.[57] The managing of mass society rested on knowledge removed from culture and emotion. To tinker with the market required only the kind of problem-oriented understanding on which one can readily act. Americans conceived of an applied social science that was quite superficial, geared toward quick results or apparently immediate relevance or, as Franz Neumann, another refugee scholar, put it, "optimistic, empirically oriented, ahistorical."[58] Lack of theory and historical depth were only two of the flaws in American applied social science.

Only a culture committed to excessive statistical objectivity could eventually produce the 1948 Kinsey report on *Sexual Behavior in the Human Male*. As Lionel Trilling remarked, the Kinsey report reduced every behavior to a statistic and refused to consider "quality" as an integral part of the sexual experience, thus "drawing sexuality apart from the general human context." As a monument to human engineering, the report saw a "fact" as a "physical fact, to be considered only in its physical aspect and apart from any idea or ideal that might make it a social fact, as having no ascertainable personal or cultural meaning and no possible consequences."[59]

By resorting to all sorts of averaging and using only what they thought were neutral categories of knowledge in a multicultural society, Americans also learned how to sanitize facts by avoiding the complexities embedded in class, gender, age, race, or ethnicity. There were good reasons to understand individuals as part of a normal statistical distribution. Although society, in all its cultural diversity, could not resemble a bell-shape curve, the modern American income structure did. With an ever growing middle class, it was bulging at the center, progressively smaller at the extremes, with some outliers. It therefore made sense for human engineers who worked for the market to search for the average worker, the average buyer, the average voter and, even if the idea sounds farfetched, the average lover in a middle-class society. In the human engineer's model society, the ideal was the middle. They pointed to the middle as the model and steered people to move themselves there. Applied social scientists, whether they worked for business or educational institutions or the government, applied their talents not to understand individuals but to manage markets. Their methods resembled their vision of what a market share should be: An individual was just a point in a statistical distribution; and the whole of society could never be greater than the sum of its individual parts.

One should not lose sight, however, of the significant role human engineers played in promoting adjustment at work, at school, at play. Most surprisingly, Adorno, smuggest among the smug critics of their naïve methods, finally admitted it in an unexpected postwar confession, "We Europeans are inclined to see the concept of 'adjustment' as a purely negative thing," only to continue, "with respect to quantitative thinking in America, with all its dangers of lack of discrimination and apotheosis of the average, Europeans must raise the deeply disturbing question how far qualitative differences matter in the present social world." The crack in Adorno's construction led him to this unexpected confession concerning his country of momentary asylum (Adorno would return to Germany after the war). Having by then adopted quantification in his own research, he concluded, very much to the point, "within the total development of middle-class civilization, the United States has undoubtedly arrived at one extreme."[60] The Nazi Germany that Adorno had once fled had reached another extreme.

By limiting their vision, human engineers could never penetrate their subjects in depth. They could predict electoral outcomes but never say much about an individual voter's motivations. They could sell a product that was only marginally different from another. They therefore became simultaneously essential to the functioning of society as their influence was felt in a greater number of bureaucratic, political, or market circumstances and marginal as they left intact the complexity and diversity of individuals hidden behind their group percentages and averages. The combination of their nonintrospective methods and limited goals, by drastically restricting their understanding of individual subjects, was the self-imposed limitation that kept them within the bounds of democracy. Despite the behaviorists' claims, these social scientists were truly "modern," as German philosopher Carl Schmitt would have it, because they downplayed the conflict and the drama of emotions, politics, and culture to promote the consensual terrain of evidence— a grid of evidence they collected dispassionately on society.[61]

The more noxious and lasting challenge to democratic ideals of individual self-realization, however, was not that of individual manipulation diagnosed by those critics committed to the abstractions of high culture like Adorno or Siegfried. The real difficulty was instead the preference for abstractions over realities. The average person took on a palpable lifelike quality, and Americans felt as if they knew him or her. If social scientists "manipulated" people, it was by conceptualizing an imaginary person who then exerted a powerful influence on the American psyche during the 1940s and 1950s and who still reverberates today as the counterpoint to our emphasis on diversity. Managing mass society amounted to turning the computing of a statistical device, the average, into an influential way of thinking about the self.

Part Two THE SOCIAL CONTRACT OF THE MARKET

CHAPTER THE SOCIAL CONTRACT OF THE MARK

CHAPTER FOUR

TURNING OUT CONSUMERS

It is in the progressive state, while the society is advancing to the further
acquisition, rather than when it has acquired its full complement of riches,
that the condition of the labouring poor, of the great body of the people, seems
to be the happiest and the most comfortable. It is hard in the stationary, and
miserable in the declining state. The progressive state is in reality the
cheerful and the hearty state to all the different orders of the society.

ADAM SMITH[1]

If Americans have been reluctant to resort to a rhetoric of class conflict in the way that citizens of other modern industrial societies have, it is because the process of inclusion has been driven by the growth of the middle class. This is a phenomenon that the social engineers who invented the concept of the average American understood. The expansion throughout most of the twentieth century of a large, urban industrial middle class of white Americans, with an extraordinary capacity for enlargement as well as internal segmentation, has facilitated the assimilation of newcomers, fostered social mobility, defused radicalism, and eased tensions among parts of society. Americans have been committed to an open class structure and have counted on an expansive and absorbing center as a key to the realization of their social contract. They have promoted a model of social integration from the middle out.[2]

In the nineteenth century, Americans had sought abundance through land acquisition and individual entrepreneurship. In the twentieth century, their sense of achievement was increasingly tied to success within complex organizations and through full participation in consumption. The unprecedented system of mass production, mass distribution, and mass communication required a large middle class of participants and consumers and stimulated social engineering and upward mobility. That shift completed the country's transformation from a society committed to local forms of voluntary associations, which Tocqueville had once visited, to a continental society dominated by national organizations. As it turned out, the new ways of accessing skills, resources, and goods translated into a greater portion of the population identifying with the middle class.[3]

By contrast to the American amalgamation of working and middle classes, much more rigid class boundaries remained the norm throughout Europe in the first half of the twentieth century. European middle classes had historically defined themselves in opposition to the rest of the population—not only the nobility but also, and equally important, the working classes. They had responded to increasing proletarianization in the nineteenth century, as Jürgen Kocka notes, by making "explicit what had gone without saying before: that they did not belong to the ordinary people." As they gained ascendancy, the European middle classes further split into two: the bourgeoisie narrowing "down to the better-off circles of property and education" while a "petite bourgeoisie" or lower middle class established itself as a separate entity.[4]

The burden of this chapter is not to revive American exceptionalism as an explanation for the more open American class structure but to examine what specific processes allowed working Americans to expand the middle class sociologically as well as ideologically in the first half of the twentieth century. However problematical the belief in an "average" American, it was a credo well suited to the new mass society. Promoting corresponding middle-class values became a priority at home half a century before turning into a tenet of Cold War foreign policy rhetoric.[5]

RESHUFFLING THE CARDS

Twentieth-century Americans derived a distinct middle-class culture from their increasing participation in the corporate and governmental bureaucratic institutions of modern mass society.[6] The so-called center firms as well as growing federal and local governments affected the class system in drastic but deceptively simple ways. At the most basic level, they imposed their internal hierarchy of managerial positions, clerical occupations, and production. But this tripartite division of work—managers, clerks, and workers—did not produce rigid strata or repeat in the United States the European segregation among bourgeoisie, petite bourgeoisie, and working class. Rather, middle-class enlargement was facilitated by the low entry point in the spreading office culture, a process C. Wright Mills described in *White Collar* in 1951 at a time when employees in that sector already made up almost 40 percent of the working population.[7] The prerequisites for corporate and government clerical work—a foundation in English grammar and proficiency in writing, as well as the ability to comport oneself decorously—limited access to these positions initially to educated native-born Americans. Immigrants, however, quickly realized that their children could enter this expanding sector of the economy if they acquired the needed education.[8]

The expanding corporate and government sectors were also responsible for the de-skilling of the working class. In the nineteenth century, the American working class was still divided between skilled and unskilled workers. That strict separation, based on membership in a craft, was reflected in the organization of the labor movement. Craftsmen could join labor unions, unskilled workers could not. The new industrial reality broke down this traditional division between skilled and unskilled workers with the creation, early in the twentieth century, of the semiskilled operative—a product of Frederick Winslow Taylor's "scientific management" and Henry Ford's techniques of assembly line production. While foremen were increasingly brought into management, the semiskilled operative came to dominate the American working class numerically and the mass unionism that would gain recognition in the New Deal.

Surviving skilled workers and artisans became members of the middle class while better-paid semiskilled operatives also aspired to middle-class membership.

But with some of the most violent labor disputes of the industrial world regularly occurring on American land, the potential for deep class divisions was real. The emergence of a democratic mass society with a large and continually expanding middle class was far from a foregone conclusion.[9] Twentieth-century Americans, nevertheless, experienced a significant blurring of the classes, with large parts of the working class slowly merging into an indefinite and loosely differentiated middle class. How the lines between these two classes have shifted, in reality and in perception, is an important dimension of economic, social, and cultural history. It was a question not simply of numbers but of culture.

EDUCATION AND MOBILITY

As in the case of immigrant children preparing for white-collar jobs, broad educational opportunities sustained the expansion of the American middle-class. At the dawn of the twentieth century, only 6.4 percent of young Americans graduated from high school. In 1950 that figure had reached 59 percent (it was about 75 percent in 1990). By way of comparison, despite the fact that we cannot establish a rigorous correspondence between the two educational systems, figures for France were much lower: Only 1.5 percent of French students completed high school in 1913, 5 percent in 1939, and 50 percent in 1990, below the American level in 1950.[10] The effects of Americans's preoccupation with testing were also less serious than other countries' mode of selection. Compared to other advanced nations, the American system of education has been relatively free from selective tracks channeling some students at an early age into long-term educational careers while holding others to limited terminal technical curricula. Primary schools, with common charters and programs, had provided a shared experience for most white students since the middle of the nineteenth century. The comprehensive high school, created during the years 1890 to 1920, was a normal extension of the nineteenth-century common school goal of forging a collective civic culture.

The pattern of education in the United States, marked by limited stratification for white students, high enrollment, and a common curriculum, reflects the middle class's and lower middle class's determination to participate in the opportunities created by the corporate reorganization of the economy. Economic elites made repeated efforts to reverse this pattern by stratifying

public education in the interest of their own children. But they were check-
mated by the extraordinary growth of the new middle class of white-collar
and skilled workers and by the powerful alliance of middle-class reformers, educational professionals, their political allies in city government, and
working-class groups.[11] As a result, American educators have been reluctant
to train students for specific jobs and guide them neatly into their appropriate
places in the labor market, thus creating distinct cultures for the young people
who would hold blue- and white-collar positions. Although the Smith-
Hughes Act of 1918 provided federal funding for separate vocational schools,
most vocational education was carried on within the comprehensive high
school where all students could be brought together for some classes and
extracurricular activities.[12]

Early in the twentieth century, John Dewey had placed much hope in the
power of education to foster an inclusive citizenry. To him, a shared experience among diverse students would infuse greater meaning into the learning
process and culture would become "the democratic password."[13] Although
Dewey's unshakable optimism and belief in progress are not always to the taste
of a late twentieth-century reader, the mass education movement to which he
contributed so much of his energies helped blur the collar line, Americanize
immigrant families, and expand the middle class as the economy grew. Education, which facilitated access to an enlarged opportunity structure, was essential to intergenerational upward mobility in the twentieth century. A generation of social historians has therefore documented in detail the career
trajectories of Americans who sought to improve their lot. These historians
settled on the image of the escalator to describe the resulting class system.
They identified enough individual failures to underscore the potential for serious social conflict, but because a large enough number of initially deprived
individuals, albeit almost exclusively white, were continually integrated into
the majority, this conflict rarely materialized. Patterns of upward social mobility for white Americans were at once an assimilation device and a safety valve.[14]

CONSUMPTION AND WORKERS' DOUBLE CONSCIOUSNESS

Shifting the economy from forces of production to strategies of consumption
has been at least as important as schooling and mobility in enlarging the
boundaries of the middle class. Common participation as consumers of same
products is what made the middle class so large—not just education and intergenerational improvement. For full participation in the mass market gave an
increasingly large number of Americans not only a distinct culture of con-

sumption but a way to achieve their "averageness" with visible symbols to announce their middle-class status. In the end, the growing pervasiveness of mass consumption accounts for much of the Americans' redefinition of the meaning of middle class.

The promise of democracy was that of plenitude. As Social Gospel political economist Simon Patten declared in *The New Basis of Civilization* (1907), "the extension of civilization downward does not depend at present so much upon gaining fresh victories over nature, as it does upon the demolishment of the social obstacles which divide men into classes and prevent the universal democracy that economic forces would bring about."[15] Arguing that the old economics were concerned primarily with the creation of wealth, Patten thought that the new had to concentrate on the moral aspects of distribution and consumption. As he saw it, invidious social and cultural differences would dim if the masses could share democratically in the new consumption.[16] His conception was but one of many from those who would see full participation in a consumption economy as the basis for a twentieth-century social consensus. In 1914, Walter Lippmann associated democracy with the right to purchase consumers' goods at low prices.[17] Democratizing abundance within an industrial economy was increasingly defined as broadening access to the products of the mass market.

Access to the market, however, was no easy proposition. Turning industrial workers into affluent consumers would require a significant overhaul of the economic system. For workers as individuals simply did not make enough money. Indeed, one of the most significant divisions traditionally separating the working class from the middle class was the need for working-class family members to pool incomes to make ends meet and eventually afford a degree of comfort and security. Income pooling was necessary for daily subsistence and long-term security in working-class families. Married women accepted piece work at home and rented rooms to boarders, while older children worked in factories. For working-class immigrants, owning a home was one way of gaining a degree of economic security, but this stability could best be gained within the framework of the household economy. The process always required money that only a firm strategy of pooled incomes could bring.[18]

Pooling incomes among household members, however, was a brake on individual mobility. With children having to chip in, the obvious and heavy toll for economic well-being was a constraint on their education. With the burden of supplementing the father's income resting on the children, the two goals of survival and intergenerational mobility were often at odds. With little effective birth control, parents came to see their initially unwanted children as future contributors to the common budget. Their hope, however, was at best uncertain given the fragility of newborn infants. Should all the children survive, the initial drain on meager resources could be too heavy and the demographic gamble turn into disaster.[19] For all these reasons, concerned social workers spent much time investigating the practice of combining income. The "family economy" was scrutinized by newly formed state bureaus of labor statistics as early as the 1870s. Family budget studies were the basis for Carroll D. Wright's pioneering work in Massachusetts and Washington. Income pooling was also a major target of the *Pittsburgh Survey,* which the Russell Sage Foundation funded in 1910.[20]

Families developed a variety of strategies to overcome the constraints of income pooling. The reliance on children's work was generally inversely proportional to the father's income. If only a modest amount of money was needed and if there was room in the house, boarders provided a form of financial relief that spared the children from working at an early age. In their attempt to improve the chances of at least some of their children, working-class families developed gendered schemes of sending their daughters to work and their sons to school. The search for middle-class status often relied on such male-oriented strategies. In Russian-Jewish immigrant families, for example, young men were often sent to the yeshiva while their sisters were on their way to the garment sweatshop.[21] In other instances, labor markets dictated an approach more friendly to young women. The massive entry of daughters of skilled workers into office work shows how working-class families responded to the increasing demand in the office sector in a manner that would ease their daughters' entry into the middle class while contributing to the collective budget for a few years. While families benefited financially, young women improved their own prospects of marrying educated men just starting out in the new corporate economy, without threatening the male domination of the workplace that lasted virtually uncompromised until after World War II.[22]

The tensions in such family schemes of income pooling between loyalty to family and the pull of individual aspirations were duplicated in workers' participation in the labor movement. Between the employers' vigorous opposition to the labor movement and the movement's concentration in skilled occupations, most workers could not count on labor organizations to provide security or comfort in their lives. But those who did had to compromise between a strategy based on pooled resources and solidarity and their individual search for a higher standard of living. That was most evident among skilled workers who were the primary beneficiaries of high wages and whose offspring were most likely to experience upward mobility. Although much labor history scholarship has exposed the oversimplifications of Werner Sombart's famous 1906 theory that "on the reefs of roast beef and apple-pie socialistic Utopias of every sort are sent to their doom," it cannot be denied that American skilled workers enjoyed comparatively high wages.[23] Their solidarity with unskilled workers was compromised by their more limited craft-based and family strategies for attaining a high standard of living for themselves and intergenerational mobility for their offspring. Skilled workers, as John R. Commons and his student Selig Perlman have shown, promoted bread-and-butter unionism and were more job conscious than class conscious.[24] For that reason, they were reluctant to make alliances with unskilled workers, often immigrants freshly arrived from eastern Europe or African Americans from the South, who would compromise their closed-shop interests. Better established and better paid workers, whose idea of mutuality did not include solidarity beyond their immediate ranks, did not willingly unite with a newer mass of unskilled immigrants.

Only occasionally did the two goals of defending large class interests or fending for one's own improvement reinforce each other. Most of the time, one weighed heavier than the other as workers walked a fine line between their commitment to mutual help within the working class and the larger middle-class ethos of acquisitive individualism surrounding them. For the mutuality of the working class, such as it was, was often yet another approach to enable their members to access available abundance.

A HIGH WAGE–LOW PRICE FORMULA FOR MASS CONSUMPTION

As workers were experiencing the contradictory pulls of embourgeoisement and class solidarity, industrialists as early as the aftermath of the depression of 1873 began rethinking the causes of recession, diagnosing it for the first time as a crisis not of overproduction but of underconsumption.[25] The problem was twofold: workers did not have enough spending money, and the market for mass-produced goods was largely unrealized. With the organizational revolution emerged the idea, so fully elaborated in the late nineteenth and early twentieth centuries, that the market not only could but should be managed. Hence the creation within the matrix of inquiry of numerous new tools to map out and manipulate the market, which we have already reviewed: marketing surveys, studies of statistical distribution of population and products, elaboration of probability theory applied to marketing, development of applied psychology, and advertising.

Late nineteenth-century economists such as Léon Walras from France and Vilfredo Pareto from Italy, who successively occupied the economics chair at the University of Lausanne, and the Americans John Bates Clark and Irving Fisher revamped their field with a new approach to computing prices that fit an age defined by mass markets. Their contribution was to revise the traditional theory of value. While classical economists had concentrated on the cost of labor, they focused instead on the prices of goods. In their marginalist theories, it was consumer demand, not labor, that gave value to consumers' goods. Having established the new principle of the primacy of consumption, they refined the connections between the utility of goods and their exchange value. They also helped expand the market by rationalizing passing on to consumers the savings resulting from decreasing unit costs of manufacturing.[26] Such efforts led to large-scale studies of market behavior and fluctuating consumption levels. Early in the twentieth century, Wesley Mitchell pioneered statistical research on the business cycle that would become a staple of the Commerce Department economic studies under Hoover's guidance.[27]

While theoreticians formalized matters, very practical manufacturers were busy turning workers into consumers. Many took their cues from the least theoretical of them, Henry Ford, who before World War I had blended the production techniques of interchangeable parts and of continuous-flow processes to mass-produce the Model T and sell it at a revolutionary low price. Even at a low price and a small per unit profit, Ford prospered. He raised his workers' wages to unprecedented levels, enabling them to become consumers of his own automobiles and other goods. Such corporate strategies were enhanced by a credit revolution in the 1920s. They were part of a larger movement in which economists, businessmen, policymakers, and union leaders sought to help workers purchase manufactured products.

Some employers paid good wages that would give workers greater access to the market not only to improve their business but also because they felt it was the right thing to do from a moral standpoint. Gerard Swope, who became president of GE in 1922, had developed a social conscience during a year in residence at Hull-House, where he was tutored by Jane Addams and where he met his wife, Mary Dayton Hill. The couple was appalled by the exploitation and hard living conditions in the immigrant neighborhoods around Hull-House and the families' need for decent housing and adequate schooling. Swope's experiences at Western Electric further persuaded him that workers should share in profits. Similarly, Owen D. Young, the chairman of the board of GE, had been impressed by the vagaries of labor markets while laboring himself on his father's farm in Schenectady. Young became especially interested in the new economic research on market performance, especially on the business cycle, which periodically threw people out of work. Young began to insist on a "cultural wage" rather than just a living wage. As he boasted in 1923, he knew from personal experience "the difference between an income which provides only an uncomfortable house, inadequate food and insufficient clothes and *no* provision for the future and an income which provides margins above suitable living conditions for education and health and recreation *and* provision for the future." Although Young was never clear about what he meant by a "cultural wage," it was enough money for a family to enjoy life and consume, not merely survive. This led to the well-known pilot programs at GE for workers' benefits and profit-sharing.[28]

A high wage–low price formula that would expand the market was thus beginning to take shape in people's minds early in the century. The idea was experimental and its application hit or miss but it was in tune with the Social Gospel, the AFL tradition of bread-and-butter negotiations for higher wages, reform efforts to expose loan sharks and to make consumer credit widely available, as well as with industrialists' strategies of implementing installment buying for workers and lowering the unit costs of mass-produced items and passing the savings on to consumers. All these notions eventually came to maturity in the 1920s. Progressive department store owner Edward Filene cut prices drastically in his bargain basement sales while sponsoring the credit union movement and creating the Twentieth Century Fund to engage in broad studies of what a high consumption society might look like.[29] Meanwhile the Russell Sage Foundation was launching a vast inquiry into credit practices with the purpose of abolishing pawnshops and making installment buying affordable for working-class families. Economists and manufacturers alike realized the effect of lowering prices on buying power. "Any economy of production will result in a glut of goods if the price advantages of the economy in manufacture are retained by the producer instead of being passed on to the consumer," a manufacturer wrote in *System,* echoing a growing sentiment. Good business and large consumption depends on prices going down, concluded a National Bureau of Economic Research study that reminded manufacturers to "think less" of their "competitors' prices and more of the consumer."[30]

As economists, businessmen, and policymakers were paying more attention to the relationship between spending power and standard of living, they were beginning to question the insistence that every penny paid to labor came out of investors' pockets. When recession hit, the immediate reaction among employers had traditionally been layoffs and wage cuts, and the recession of 1921 was no exception. Over 300 articles published in specialized magazines read by management told of ways to cut wages and suggested how low they could fall. But as times got better, employers were told they could become more generous. Such cautionary articles had practically disappeared by 1922, to be replaced by essays on wage incentives. By 1926, a commitment to high wages reflecting the buoyant economic times was widely held.[31]

As the new high wage–low price formula for national prosperity began to emerge, with it came a new perception of class. Although the President's Conference on Unemployment in 1921 appears to have focused largely on gathering statistics and understanding the interrelationships of production and price cycles, there was discussion (primarily outside the conference's formal venue) of the need to increase the purchasing power of consumers. At the conference, both AFL representatives and businessmen defended a policy of liberal remuneration. Particularly revealing was the discussion among conference participants generated by Roy Dickinson's articles in the trade magazine *Printer's Ink*.[32] To combat underconsumption, Dickinson advocated high wages, low prices, and aggressive advertising as the key to maintaining full production even in a recession. He promoted the idea that high wages and sustained production went hand-in-hand. His main point was that workers were also consumers. As he put it, "lower wages reduce purchasing power; men on starvation wages do not buy phonographs, clothes, shoes, etc. The key is to make goods to sell to the largest number of purchasers, and most of those are farmers or men who work for wages in industrial plants."[33] The purpose was to stimulate the economy by enlarging the pool of buyers; the consequence was to establish a more widely held middle-class standard of living. If manufacturers wanted to make more money, they needed to pay their workers well and pursue volume production and selling through low prices and smart marketing techniques rather than wage reduction. They had to view wages as purchasing power rather than as something subtracted from capital's stake in a business.

Meanwhile, proto-Keynesian writers like William Trufant Foster and Waddill Catchings also spread the idea that recessions were caused by underconsumption and that the government needed to take steps to encourage purchasing power. As they put it, increasing the standard of living could take place "only so long as increased per capita production induces a flow of money to consumers sufficient to enable them to buy the increased output."[34] Workers should share in profits generated by increases in productivity. All of this added up to something larger than anybody had really anticipated. Wesley Mitchell, after noting the fall of costs and growth of new products like rayon, radios, automobiles, cigarette lighters, watches, electrical appliances, and other goods throughout the 1920s concluded *Recent Economic Changes* by summing up the decade-long trend of higher productivity, wages, and consumption:

> At the close of the war, when a fall in the price level like that of 1865 was expected by many, business executives frequently said that the first task of reorganization was to "liquidate labor." The great buying campaign of 1919 and the accompanying uprush of prices caused a postponement of this program. For a time it was hard to get men enough, even at rising rates. When prices fell precipitously in 1920–21 and unemployment was rife, the moment to insist on wage reductions seemed to have come. But the trade unions offered strenuous resistance, despite the number of the temporary idle. Their resistance was more effective than it could have been had not the growth of population been retarded for some years. The prices of labor were cut, to be sure, but not cut as much as the prices of consumers' goods. Hence when employment became tolerably full again toward the close of 1922, wage earners found themselves in possession of relatively large purchasing power. Then the economic advantages of a broad consumers' market began to appear. Employers discovered that their inability to "liquidate labor" had been fortunate for themselves as well as for their employees. The doctrine of high wages found conspicuous champions among the business leaders, and their formulations favored its spread. Discoveries in science, as well as in practical life, have often been made thus by observing the consequences of a thwarted effort.[35]

The idea of the twentieth-century American middle class became thus closely tied to that of consuming the products of the mass market. As an enhanced standard of living tied to rising productivity was becoming its hallmark, it was difficult to disentangle middle-class status and ability to consume. Indeed, after a brief post–World War I recession, a growing number of Americans did begin to enjoy the benefits of mass production, mass consumption, and innovations in consumer credit. Only 8 percent of American households had washing machines in 1920, but by 1930 this number had grown to 24 percent; 26 percent had cars in 1920, a percentage that had soared by some estimates to 60 percent in 1930. Earnings grew and unemployment declined. In 1914 dollars, average income rose from $546 in 1910 to $793 in 1929, just before the stockmarket crash, while unemployment declined from 5.9 percent to 3.2 percent.[36]

Everybody, including workmen, "ought to be rich," claimed John Raskob, the Du Pont executive who managed Al Smith's campaign in 1928.[37] Although his prescription to invest in the market at a time of freewheeling speculation must have sounded insane to the mass of working people who still had to pool family incomes to make ends meet and who borrowed from credit unions just to pay for medical bills and coal, Raskob's pronouncement reflects the faith many held in the redistributive power of corporate capitalism and its potential for abolishing class divisions. An enlarged middle class of consumers, as its standard of living rose, strengthened its class position through acquisitive individualism. Encouraged by social engineering and marketing strategies, it welcomed an ever larger segment of sons and daughters of the working class. But such a trend, as it germinated in the twenties, was suddenly interrupted by the Great Depression.

RESPONDING TO THE DEPRESSION: RESTORING PURCHASING POWER?

When the country was thrown into the Depression, the immediate danger was a hardening of class lines. It was happening elsewhere. Thus the German lower middle class, badly hit by the drastic turn of events and eager to hold on to its middle class status and to keep its distance from the working class despite a loss of income, swelled the ranks of the Nazis.[38] Other European Fascist movements were fueled by the same fears. Could similar crusades from left and right have any real effect in the United States, where a middle-class position had been so much easier to achieve?

The Depression did provoke a surge of class consciousness among American workers. By then, the dramatic reduction of immigration in the 1920s had altered the composition of the working class. The labor movement was overcoming its most profound cultural divisions, and class consciousness was stimulating solidarity as ethnic boundaries loosened. Technologically driven demand for semiskilled workers was also helping the labor movement dissolve the traditional barrier between the skilled and the unskilled. Although still quite diverse, the increasingly homogeneous working class could fight the open shop, join the newly created CIO, organize the sit-down strikes of 1936–37, and finally gain recognition in the New Deal. Workers therefore partly overcame their parochialism to unite in a mass movement. Even issues of race became closely linked to issues of class. The more open minds among labor leaders looked to the condition of African Americans as a product of the class struggle and attracted black intellectuals to fight the class war on behalf of all workers.[39]

The middle class was also deeply affected by the Depression. For the workers who had already experienced poverty, the Depression was a more dramatic replay of a known scenario, but for middle-class Americans who had shared in the prosperity of the twenties, the decade that followed was a period of great fear and adjustment as they wrestled with poverty. Millions turned temporarily to Huey Long's "Share Our Wealth Campaign" or the populist formulas of Dr. Francis Townsend or Father Coughlin. Long's, Townsend's, and Coughlin's supporters were a mixture of lower middle-class Americans and better-paid skilled workers in craft unions who sought to reconcile their self-image with their eroding purchasing power.[40] They sought to maintain an American way of life they feared losing, that is, in Long's words "a home and the comforts of a home, including such conveniences as automobile and radio," all "free of debt."[41] They felt estranged both from the rich and the working class. It was plausible for a while that they might identify themselves as a separate class, as in Germany.

Many contradictory policies were attempted in the short span of a few years to restore mechanisms of social cohesion that only affluence could bring. The two main alternatives were to generate wealth by stimulating market mechanisms or to engage in the politics and programs of redistribution in the name of social justice. Although most schemes emerged as compromises between these two objectives, the New Deal programs favored means of generating wealth instead of redistributing it. To do so, the underconsumptionist argument that was initially popularized in the 1920s ultimately won the day among politicians, policymakers, businessmen, and union leaders alike. And the solutions tried during the Depression contributed to further definition of the social contract in terms of easy access to the mass market. By boosting consumer spending, FDR's "economic bill of rights" promoted essentially the right to consume and turned into national policy a process already well underway.[42]

Efforts to promote the social justice solution quickly lost steam. Early in the New Deal, the movement to "share the work" scored a temporary victory when the Senate passed Alabama Senator Hugo Black's bill to reduce the work week to thirty hours.[43] Partisans of the bill, including AFL president William Green and his allies primarily in labor-intensive industries such as clothing and textile, argued that such a measure was needed to reduce unemployment as well as to eliminate overproduction.[44] But the ultimately defeated legislation faced fierce opposition from Roosevelt, as well as the larger business community, who preferred economic stimulation over income redistribution. They believed that public works and pump priming measures were more hopeful means of recovery.[45] With the help of Senator Robert Wagner, FDR and his cabinet offered the National Industrial Recovery Act as an alternative to the zero-sum game of rationing work. NIRA was conceived as a major effort in planning work, wages, and consumption. Part of it was aimed at industrial stabilization through wage-price formulas theoretically designed to restore purchasing power. Another part emphasized cooperation between capital and labor (section 7a guaranteed union organization and collective bargaining and outlawed yellow-dog contracts). Title II of the act created the Public Works Administration for employment in public projects.[46] Generating new resources seemed more satisfying than sharing existing ones.

The short-lived National Recovery Administration (1933–35) that the bill created was therefore predicated at least in part on the idea that the government had to promote purchasing power, four years before the New Deal openly embraced Keynesian principles. The 1934 review of *Current Economic Policies* and the 1937 presidential review of the NRA both contain the decisive statement that the NRA was built around the theory that depressions were caused by inadequate mass purchasing power. There was also some recognition within the administration, emerging from the evolution of antimonopoly thinking that some forms of producer combination (trade associations, for example) could be useful in controlling prices and preventing the unpredicted and sometimes disastrous effects of cutthroat competition. The main thrust of NRA policies aimed at restoring mass purchasing power, however, gave the advantage to large Northern "center" firms best prepared for working out partnerships with labor. These policies prompted fear, resentment, and noncompliance with codes from low-wage Southern firms and more generally "peripheral" industries.[47]

From his office at the Works Progress Administration, the "world's greatest spender" Harry Hopkins looked at public projects as a means of putting paychecks in the hands of people who would immediately spend their money on consumer items.[48] His rationale and hopes were shared and articulated by a number of economists. Undersecretary of Commerce John Dickinson described the New Deal in 1934 as an effort to increase farmers' and workers' ability to pay.[49] Although NRA codes and compliance varied greatly among industries and regions, many politicians, business leaders, and economists saw decent wages as the most direct way to boost the "inadequate mass purchasing power" on which they blamed the Depression.[50] In the end, the NRA's opponents brought its demise precisely by arguing its failure to live up to such initial goals.[51]

MASS CONSUMPTION AS THE AMERICAN MEANS OF SOCIAL COHESION

Several groups of businessmen, led by the Business Advisory Council (BAC), recognized the failure of laissez-faire capitalism and the need for greater federal intervention in the economy. When the BAC was formed in 1933 by investment banker and railroad heir W. Averell Harriman, it was a real Who's Who of big business top executives who wanted to promote purchasing power: Gerard Swope of GE, Alexander Legge of International Harvester, Walter Teagle of Standard Oil, Alfred Sloan of General Motors, and Boston merchant Edward Filene (who had pioneered the credit union movement in the 1920s). BAC became a backer of the social security system, and a voice for planning among businessmen, as well as a source of top managers in mobilization agencies during World War II.[52] BAC first articulated the postwar program for "corporate liberalism."[53]

Within BAC, Edward Filene promoted a fiscal policy influenced by British economist John Maynard Keynes's ideas on deficit spending. Filene's advocacy of Keynesian principles was seconded by other businessmen, particularly Beardsley Ruml, who was a pioneer of social engineering. Ruml had abruptly left his job as dean of the social sciences at the University of Chicago to become the treasurer of Macy's department store. Ruml's unexpected departure from academic life took his colleagues by surprise. It prompted the wife of the University of Chicago president to quip that Ruml was giving up "ideas for notions." This remark was spirited but missed the point. At Macy's, Ruml learned much about the ways mass consumption was reshaping American society. And when named a director of the Federal Reserve Bank of New York in 1937, he renewed close ties with New Dealers like Charles Merriam and Frederic Delano of the National Resources Planning Board and came to know many of those in the administration who were moving toward Keynesianism.[54] Feeling that the country was drifting toward another economic collapse in 1937, Ruml worried that the government might repeat the 1933 mistake of attempting to balance the budget rather than engaging in deficit spending. He too began to formulate a Keynesian approach to what the government should do. Ruml was unexpectedly called upon to elaborate on these arguments for the president, and his intervention proved to be decisive.

In March 1938, FDR retired to Warm Springs, Georgia, to formulate his strategy to stop the so-called Roosevelt recession, which was prompted by his abrupt brake on deficit spending. Treasury Secretary Morgenthau urged him toward a balanced budget to restore business confidence. To counter the secretary, head of WPA Harry Hopkins went to Warm Springs to make the case for a renewed spending program.[55] Hopkins asked two of his own advisors, Leon Henderson of the Commerce Department and Aubrey Williams, director of the National Youth Administration, to stay in nearby Pine Mountain to counsel him while he was visiting with the president. By sheer coincidence, Hopkins's associates met Ruml on the train as he was on his way to visit Macy's store in Atlanta. Ruml agreed to go to Pine Mountain instead to help make the case for spending.[56]

With Henderson's and Williams's help, Ruml drafted the main memorandum that gave Hopkins the winning argument. The three developed a historical perspective on government spending. As economist Herbert Stein tells the story, they argued that the federal government had always created purchasing power through the somewhat indirect process of alienation of the national domain. Land grants to railroads were a perfect example; the unlimited coinage of California gold another; franchises and tariffs more evidence of federal action. Pushing mass consumption was only one additional step in a well-established historical process. "It follows," Ruml concluded, "that the competitive capitalist system has been sustained from the beginning by federal intervention to create purchasing power."[57] This argument for historical continuity swayed Roosevelt. The next logical step was to turn to borrowing to create purchasing power.

New Deal deficit spending reached about 5 percent of GNP (Reagan deficit spending peaked at 6.0 percent of GNP in 1984).[58] The conceptual breakthrough was real and its implementation generated an array of American Keynesian views. Some Keynesians emphasized only monetary policies, mainly low interest rates; others, dubbed pump-primers, occasional doses of deficit spending; still others, labeled compensatory spenders, viewed capitalism as capable of only short periods of stable growth on its own. The most radical wing, termed the stagnationists, pushed for constant government intervention in the economy.[59] Harvard economist Alvin Hansen, who had initially resisted Keynesianism, led the stagnationists in the late thirties. He was especially persuasive after the recession of 1937–38 in pushing the state to take the lead in the "bold steps" Keynes had advocated in his 1933 open letter to FDR. By the time of his 1938 presidential address to the American Economic Association, the formerly reluctant Hansen had translated the *General Theory* into "an American idiom."[60] In his *Full Recovery or Stagnation?* he developed a stages theory of economic development in which he argued that the time had come for government's intervention in the economy on a permanent basis.

With economic adviser to FDR Lauchlin Currie, he argued that "public policy should aim at moving the United States to a 'higher-consumption and lower-saving' economy."[61]

The national policy of sustaining mass consumption as the basis for American democracy was emblematic of the "American century" as liberals saw it. Liberal policymakers were increasingly supported in their endeavor by a new labor movement representing a number of workers much larger than those previously affiliated in the AFL. Big business executives and neo-Keynesian economists were joined by labor leaders in stressing mass consumption as part of a renewed social contract of abundance. Clothing workers' leader Sidney Hillman was convinced from the beginning of the Depression that a high standard of living was "no more a question of mere justice." It was instead "essential to our system of mass production to create a consumer's demand for almost unlimited output."[62] Although such key CIO figures as Hillman, the coalminers' John Lewis, the autoworkers' Walter Reuther, and many others intimately knew the meaning of class struggle, their victories brought an ever greater segment of the working class of mostly semiskilled workers into the society of consumers. The nationalism of World War II that shattered both radical unions and ethnic particularism combined with the vast array of New Deal and post–World War II neo-Keynesian policies to finish the job.

Recognizing this trend, recent interpretations of working-class history have departed from an older emphasis on class consciousness to focus instead on labor consumerism. Some, who perhaps would have preferred to see John Lewis's radicalism prevail, have condemned Hillman for giving up confrontation for consumption.[63] Others have accused UAW's Walter Reuther of the "Faustian bargain" of trading mutualism for acquisitive individualism. Reuther's efforts climaxed with the May 1950 "Treaty of Detroit," as Daniel Bell called it, that gave GM's workers unprecedented high wages and benefits but kept full managerial prerogatives in the hands of managers.[64] It was the beginning of a postwar era of conservative prosperity. Rather than foreseeing a country polarized with antagonistic classes, policymakers saw a trend toward a congeries of middle classes, unionized workers among them, with only relics of obsolete classes standing above and below. In contrast to the situation in Europe, consumption, not welfare, was the American means of social cohesion.

American consumers of the 1950s emerged as the "people of plenty," as historian David Potter called them.[65] The so-called consensus of the postwar era, echoed in the voices of social scientists who provided policymakers with the tools to manage abundance, revealed Americans' massive commitment to a consumption economy. "Consensus," however, is a very unsatisfactory word. But if there ever was something approaching a shared communal myth in the postwar era, it was reflected in the debates on what I have called the high-low principle and the subsequent formulas for high wages and low prices that promised to give the largest possible number of people middle-class status.[66] With a growing agreement on consumption in a middle-class society, the task of economic policy concentrated on giving an ever larger majority of the population full access to the market. Such became the overriding goal of American economic policy—a goal that both capitalists and labor leaders shared. There was never a consensus on protective legislation, welfare measures, the safety net, health insurance, or employment policies. But there was one on the need to nurture a society of consumers.

An affluent consumer society with numerous possibilities for personal advancement has had enormous psychological implications for twentieth-century white Americans. It has made each individual appear so much more responsible for his or her own fate. As Marie Jahoda, a psychoanalyst and refugee scholar from Vienna who lived both in the United States and England since the late 1930s, has observed from the front row:

> Before J. K. Galbraith popularized the phrase, America was an affluent society in which the belief that everybody could reach the top was widespread, almost universal. . . . In England before the war the ambitious working-class youngster knew that the class structure was holding him back. He could join a labor movement and find satisfaction in collective experience; though his individual fate was frustrating, he did not need to lose self-respect. Society was at fault, not he. His counterpart in the States, even in the relatively rare instance in which he joined a political movement, was confronted with the powerful ethos of his society: he believed in his heart that he had nobody to blame but himself.[67]

Under such circumstances, the psychoanalysis that Jahoda practiced in her adoptive America helped relieve individuals from full responsibility for their failures, which may have been beyond their control.

Postwar prosperity seemed to reaffirm the many advantages of a consumer society, but it also led to two assumptions that unfortunately did not bear close scrutiny. The first was that abundance would be recreated *ad infinitum*. Postwar Americans, who faced no real economic competitors around the globe, were generally confident that they could always find the means to generate prosperity. The possibility of a Great Society emerged from that assurance.

The second was that everybody could share in the prosperity. Liberal policymakers, to be sure, were conscious of racial discrimination. But the culture of abundance and growth they promoted left little theoretical space for poverty. Alternative cultures were blamed for causing the problems that created them in the first place. But no matter the problems at home, an expansive middle class of average citizens, defined by access to abundance, became the emblem of the American century. It was the forerunner of social change in other industrialized economies, as Americans made their power felt around the world and, wherever they could, advocated their vision of society.

CHAPTER FIVE

DERADICALIZING CLASS

The Lord prefers the common people. That is the reason he makes so many of them.

ATTRIBUTED TO ABRAHAM LINCOLN[1]

What made American corporate capitalism distinctive was not its superior technological prowess, for competition with Europeans for technological innovation was fierce. It was instead the ability of American managers to put technological innovations to the service of an organizational revolution promoting mass consumption.[2] In this endeavor, the difficulty was to reconcile mass and class. Satisfying a fictional average customer was one procedure; producing different versions of the same product for average consumers in specialized markets another. To reach as large a mass as possible, American marketers sought to meet people's real expectations while downplaying the significance of their class divisions. Whereas nineteenth-century plutocrats had looked to the workings of the market to justify social inequality, twentieth-century marketers saw themselves as modern-day levelers who could accommodate different groups within a single deradicalized class.[3]

Their vision of a market society at once homogeneous and diversified developed during the interwar years just when pollsters and other applied psychologists attempted to bridge the ideas of the average American and of social stratification. Historian David Potter expressed this effort well in suggesting that if "the American class structure is in reality very unlike the classless society which we imagine, it is equally unlike the formalized class societies of former times, and thus it should be regarded as a new kind of social structure in which the strata may be fully demarcated but where the bases of demarcation are relatively intangible."[4] People move rather easily from level to level. This vision of stratification reached its highest level of popularity after World War II, for it allowed marketers, policymakers, and social scientists to talk about an American middle class that was both uniform and divided.

SOCIAL STRATIFICATION: ALFRED P. SLOAN'S BREAKTHROUGH

The movement to segment the entire mass of American consumers took off when president of General Motors Alfred P. Sloan sought ways to compete with Henry Ford in the early 1920s.[5] While most car manufacturers had heretofore sought the attention only of upper-class buyers, Ford sought to capture the mass market with his Model T. In 1921, Ford sold 845,000 vehicles, more than 55 percent of all automobiles purchased.[6] Furthermore, he was selling the popular car practically at cost, making a profit of only $2 per unit.

In approaching the challenge of competing with Ford, Sloan reconceptualized the entire relationship between the market and consumers. Dismissing the dichotomy between upper-class taste and mass taste, he discarded established class boundaries and concentrated instead on the car buyers' ability to consume. Sloan's major breakthrough was to erect a ladder of consumption that consumers could learn and climb. His new product policy specified a line of cars in each price area, with small price steps and no duplication. By manufacturing "a car for every purse and purpose" along a critical consumption ladder, Sloan broadened consumer choice. As *Fortune* described the new GM five-nameplate product series, Chevrolet was redesigned "for the hoi polloi," Pontiac "for the poor but proud," Oldsmobile "for the comfortable but discreet," Buick "for the striving," and Cadillac "for the rich."

At the time Sloan implemented this marketing strategy, GM was still an aggregate of the various companies assembled by William T. Durant and now controlled by Du Pont. "Each division," Sloan later recalled, "in the absence of a corporation policy, operated independently, making its own price and production policies, which landed some cars in identical price positions without relationship to the interests of the enterprise as a whole." In 1921, all lines except Buick and Cadillac were losing money.[7] Sloan needed the principle to reorganize them. He was also helped in his task of redefining GM by Henry Ford's unwillingness to adjust his Model T to reach an increasingly sophisticated mass market.[8] While Ford took aim at what he perceived was the fat middle of the market, Sloan went after the whole population of potential buyers. In addition to a choice of automobiles, he initiated a color option and the annual model change. While all Model T's were black, Sloan introduced Dupont's quick-drying "DUCO" for the "true blue" Oakland, which was renamed Pontiac in 1924. Moreover, model changes helped differentiate purchasers of new and used cars.[9]

If I am recalling this story famous in the annals of American business, it is because Sloan envisioned all of American society as potential customers. He targeted different versions of the same good to specific market strata. His idea was that Americans would not buy just a means of transportation but an emblem of their status and/or aspirations. Sloan envisioned a mass market where all Americans could think of their purchases as part of their larger quest for social mobility.

Sloan's policy disrupted not just the market but the conventional way of thinking about society. As Sloan himself put it, "the idea of this policy seems pretty simple, like a shoe manufacturer proposing to sell shoes in more than one size. But it certainly did not seem simple" in 1921.[10] It meant breaking down the mass of consumers into niches that reflected economic and social-psychological realities. In doing so, however, the GM board acted on its intuitive perception of society. There was never any mention of formal research. Rather, GM executives relied on their crude sense of income differences and their intuition of customer taste.

Soon, however, the GM sales section refined techniques for estimating demand. By 1923, Albert Bradley of the financial staff formulated the idea of a "pyramid of demand." He pushed for "the analysis of market potential by price class" to understand the "relationship between potential automobile demand and the distribution of income in the United States."[11] Under his guidance, GM executives began experimenting in collecting and interpreting relevant sociological data. With time, GM refined its sales strategy not only for cars but also for its other product lines.

GM executives reconciled mass and class. Thus when it came time to market Frigidaire, the refrigerator produced by a GM subsidiary, executives sought to satisfy both the average consumer and the various consumption strata. They were ably advised in this matter by Lord and Thomas, the advertising agency they hired to tackle the problem.[12]

Lord and Thomas advertisers explicitly defined for their client the marketing compromise between mass and class. Although their work was not yet informed by any scientific principles of social stratification, they presented their client with a few powerful principles of marketing that would eventually reinforce the social tendencies they were diagnosing. First was their keen awareness of a mass market governed not by the taste of the elites but by that of the average American. As advertisers put it, "when you have sold four million of anything, as Frigidaire has, and with say 7,500,000 electric refrigerators in use, it is obvious that somebody else besides the [upper] classes" is buying them. Then added: "If there is any change that has come over the profession, it is a change from talking to the two yacht family and showing ordinary people instead." "Ordinary," in this instance, meant the average middle-class consumer.

Second came a basic psychological rule of merchandising: the need to market products in ways that made customers feel good about themselves when buying them. An advertisement, they said, should be like a flattering "mirror" where a consumer "sees himself reflected."[13] Third was market expansion: the imperative not to neglect any potential customer, especially among the working class, in a sales campaign. Advertising agents suggested that their campaigns "must not exclude the important and growing wage earner market." Bypass only those members of society clearly without access to spendable income or credit.

Fourth, the ladder of consumption had to be realistic. People should be asked to aspire to products they could eventually afford: "If we show a man someone in his class of life whose standards are just a little better than his, he will probably want to emulate him; but if we show him a millionaire, and he makes $20 a week, he knows better than try to compete." Therefore, steps in the ladder of consumption had to be high enough to be appealing but small enough to be attainable. The art of merchandising was to grant prestige to customers by tying their purchases closely to their quest for higher status.

The fifth and last principle, however, would turn out to be the most important in thinking of the mass of consumers as middle-class Americans. It was the advertisers' diagnosis that the best way to penetrate the ladder of consumption was at the point of least resistance, that is somewhere in the fat middle of the market. Not only did the advertisers know that in appearance the bulk of the advertisements "must not be Fifth Avenue, but that they must be middle class," they also realized how crucial the market level of entry was to the success of any campaign. By the 1930s, advisors to Frigidaire were proposing that their client envision a large middle class market. They questioned the wisdom of "the theory of penetration from the top down," and suggested instead an alternative theory of market penetration "from the middle class down and perhaps also up."[14]

From market penetration to middle class expansion, there was a tempting short conceptual step. The trick of rethinking the market according to both mass and segments could not be separated from larger efforts of reconceptualizing society. As Americans found themselves purchasing goods that were both mass produced and designed for their market strata, they learned to manage the sleight of hand of simultaneously thinking of themselves as lost in the growing mass of consumers, as part of a group with a special taste, and as upwardly mobile.

THE SOCIAL SCIENCES

Marketers defined boundaries between segments of the population to the extent that it helped them sell products. They did not care about class except as an indication of consumption. But so successful had marketers been at creating a national ladder of consumption for mass-produced goods that the social scientists saw in consumption a new way to measure class. Social scientists formalized some of the distinctions marketers were advancing and made them a function of class. They eventually handed back their research to the marketers and gave them a scientific justification for their practice.

Many social scientists interested in the development of consumption pat-

terns were at first ambivalent about business efforts aimed at remapping class
for marketing strategies. It had been the intensity of labor conflicts that, by
prompting a vigorous regulatory response from local, state, and federal governments, had given social investigation and social science much of its raison
d'être in the Progressive Era. As a result, many still viewed class relations
through the prism of labor. Former Presbyterian minister and muckraker-
turned-sociologist Robert Lynd's inconsistent approach to class was in this
respect typical. While serving as secretary of the Rockefeller-funded Social
Science Research Council, Lynd accepted an appointment from Rockefeller's
Institute of Social and Religious Research to explore social trends in Muncie,
Indiana, which resulted in the classic 1929 study, *Middletown: A Study in
Modern American Culture,* co-authored with his wife Helen. While the
Lynds diagnosed consumption as a major preoccupation in Middletown, they
yearned for the producer ethic they saw the American working class losing.
Holding on to still relevant but older categories of class analysis, they identified citizens of Middletown either with the business class or the working class
and posited a dialectic of class consciousness and conflict. But in his contribution the same year to Herbert Hoover's report on *Recent Social Trends* entitled
"The People as Consumers," Lynd fully acknowledged the scale of the consumer revolution. He reported that very little that Americans had consumed
in the 1920s had been made at home or bartered; virtually everything had
been bought. Pointing to the increasing consumption that goes along with
greater amounts of leisure, he called for research on the "personality adjustment of the individual consumer."[15]

That call was being answered around him. Among the social scientists who
pioneered the study of the connection between purchasing and class was F.
Stuart Chapin, a student of Edward Thorndike and John Dewey at Columbia.
Chapin believed that industry and commerce should expand abundance and
bring more harmonious social relations. At Minnesota, where he spent most
of his teaching career, Chapin created a center for the new quantitative efforts
in social science. Very much a navigator of the matrix of inquiry, he was asked
to become one of the first directors of SSRC, where he was an effective advocate for his university.[16]

Chapin's main contribution to marketing was to conceive of class as a function of consumption. In 1927, Chapin invented what he called a living room
scale, which came out of his growing interest in behaviorism and his belief
that the best way to measure class was to observe consumer behavior.[17] Supported with Laura Spelman Rockefeller Memorial research money, he constructed an index of class from the observations of living room furniture. His

main goal was to use his living room scale to a establish a middle-class standard against which to compare the other classes. He therefore selected a large number of "middle class" or "upper middle-class" families and reviewed and rated four categories of items available on the mass market in their living rooms: fixed features (items such as floors, wall covering, windows and window covering); built-in features (book shelves, window seats); standard furniture (tables, chairs, sewing machine); furnishings and cultural resources (lamps, clocks, newspapers and periodicals, pottery, pictures)—the higher the rating, the higher the socioeconomic status. He then correlated the results with the parents' education, their occupational status, as well as the IQ and vocabulary level of their children. To him, the living room reflected "cultural acquisitions, the possessions, and the socioeconomic status of family." Working toward reconciling objective with subjective measurements, he defined socioeconomic status as the "position" an "individual or family occupies with reference to the prevailing average standards of cultural possessions, effective income, material possessions, and participation in the group activity of the community."[18] To merchandisers who wanted to understand the range of consumer behavior, Chapin's efforts in the 1920s and 1930s marked the beginning of significant empirical work on the matter within academic circles.

Among social scientists, it was W. Lloyd Warner, an anthropologist-turned-sociologist, who eventually did the most in the 1930s and 1940s to reconcile social scientists' conceptualization of class with marketers' ladder of consumption. Warner gave a tremendous boost to marketing efforts not only by tying class closely to consumption but by grasping and publicizing Americans' understanding of social standing. Warner provided analytical tools to those who needed them in the marketing world while directing academic research away from issues of class conflicts toward questions of status and prestige.

As an outsider to the field, Warner had a fresh approach. He did not share the Social Gospel, pro-labor background of most reformers of an older generation. He had trained as a social anthropologist at Berkeley and spent three years studying the Murngin people of northeastern Arnhem land in Australia. But when he joined the Anthropology Department at Harvard in 1929, he took a keen interest in the new work in industrial psychology Elton Mayo was conducting at the Harvard Business School and contributed to Mayo's experiments on workers' motivation at Western Electric. When Warner decided to investigate issues of class and community in the United States, Mayo helped him launch his Yankee City studies, conducted at first from Harvard, then after 1935 from Chicago; the first volume appeared in 1941.[19] As he was associated with Mayo, Warner could have concentrated his fieldwork on

Cicero, the site of the Western Electric Hawthorne plant where Mayo had many contacts. But Cicero was too well known as a teeming city of immigrants and also gangsters; Al Capone had established his headquarters there.[20] Warner's idea was to concentrate on a more traditional community to measure class. He chose the seemingly more homogeneous and Protestant Massachusetts town of Newburyport.

Warner developed a method of measurement that completely ignored the relation of power at the production site and relied entirely on a measure of status, conferred mostly by consumption, to rank order people in a given community. He divided the population of the community into six classes he labeled "upper-upper"; "lower-upper"; "upper-middle"; "lower-middle"; "upper-lower"; and "lower-lower." Like Sloan, Warner saw each class as a step on a status ladder. For Warner the top 3 percent of any community were in the first two classes, those he called "upper-upper" or "uu" (1.4 percent) and "lower-upper" or "lu" (1.6 percent). They comprised the "old aristocracy" as well as the "new families being fortunate enough to participate with the top group in their clubs and cliques." He felt, however, that the "new families" were "socially inferior to the old ones," even though they had "more money, better houses, more expensive automobiles, and other material goods that are superior in dollars and cents to those of their social superiors." "If the success of the new families is due to wealth, their money is felt to be too new; if due to occupational triumph, their achievement is too recent."

At the "upper middle" or "um" level, just below the "lu," Warner placed the "solid citizens who are the active civic leaders of the community." Warner estimated them to make up 10 percent of the population, and he remarked that, for the most ambitious of them, "the presence of an upper class sufficiently open to make it possible for some of their level to climb into it is a source of continuing frustration or anxious anticipation." Altogether, "uu," "lu," and "um" (13 percent of the population) constituted "the level above the common man" in Yankee City.

Warner wanted to show that his placements of people in the upper classes were supported by the keen observations of such talented watchers of the social scene as Sinclair Lewis. He therefore applied his Index of Status Characteristics (ISC), which rated four "objective" social characteristics (occupation, source of income, house type, dwelling area), to Lewis's *Babbitt*, the American novel of the 1920s portraying consumption in the greatest detail, and easily confirmed Lewis's perception of upper-class Zenith.[21] Thus the ISC for William Eathorne, an old-family, upper-class character Babbitt wanted to associate with, was easy to compute. Warner explained:

He is director of several large corporations including a bank. His principal source of income is from several generations of inherited wealth giving him a 1 for this characteristic. He lives in a mansion in Floral Heights, for which he scores a 1 in house type and a 2 for the area in which he lives. After multiplying each score by its proper weight he achieves the total of 14, only two points below a perfect 12. The fact that he and a few others like him preferred to live in Floral Heights after it had become a new development filled with Babbitts and their Dutch Colonial bungalows pulls down his ISC, but not sufficiently to change his score from near the top of his upper-class range.

Babbitt, however, scored only 26, "putting him at the high end of the ISC range for upper-middle class." Babbitt received "a 1 . . . as a proprietor for occupation; a 3 for profits as his source of income; a 3 for his Dutch Colonial Bungalow, which is above average but not a 2, and he rates a 2, as did Eathorne, for living in Floral Heights." In addition to ISC, Warner computed a second index of class in "Yankee city," which he called evaluated participation. That measure was constructed from interviews with Newburyport residents placing other residents in his classification schemes.[22]

Resorting to an old phrase to describe a new reality, Warner's description of the next two classes focused on "the common man." Warner's common man, like that of Vice President Henry Wallace, was the average man—the center of gravity—of the new consumption society.[23] In Wallace's words, the "common man" of 1941 was a "middle class American" enjoying all the comforts of a "home of his own with all the conveniences that modern science has made possible: electric light, central heating, modern plumbing, electric washing machine, electric refrigeration, radio, comfortable furniture and rugs" as well as "ample food," "a car neither old nor ramshackle, decent clothes and books," some recreation including "movies or theater, trips, vacations, horse-racing, football, golf, or tennis, as his taste is inclined," and "high school and college for his children." This would become "the American way of life" for "the great mass of our people," FDR's vice-president predicted as soon as Americans could apply their energies to peacetime prosperity.[24]

Warner's "common man level" included as much as 61 percent of the population distributed between 28 percent lower middle class ("lm") and 33 percent upper lower class ("ul"). In Warner's words, "the lower-middle class, the top of the common man level, is composed economically of small businessmen, a few highly skilled workmen, and a large number of clerks and other workers in similar categories. Members of this class tend to be extremely

proper and conservative. They belong to patriotic organizations, fraternal orders." They live in the little houses, "with well-kept but cramped gardens and
lawns." Warner saw the men and women of this class as approaching "the
ideal typical of the Protestant ethic, being careful with their money, saving,
farsighted, forever anxious about what their neighbors think, and continually
concerned about respectability." He understood the second tier of the "common man level"—"the semiskilled workers, the small tradesmen, and often
the less-skilled employees of service enterprises" to be "highly respectable,"
albeit "limited in their outlook on the world around them."

In Warner's scheme, the bottom 25 percent of the city's population were
considered to be lower-lower class, that is, at a "level below the common
man." Warner estimated this quarter of the population to be a grab bag of
"pitied unfortunates," "greenhorns," and "ethnic peoples." "Starting at the
bottom, they begin their slow ascent in our status system," if they moved at
all.[25]

If I have gone on at length about Warner, it is not because I subscribe to
his explicit or implied value judgments. It is instead because Warner's work
gave marketing and advertising executives a tool to apprehend and quantify
society as a whole. The *Journal of Marketing* heralded Warner's 1948 book
Social Class in America as "the most important step forward to market research in many years." For merchandisers, the bulk of the market resided in
Warner's fourth and fifth classes which "constitute, together, about 65 percent of the population in a typical community and make up a great concentration of the nation's purchasing power."[26] Marketers were busy turning
Warner's "lm" into enthusiastic buyers. They recognized the third of the
population in the "ul category" as the core of an expanding mass market.
Above them, the top three classes were the "so-called 'quality market.' " The
25 percent at society's bottom were unpredictable.

Within academia, Warner's scheme fared well but met also with resistance.
Chief among the critics was C. Wright Mills, who reviewed volume 1 of *Yankee City* in 1942. To Mills, who was attached to individual entrepreneurship
and the producer ethos and who did not like the idea of mass consumption,
Warner's *Yankee City* was no substitute for Lynd's *Middletown*. Mills took
Warner to task for his failure to define "class" adequately and to appreciate
the significance of class conflicts. The words Warner used, Mills charged accurately, came closer to looking at "status" than class. If they conveyed economic
and power relations at all, it was only as "sponge" terms, which absorb a
host of meanings and are difficult to use precisely. Furthermore, Warner's

anthropological background led him to overgeneralize "community" and confuse it with "society"— allowing Newburyport to stand in for the United States (a distortion the Lynds also made with Muncie, Indiana as Middletown).[27] The Texan sociologist turned New Yorker who would conceptualize *The Power Elite* (1956) made some important points against Warner. The power elite, however, had no need for him. They throve instead on Warner, whom they read. What especially excited businessmen in Warner's work as they adapted it to their purpose was precisely what turned Mills off: that the social structure had a huge center and could be at the same time stratified and fluid.

THE INFUSION OF SOCIAL SCIENCE INTO MARKETING

While marketers and social scientists had initially followed distinct paths, they increasingly merged their efforts in the years following World War II under the large heading of "motivation research," billed by its advocates as a new trend in social engineering. Its purpose was to give people "the sanction and justification to enjoy" a life of abundance. Researchers like Ernest Dichter and Burleigh Gardner wanted to make "democracy" accessible simply by making it easier for people to buy goods. Although Dichter readily admitted that "material possessions cannot satisfy us completely," he nonetheless argued that "the surest sign of unhappiness" was "the lack of things to enjoy." Dichter, following Warner, had no qualms asserting that it would become "customary," if present marketing trends were sustained, "to describe an individual's personality not by referring to him as one who is timid or self-conscious or characterized by other traits, but rather, for example, as one who wears an Adam hat, drives a Plymouth car, drinks PM whiskey, and wears Arrow ties and shirts."[28]

Motivation researchers were busy putting social science to the service of the market. Pierre Martineau, director of research of the marketing division of the *Chicago Tribune* in the 1950s, refined methods borrowed from studies of mass consumption funded by the Twentieth Century Fund (the research foundation created by merchant reformer Edward Filene) to survey the Chicago area. He exchanged data with the newly created Survey Research Center at the University of Michigan. The most influential figure in Martineau's life was University of Chicago sociologist Lloyd Warner. The two men were friends; Warner had informally tutored Martineau in the social sciences. He also reinforced Martineau's belief in social mobility. The marketing executive remembered Warner as infusing in him the idea that every American should act as if he were "free, white, and twenty-one, completely able to handle the world, and perfectly willing to gamble on himself as a sure bet to succeed."[29]

Another key personality of the movement came directly from Warner's team and was also close to Martineau. Burleigh Gardner had studied at Harvard with both Warner and Elton Mayo. He had assisted Warner in the Newburyport study. Upon completing his doctorate in social anthropology in 1936, he worked in human relations at the Western Electric Hawthorne works, where Mayo had conducted his investigations. In 1943, Gardner was appointed assistant professor in the University of Chicago School of Business but he left teaching in 1946 to create his own marketing firm, Social Research, Incorporated.

Gardner's goal was "to sell the U.S. by class" following the concepts of the status-symbol school of sociology, as the Warner group came to be known. That brand of marketing was premised on "the old American urge for self-betterment and self-expression." As a status-symbol sociologist, Gardner held that people expressed "their personalities not so much in words as in symbols (i.e., mannerisms, dress, ornaments, possessions)" and that they were increasingly concerned about the "symbols of various social positions." Businessmen, who are more practical than academic sociologists, want to understand class, explained Gardner to *Fortune*. While the latter have sometimes been prone to deny the existence of class for ideological reasons, businessmen "find that a knowledge of the social structure enables them to organize lots of facts about consumer behavior." They want to understand "complex set[s] of symbols" that are involved every time they "advertise, or merely package a product." For, as the ad executives working for Frigidaire had asserted in the 1930s, the key was to make the ladder of consumption an instrument of class emulation. The new motivation research school insisted that "group boundaries" were not the "boundaries of people's aspirations." Rather, the "urge of self-expression and self-betterment shared by nearly all Americans take[s] the form of aspiring to higher status. Thus people tend to buy things that symbolize their aspirations—a certain make of car, a certain style of house, a certain mode of dress. Their very status aspiration, in other words, drives them to emulate 'better' taste and upgrade their own."[30]

By extending from the luxury to the mass market the conceptual linkage between purchasing and status, Warner and his students had opened possibilities for analyzing consumer behavior on a large scale. Martineau and Gardner were putting social science to the service of marketing. At the same time, university-based scholars were beginning to view market research as central to social science's pursuit of basic knowledge. This enlarged emphasis was the significant contribution of refugee scholar Paul Lazarsfeld, who, with Talcott Parsons and Robert Merton, is today widely considered a major figure of the postwar generation in the then increasingly influential field of sociology. Lazarsfeld's studies of purchasing behavior led to methodological contributions to survey research and quantitative social science that were enormously influential across the entire institutional matrix of knowledge.

In Vienna, Lazarsfeld had been greatly impressed by Alfred Adler and the Gestalt psychology of Karl Bühler that would allow him to move beyond behaviorism. Trained as a social psychologist, he had pioneered some market research in Austria and developed a keen interest in understanding *Handlung*, or "action." When Lazarsfeld moved to the United States in 1933 with assistance from the Paris office representative of the Rockefeller Foundation, he discovered a climate where his "interest in more concrete work" than allowed in European intellectual circles could flourish. Robert Lynd took a liking to the young scholar and helped him find a position in survey research. Lazarsfeld would soon direct the Rockefeller-funded Princeton office of radio studies, where he hired Theodor Adorno (see chap. 3), before moving his research organization to Columbia University.

Shortly after his arrival, and according to his own immodest evaluation of it, Lazarsfeld wrote "a fundamental paper on language as a special form of action" entitled "The Psychological Aspect of Market Research." That paper prefigured the rest of his career in that it combined theoretical considerations on "the structure of the act of purchasing," presented diagrams, proposed new terms ("Accent on Motivation") and intermingled these theoretical points with, as he put it, "interesting examples on the purchase of sweaters and soaps."[31]

Perhaps Lazarsfeld is most fondly remembered in the world of social science for his aphorism that circulated in the 1950s that there was a "methodological equivalence" between finding out why people voted for the socialist party and finding out why they bought a certain brand of soap.[32] That maxim reflected the view that consumption is a basic human enterprise simultaneously at the heart of everyday activities and social change. In 1906, when German economist Werner Sombart asked "Why is there no socialism in the United States?" he answered his question by pointing to the American worker's already superior purchasing power.[33] There was no possibility in 1906, however, of applying a "methodological equivalence" between voting for the socialists and purchasing soap. The two types of behaviors were not seen as comparable when employers were still enforcing blacklists of unionized workers, playing on the ethnic divisions of the working class, and appropriating the police and judicial power of the state.

But times had changed. In 1947, Dichter, whom Betty Friedan would single out as one of the master manipulators of his generation, could keep a straight face when arguing that soap had become "an important element in the psychology of everyday life":

> The number of friends we make, the amount of romance and adventure in our lives, the success of our marriage and of our business, all depend on soap. . . . Not only magazine and newspaper columns but also radio programs are used to propagandize the miraculous effects of soap. More than twelve percent of the income of the major radio networks is derived from sponsors of daytime serials. Because of their sponsorship, the stories are popularly known as "soap operas." . . . The characters experience friendship and romance, marriage and love, in some form or another. By association with the program, the soaps advertised take on a similar romantic aura.[34]

Dichter, like Lazarsfeld, had left his native Vienna to escape the Nazis and was Lazarsfeld's protégé.[35] As a new American, Dichter embraced market culture with unusual enthusiasm. The fact remains that purchasing for daily consumption on the mass market was becoming as important an indicator of Americans' collective identities and mores as the vote. As a consumer product, soap was actually more popular than democracy. The number of Americans who exercised their voting rights had been declining steadily from a high average of 77 percent for presidential elections between 1876 and 1900, to 60 percent between 1900 and 1916, to 50 percent between 1938 and 1960. The mass market for soap and a host of related products had instead become pervasive.[36]

By being so ubiquitous, the mass market generated a new consumer activism, initially but only temporarily tied to the labor movement. Middle-class women, who became increasingly instrumental in launching this new form of collective action, had become neither free from domestic drudgery nor social equals to men by being major consumers on the mass market. They played their part, however, in closing the gap between the sophisticated art of making money and the backward art of spending it, to borrow economist Wesley Mitchell's formulation.[37] As the young Walter Lippmann predicted in 1914, "the mass of women do not look at the world as workers; in America, at least their prime interest is as consumers. It is they who go to market and do the shopping; it is they who have to make the family budget go around; it is they who feel shabbiness and fraud and high prices most directly. They have more time for politics than men, and it is no idle speculation to say that their influence will make the consumer the real master of the political situation."[38]

Consumer consciousness began as a reformist drive to alleviate the plight of the working class. When the National Consumers' League was organized in 1898, its main purpose was to protect *not* consumers but workers. Florence Kelley, who represented the local Chicago Consumers' League at the May 1898 founding meeting of the national organization, could boast of her league's great work in teaming up with cigar workers to eliminate tenement sweatshops. She promoted a "consumer label" as reward to those industrialists who were fair with their workers and as retaliation against those who mistreated them, especially if the latter were women and children.[39] But soon middle-class women adopted the consumer banner to suit their own needs as customers. *Good Housekeeping* published a honor roll for the food products it approved a year before Congress passed the 1906 Pure Food and Drug Act and the Meat Inspection Act.

From that point on, women and men around the country organized an array of consumer clubs and voluntary organizations watching over manufacturers's shoulders for quality products in addition to workers's protection. They were ably helped in that task by the National Bureau of Standards's testing program and the diffusion in American homes of its instructional brochure *Care and Repair of the House*.[40] By 1927 these consumers were among the readers of the Book-of-the-Month-Club best-selling *Your Money's Worth* by Stuart Chase and F. J. Schlink. Encouraged by success, the two authors turned the suburban White Plains, New York, consumer club into Consumers' Research, Incorporated, of New York City and launched the publication of Consumers' Research Bulletin. They gained 42,000 subscribers in five years. By the time of the rival *Consumers Union Reports'* first issue in 1936, consumer consciousness had become widespread. The movement never abandoned concerns with factory conditions but focused primarily on the qualities of the goods themselves.[41]

PERSISTING BOUNDARIES

The relationship between consumer and class consciousness was partly a function of economic cycles. In the prosperous 1920s, the creation of a ladder of consumption that linked the mass market to the more luxury market had helped blur the line between blue- and white-collar workers. Turning the workers into consumers in the 1920s created the potential to integrate them into the middle class. At the same time, common participation in the mass market that softened the cultural divisions of an ethnically fractured working class also helped unite class-conscious workers. This is partly what took place as the Depression hit.[42] In the postwar era, a more prosperous working class invested again in the soothing effects of consumption.

The stratification models of marketers and sociologists alike were meant to describe a mass-market society where no cleavage was hard, no stratum sealed. Researchers were refining ways of measuring its gradations in fine detail: a continuum of subclasses according to such characteristics as access to education, income levels, patterns of friendship and association, habits of consumption and other variables. A vision of a classless society, that is, one where class becomes irrelevant because it is deradicalized by participation in the mass market, directed their work.[43] But how realistic was it to confuse, as they did, market stratification and social organization? Market researchers acknowledged the persistence of discrete class identities while denying class its radical potential. Thus Martineau and Gardner, who saw the extraordinary growth of the postwar unionized industrial workforce, witnessed not only the strikes caused by production readjustments but the settlements that turned unionized workers, teamsters, assembly line autoworkers, and steel workers into affluent suburbanite consumers. Yet they sensed a tension between working-class and middle-class versions of consumerism.

Martineau and Gardner attempted to figure out why affluent workers were still behaving more like workers than middle-class Americans. Martineau put the problem most succinctly: "We speak of America as a middle class society; but the middle class value system stops here." Looking at industrial Chicago in the 1950s, Martineau argued, "two-thirds of the society are *not* middle-class." Martineau counted as much as 44 percent of the Chicago population as part of a working class of consumers ready to be courted by capitalists. On the strength of that figure, he insisted on the power of class cohesion that held together "factory production workers," the "labor union-groups," the "skilled workers," the "service workers" and also the "politicians and union leaders who would lose their power if they moved out of their class."[44] He suggested a revised class pyramid where the bulk of the market was working class.

Relying on extensive probability sampling and survey research, Martineau concluded, "we must realize that between us (the upper middle class) and the vast majority of the market there are differences in communication skills, differences in moral viewpoint, differences in what constitutes humor, differences in sophistication, differences in the reception of advertising itself. The symbols we use for communication are often completely meaningless to the class we are trying to sell [to]."[45] Martineau then proceeded to draw important psychological distinctions "between the middle-class individual" and the "individual who is not a part of the middle-class system of values." Save for a small transitional group of people he labeled, in Warner's fashion, the "upper-lower 'stars' " or "light-blue collar workers," who have the income for more ostentatious living than the average factory worker but who lack the "personal skills or desire for high status by social mobility," Martineau rejected the notion that "a rich man is simply a poor man with more money."

Martineau understood mid-century well-paid industrial workers as primarily "savers," nonmobile people who rationalized their purchases "in terms of the savings involved" and their desire for financial security over risk. Analyzing the market for appliances, he combined his understanding of class with his theory of the workingman's search for security: "The upper-lower class man sees his home as his castle, his anchor to the world, and he loads it down with hardware—solid heavy appliances—as his symbol of security." Selling to the working class was therefore a completely different proposition from selling to the middle class, for "the kind of super-sophisticated and clever advertising which appears in the *New Yorker* and *Esquire*" was "almost meaningless to lower-status people. They cannot comprehend the subtle humor; they are baffled by the bizarre art." By contrast, Martineau characterized the middle class "mobile individual" as "spending for various symbols of upward movement" as well as "for display and consumption." Middle-class buyers bought stocks because they were risk-takers. They spent money on "hobbies, recreation, self-education and travel" because they were seeking new experiences.[46]

Market researchers like Martineau were far less willing to forego the concept of class than more ideologically oriented social scientists and politicians. Market researchers, however, wanted to deradicalize the concept. They intended to identify working-class taste in order to please it, but they had no need to think of class as anything more than a mere market stratum. They wanted a working class without Marxism and a conservative labor movement that turned workers into consumers. The irony is that marketers cultivated a class/stratum consciousness as a tool to penetrate the market but feared its disruptive potential. They did not want class consciousness but they could not do without it.

If workers in the country's industrial heartland did not use the ladder of consumption as marketers had initially intended, African Americans, by being excluded from the mass market, could feel neither the equalizing nor the up-lifting effects of consumerism. A mass-market society rests on maximizing freedom and mobility, two qualities American society denied its black citizens. Not active participants in the mass market, African Americans were not part of the polity. Although segregation precluded any effective use of market solutions for racial justice, the group of liberal businessmen and market-oriented social scientists revolving around Lloyd Warner attempted to assess the potential effects of the new mass market on the internal class structure of black communities. By joining the faculty of the University of Chicago in 1935, Warner found himself immersed in a great academic center of racial integration with a strong commitment to sociological studies of race. It was at Chicago that Robert Park, once Booker T. Washington's secretary and the leading figure in the burgeoning field of urban sociology, had taught E. Franklin Frazier the techniques of urban research. Warner was to build on the Park-Frazier tradition and help a new generation of African-American scholars conceptualize the peculiar class system of segregation in the new age of mass consumption.

Frazier had already done much to challenge the customary categorization of 90 percent of the black population in a lower class. Standard notions of occupational stratification did not apply to African Americans trapped in the Northern ghetto, Frazier argued in his studies of black occupational structure after the great migration. These categories were too vague to convey the finer sense of social structure that existed in black communities cut off from main channels of mobility and consumption. Frazier's findings were refined by St. Clair Drake and Horace Cayton's 1946 classic *Black Metropolis,* an investigation of the rapidly developing class structure among Negroes in "Bronzeville," the inner-city of Chicago. Warner advised the two black authors and wrote in appendix to their book a methodological note on the concept of caste. He defined caste as a social system "which organizes the lives of Negroes into a subordinate level and of whites into a superordinate level" and lasts "throughout the lifetime of an individual and throughout the lives of his descendants."[47] In their study, Drake and Cayton estimated that after just a few decades of rural to urban migration, 5 percent of the African Americans in Bronzeville were in the upper class, 30 percent in the middle class, and 65 percent in the lower class. But under the special conditions of caste that forced all African Americans to live together, the black upper class was penetrated by the leaders of the underworld. Drake and Cayton therefore felt they had to separate the "true" leaders of the race from the "gentlemen racketeers." They also distinguished the honest lower-class majority living a decent life organized around churches and clubs from the "disorganized segment of the lower class" and the criminal underworld.

In the ghetto, most African Americans did not have full access to the market. Those who did, Drake and Cayton pointed out, could neither turn the ladder of consumption into an instrument of racial assimilation nor, if the source of their wealth could not be disclosed, unequivocal prestige within their own group. To make things worse, ordinary people's participation in the mass market was perceived as a threat to the welfare of the black community because it jeopardized the few opportunities segregated elites had. These elites actually pressured ghetto residents to support black businesses under the doctrine, often heard at Sunday sermons, of the "double-duty dollar." But as a woman typically reported, "I buy at the A & P where I can get food cheapest. I try to patronize my race, but I can't on my husband's salary."[48]

The liberal sociologists and market researchers around Warner understood the dilemma and took a genuine interest in exploring ways in which marketing tools might break down racial prejudice. Gardner believed from the studies of caste in the Deep South he had co-authored in 1941 with black sociologist Allison Davis, another Warner student, that "economic behavior" was "the only type of behavior" by which a segregated society allowed "a colored person to express superiority to any white individual."[49] This small group of marketers realized the growing demographic presence of African Americans in industrial America (25 percent of babies born in Chicago in 1954 were blacks, remarked Martineau) and predicted their buying power would eventually increase and help them fight back. They viewed consumption as a weapon and optimistically imagined "the Negro" as "forging ahead" faster than the "average American citizen" and were bothered by the exclusion of 10 percent of the American population from daily vital economic relationships.[50]

But as marketers explored the possibilities of a growing African-American presence in the mass market, it became clear to them that, no matter their personal inclinations, they could not touch the evil effects of segregation. Their theory of uplifting abundance turned into deceptive abstraction in the absence of integration and freedom. If mass consumption did not bring about the bland middlebrow homogenizing culture its critics saw invading American society, its claim of making society more democratic was unwarranted when it came to minorities who suffered from discrimination. Marketing strategies left inequality, segregation, and prejudices largely untouched. The barriers of discrimination would have to be broken down for the democratizing effects of consumerism to be felt among African Americans. For no matter how hard we try, market and society cannot be made fully congruent.

Part Three EMBATTLED IDENTITIES

CHAPTER SIX

FROM VOLUNTARISM TO

PLURALISM

_____

The idea of the kingdom of God [has] indeed been the dominant idea in American Christianity . . . but it [has] not always meant the same thing. In the early period of American life . . . "Kingdom of God" meant "sovereignty of God"; in the creative period of awakening and revival it meant "reign of Christ" and only in the most recent period [has] it come to mean "kingdom on earth."

H. RICHARD NIEBUHR[1]

Finding a way to preserve the cultural richness of America while implementing social engineering was an important preoccupation of a generation of American intellectuals and public figures as the twentieth century dawned. These pluralists, including such diverse personalities as philosopher John Dewey, Supreme Court Justice Louis Brandeis, social worker Jane Addams, and political scientist Arthur Bentley, were liberal reformers who understood that the new corporate economy, relying on bureaucratic systems, and promoting a large assimilative center, could impose an unprecedented uniformity upon American life. In a new world of consumer democracy and average Americans, they struggled to find a context that would balance the right to be different with the right to participate in mass society. As it became clear they could no longer take for granted the variety of situations they knew and cherished, they embraced pluralism.[2] They attempted to write into national consciousness the diversity that had been heretofore embedded in local fragmentation. The more social engineering unified the country and flattened differences, the more they promoted pluralism as a defining principle but the less it comported with the daily experience of Americans.

The liberal elites' brand of pluralism had an abstract quality one would expect from established intellectuals who stood firmly at the center of society. Committed to the idea of America as a unified whole, these pluralists formulated an ideology of limited difference. They envisioned the world around them as fractured and refused to accept the existence of any one truth; they saw in the country's pluricultural character a means of guaranteeing freedoms. They sought also to protect minorities. At the same time, their pluralism required a sense of common ground. Bound to the center, they struggled to achieve an ideological framework capable of responding to the fragmentary possibilities of American society while simultaneously keeping them in check. Their idea of pluralism was to promote an appreciation of real-life differences, but in practice its effect was to diminish these differences and encourage Americans to seek the average.

Pluralist ideology, as I have just defined it, cannot be confused with "ethnicity," that is, the cultural autonomy of ethnic groups persisting in the twentieth century.[3] Those on the social periphery, usually leaders of ethnic communities, responsible for foreign-language religious services and newspapers, parochial school systems, and other minority institutions, only occasionally could afford to share the global pluralist viewpoint of liberal reformers. They were instead on the defensive when highlighting their special contributions to American culture.

NINETEENTH-CENTURY POLITICAL FRAGMENTATION

Pluralism as the modern ideology of tolerance was a distinct creation of the twentieth century. It could not have been elaborated as an intellectual project in the highly localized politics of nineteenth-century America. There was no real possibility that the whole could conceal the parts and consequently almost no call for a pluralist ideology.[4] It is symptomatic that the only explicit debate in the early nineteenth century on a concept similar to pluralism in a political and territorial sense came from the South, where the elites felt embattled. Seeking to defend the rights of the South, John Calhoun proposed replacing a majority government by one that would represent organically both the majority and minorities.[5] Since governments' legitimacy depended solely on majority vote and did not take into account the economic interests and the geographic and functional divisions of the nation, the only way to prevent suffocating the minority was for the Constitution to protect the interests of the different "orders, classes or portions of the community," thereby avoiding conflict among them.

Local autonomy otherwise flourished throughout most of the nineteenth century and encouraged not only the independence of local politics but the expression of many cultures. The cohesiveness of semiautonomous ethnic communities suggests that their self-government, the socioeconomic reliance achieved by ethnic business, and their freedom to express themselves culturally and religiously compensated their members, at least in part, for the inequality and persistent discrimination they often had to face outside their own communities. Moreover, unfair treatment in one place could be compensated to some degree by freedom in another. If on the East Coast immigrants had difficulty finding a niche in an already established social structure, they could become pioneers in the West where they were often the founding groups.

Intense localism encouraged a rich associational life in communities of native-born Americans as well as in immigrant communities. As early as the 1830s, this fragmented society had fascinated Alexis de Tocqueville, who came from a country where no equivalent to American voluntarism existed. It was Tocqueville's genius to capture Americans' commitment both to individualism and to community and to highlight voluntarism as the mechanism for their mutual reinforcement. Tocqueville did it with such brilliance that he helped later Americans make sense of their own practice.[6] Seeing in the resulting localism a prerequisite for American democracy, Tocqueville became one of the first theoreticians of America as an archetypical society built on the voluntary associations of free individuals in a weak state. He expressed better than any other contemporary the American commitment to pursuing individual freedom through voluntarism with few encroachments from authority.

The process by which nineteenth-century Americans willingly assembled to form associations is often confused with pluralism. Tocqueville's work forces us, however, to differentiate sharply between nineteenth-century voluntarism and twentieth-century pluralism. What interested Tocqueville was the relationship between individual aspirations and the associative drive that helped Americans construct a civil society. When he talked of associative life, Tocqueville was insisting on the ad hoc, practical, indeed changing character of these associations, which were generated from a multiplicity of projects and created competing spheres of actions. Their animating principle was that of loyalty to like-minded people. Voluntarism was the process by which a multiplicity of groups created an array of distinct circumstances. The resulting contrasts of people and situations was an unintended consequence. By contrast, twentieth-century pluralism was conceived as an ideological movement that could preserve an appreciation of diversity while local autonomy dramatically declined.

The autonomy and voluntarism of nineteenth-century local life prompted an active search for a sense of national institutions. Semiautonomous communities, whether from the majority or the minority, were under pressure to build large coalitions around which to organize ideas and policies. Regrouping disparate elements was an essential means of integrating religious and ethnic groups as well as classes into political alignments. Local voluntarism created the building blocks for larger political coalitions. Thus a growing number of Americans with a variety of local allegiances participated during the Jacksonian era in the founding of political parties. Although the fluid nature of these alliances shows how unstable the system was, these new mass parties drew their strength from their ability to form coalitions of otherwise geographically, religiously, and culturally divided electorates. The Democrats enlisted groups committed to individual freedom, moral tolerance, and the absence of government intervention, while their Whig, later Republican, opponents were associated with Protestant morality, government intervention in the private domain, and a tendency toward cultural homogenization.[7] To these political ideological dualisms must be added the sectional dualisms of North and South and that of the settled East and the frontier West.

RELIGIOUS VOLUNTARISM AS FRAGMENTATION WRIT LARGE

The Pan-Protestantism movement was another expression of the need to create national coalitions of local groups. Nineteenth-century American Protestantism was fragmentation writ large. The sociological and ideological consequences of a religious tradition that granted great latitude to individual interpretations and the assembly of like-minded people are easy to see. The absence of centralizing religious institutions exacting orthodoxy and of an authoritarian clergy busy enforcing it, like that at work in England, Scotland, the German states, and Scandinavia, had made it possible for American Protestants to form small groups of worshipers among individuals sharing affinities. Furthermore, the little formal knowledge required of leaders encouraged the founding of many unrelated congregations. This principle of easy entry for leaders, irrespective of quality or length of training, has proved essential in generating religious sectarianism.

As William James explained in the lectures on the "varieties of religious experience" he gave in Edinburgh in 1899–1900, the American creed had been one of personal choice that rejected elaborate theology, a kind of culmination of "the idea of an immediate spiritual help, experienced by the individual in his forlornness and standing in no essential need of doctrinal apparatus."[8] No theological machinery was to interfere between God and his subjects. Like Emerson before him, James stressed that Americans best experienced God when left to their own solitary devices. He enumerated and classified an impressive assortment of them.

The "varieties of religious experience" were reflected in the many covenants of like-minded proselytes who assembled around their preferred version of Protestantism. Once together though, they tended to fragment further over points of doctrine. Thus Presbyterians debated the Westminster Confession and Methodists John Wesley's writings. Others even dispensed with a canon altogether. The southern Baptists' trust in their own "soul competency" exemplified the gnostic tradition on American soil. Baptists have had no person, date, document, or event which defines them—except respect for the Bible, individually interpreted. Their most vivid expression of a Christian community is the local congregation where similarly inclined individuals follow the light of their own conscience. They are the product of voluntaristic fragmentation and at the same time a perfect example of antipluralistic intolerance.[9]

Some groups were open but others were exclusionary. Tolerant and intransigent sects drew and redrew boundaries as they coalesced into a system where local fragmentation remained the best guarantee of individual freedom. When the conditions for this local fragmentation became severely restricted, pluralism emerged as an attempt to maintain freedom.

Among twentieth-century theologians and scholars, we owe a discerning analysis of the conflict between tolerance and the search for religious purity in American life to H. Richard Niebuhr. Because he disapproved of the new pluralistic tendencies he saw emerging around him, which he blamed for watered-down spirituality and an impediment to spiritual unity, and because he struggled over time with seemingly contradictory methods to clarify his thoughts, he is an especially valuable guide to understanding not only nineteenth-century voluntarism but why the shift to modern pluralism was traumatic for so many white Protestant Americans. Although remembered primarily in the shadow of his more liberal older brother, Reinhold Niebuhr, who electrified Americans of the 1930s by taking on the secular problems of his day, Richard Niebuhr has left us with an important body of theological work that sheds light on the ways in which Americans have redefined tolerance in shifting from voluntarism to pluralism.[10]

Although the voluntary association of like-minded individuals is often considered a source of vigor in communal religious life, Niebuhr questioned its merit. Instead of seeing, as Tocqueville had, a vast network of loosely connected congregations within which Americans expressed an endless diversity of affinities and purposes, Niebuhr saw fragmentation as the proof of the ethical failure of Christianity. He granted an exception only if fragmentation generated a new level of religious intensity. Coming from the Old World, where religion was tied to absolutism and hierarchy, Tocqueville and other European visitors discovered in American voluntarism a close alliance between the spirit of freedom and the spirit of religion.[11] Reflecting on the American past a century later, Niebuhr pointed instead to the essential hypocrisy of voluntarism: practicing divisiveness while preaching brotherhood.

Nonetheless, Niebuhr saw in the fragmented communities the only possibility of spiritual renewal. In *The Social Sources of Denominationalism* (1929), a book written in the social and institutional tradition of Max Weber's *Protestant Ethic and the Spirit of Capitalism,* Niebuhr studied community formation. He argued that fragmentation could be justified when it brought about renewed purity, a process he denied to established churches. With Ernst Troeltsch, he argued that "the really creative, church-forming, religious movements" could be "the work" of only "the lowest strata" and maintained that this was as true of modern America as it had been of the Renaissance. Bothered by the weak religious commitments of his contemporaries, Niebuhr talked with emotion of the great religious conflicts of the distant past as well as of the great American revivals of the nineteenth century, coming as they did from below and uniting the people in a Christian spirit. Before historians identified similar outbursts in Eastern cities, he pointed to the originally freer, more emotional and less liturgically minded environment of the frontier.[12]

Niebuhr denounced the process of embourgeoisement that, in his view, inevitably took over all sects with time and weakened faith. He pointed, for instance, to Methodism as a sect that had drawn its evangelical strength from the great revivals of the early nineteenth century that helped keep American religion one of individual experience. He saw Methodism as an example of the increased impulse to stress free will, or Arminianism, that had over the years blunted the harshness of Calvinistic predestination. It was up to dissenters like the early Methodists to keep alive the experiential, anti-intellectual, and anti-establishment religious spirit.[13]

Although Niebuhr invested his hopes in dissenters, he knew that purity, no matter its origins, was bound to be short-lived. Methodism had rapidly lost its appeal to the uneducated. By the time Methodists created colleges, they had already reconciled themselves enough with formal learning to become part of the establishment. Methodism, then, ceased to be a popular sectarian religion of direct experience, with little institutional structure, to become another undemanding middle-class denomination. Niebuhr feared the negative consequences of embourgeoisement on religious intensity as much as the racial and ethnic divisions that stood in the way of brotherhood.

But no matter where Niebuhr turned in his historical investigation, he found the same tension between purity and unity. Niebuhr inquired into sectarian formation among small groups of native-born Protestants. He scrutinized also such national Protestant churches of immigrants as the Lutherans. He noted the appearance of Lutheran synods in the United States and observed that each one had been anchored in local cultural and social traits as well as points of theology.[14] Although he dealt with Catholics and Jews superficially, he extended his analysis to them by pointing out that national churches of immigrants were recreated in America following the "sectarian principle of voluntary membership."[15] He saw that the voluntary principle was by no means operating only within the communities of the majority or within the boundaries of Protestantism.

Voluntarism also operated in the communities of Jewish and Catholic immigrants, which have traditionally displayed a strong associational life. Even though the religious practices of immigrants have been generally respectful of hierarchical authority, immigrant voluntarism became key to the growth of ethnic churches. Among Catholics and Jews, like-minded parishioners exercised their right to pray together by sharing the same native tongue or the same inclination toward socialism and other communal bonds. Therefore one might say that the immigrant and native worlds, although still distinct in most ways, had developed along parallel lines. Among Catholics, the Italian and Polish churches approximated the denominational model.[16] Even Judaism was increasingly divided along denominational lines.

Recent scholarship has confirmed Niebuhr's analysis of the extension of the voluntary principle to non-Protestant faiths. The immigrant adoption of this native trait became more significant as the number of Catholics grew twice as fast between 1890 and 1906 as the number of Protestants, and the number of Jewish synagogues quadrupled. As top-down ritualistic practices, tied as they were to Old World hierarchies, eroded, immigrant voluntarism gained in importance. While some Catholics, Lutherans, and Jews remained subservient to hierarchical theological authority, others did not. One can therefore agree with R. Laurence Moore that not only did indigenous sects on the margins of Protestantism keep American experiential religion alive, but so did those "outsiders" who became "insiders" by shedding much of the ritualistic practice imposed by church authority.[17] As outsiders embraced voluntarism, minorities proved capable of representing authentic national values as well if not better than the majority. It is therefore in the multiplicity of small groups willingly assembling to pray, without coercion, that Americans of all origins turned the "British sociological invention" of the dissenting denomination into a universal principle.[18] Voluntarism flourished in the nineteenth century within established as well as new denominations.

THE CONSTRAINTS OF VOLUNTARISM

Voluntarism, however, generated fragmentation, not pluralism in a modern sense. If native white Protestants practiced what Hector Saint-John de Crève-cœur called "indifference" and John Locke "tolerance," it was primarily to allow their own denominations to coexist within the same extended family—only secondarily and intermittently to tolerate Protestant African Americans, Catholics, or Jews. There was actually a dark side to Protestant hegemony. In his authoritative interpretation of the "national religion," Henry May emphasizes the fact that native-born white Protestants' evangelical zeal only served to reinforce their nationalist convictions.[19] Majority coalitions often castigated minority visions in an attempt to impose conformity. Pan-Protestantism, strengthened as it was by the belief in the manifest destiny of the Anglo-Saxon "race," was often intolerant. Exclusionary "racial ideology" was invoked, in Reginald Horsman's words, "to force new immigrants to conform to the prevailing political, economic, and social system," "to justify the sufferings or deaths of blacks, Indians, or Mexicans" and to assuage "feelings of guilt" with a sense of "historical and scientific inevitability."[20]

Protestants, if they did not adhere to "racial Anglo-Saxonism," and if they thought at all positively of their relationships to non-Protestants, were likely to practice not pluralism in the modern sense of accepting differences but mutual avoidance. As long as members of different cultures refused to abandon their distinct way of life, they were to be shunned. Minorities reciprocated. They avoided white Protestants as well as other ethnic groups. As a result, the most common pattern was for members of abutting communities to avoid one another rather than to seek mutual understanding.[21] Worse even, periodic waves of xenophobia led to regular outbreaks of violence against, and sometimes among, minorities. It is therefore quite hard to apply our understanding of pluralism as an appreciation for difference to nineteenth-century voluntary fragmentation. The closest we come to pluralism in the nineteenth century could be found in the white Protestant denominational world, and here it was limited to them. That restriction would have to be lifted for modern pluralism to gain the status of a modern national value.

DEFINING TWENTIETH-CENTURY PLURALISM

Pluralism was an attempt to redefine tolerance in a society that increasingly restricted local autonomy. In that effort, the minorities who contributed to the emerging debate on pluralism often spoke from a position of defensiveness. From their religious covenants as well as Free Thought associations, the German Americans were the first to reflect on the relations between their communities and American society in a pluralistic way by asking as early as the mid nineteenth century the question of the future of the "Teutonic race" in the New World and demanding that the larger society be tolerant of their folkways. The exiles of 1848 were responsible for an important theoretical attempt to define a new group identity, one that went against both the assimilation norms of the host country and Crèvecœur's vague model of a "melting pot."[22] The German Americans innovated in defining a collective identity reinforced by group institutions, whereas Anglo-American ideology took only individuals into account. Certain German intellectuals even went so far as to propose separate communities, although complete isolation was rare. Finally, the German theoreticians opted for "an aggressive doctrine designed not only to reassure German-Americans that it was possible to survive as Germans in the midst of American society but also to assert the German right to enter the melting pot collectively and on their own terms."[23] But the efforts of the German immigrants were ultimately stifled by the shock of World War I, when the German-American community gave up any attempt at self-definition that could be interpreted as betraying the national interest.

If the Germans were the first to test the ground of modern pluralism, all ethnic groups have felt the same need, in varying degrees, to measure their distance from and to define the terms of their integration into American culture.[24] But minority pluralism remained fragile. Minority life could not of itself give birth to a commonly accepted pluralist ideology. Rather, immigrants and their children became masters of divided consciousness as they shared their loyalties and energies among their several worlds. Assuming complementary identities was their way to answer assimilative pressures positively. Most often, they adapted to the economic demands of an increasingly unifying market while retaining some of their folkways to pray, to court their loved ones, to eat, and to raise their children, and protecting their mores by practicing them from within their own institutions.[25] Although their balancing act always affected the common national culture, minorities could claim their distinctiveness only when more centrally located advocates of pluralism took the lead in voicing their own pluralistic formulas and, in the process, created spaces in the national consciousness for minority groups.

National circumstances contributed to the movement toward twentieth-century pluralism. After the crisis of the secession and the loss of so many human lives, northern Americans preached moderation toward the South and oneness among whites, even if that meant reaffirming the color line. The plurality encouraged by geographic isolation diminished with the joining of the Atlantic and the Pacific by the railroad and the closing of the frontier. In business, science, technology, and law, the trend toward integrating knowledge on a national scale led to disenclosure; and disenclosure increased pressure for homogenization. Across the nation, communities were restructured according to the classifications of science, the requirements of newly minted national professional associations, universities, corporate bureaucracies, and a bigger state. In the late nineteenth and early twentieth centuries, the many independent organizations based on voluntarism, such as community hospitals, parochial schools, or mutual aid societies, that continued to cater to the needs of a multiethnic population became increasingly labeled by participants in the larger institutional matrix of inquiry as minority institutions.

This context of economic and cultural unification stimulated a strong sense of interwoven national obligations. Pluralism's most influential spokesmen emerged not among minorities but in the heart of America. Although German Americans had to abandon all pretense of dual allegiance when the United States joined the Allies against Germany, Anglo-Americans were unlikely to be suspect in their loyalties and felt freer to speak for the right to be different. The keenest observers of social change among them established the main tenets of modern pluralist theory. Intent on resisting uniformity, they reformulated in their own terms much of the tension minorities felt between conflicting cultures. They made assimilation and pluralism not the mutually exclusive categories they are too often thought to be, but the two sides of the same coin.

A small number of intellectuals around William James and his pragmatist philosophy elaborated pluralist ideology initially as part of a philosophical and epistemological revolt against formalism and adoption of cultural relativity. At a time when the multiplicity of nineteenth-century society was threatened, they constructed a new intellectual world, no longer sure of any one truth but eager to espouse many. In the preface to *The Will to Believe* (1897), James stated that "*prima facie* the world is a pluralism," and that "he who takes for his hypothesis the notion that [pluralism] is the permanent form of the world is what I call a radical empiricist." James spent much of his philosophical career thinking about the variety of choices individuals make to construct a "pluralistic universe." James combated the monistic systems that characterized nineteenth-century philosophy, the absolutes of Spencerian determinism or Hegelian idealism.[26] Content to follow his metaphysical penchant and talent for cosmic formulations, James pointed to the "enormous diversities which the spiritual lives of different men exhibit."[27] He thought of pluralism mostly as an alternative to nineteenth-century philosophical monism.

John Dewey, however, remained closer to mundane realities. Dewey stressed participation in democratic institutions and the cumulative enrichment that the recognition of social and cultural multiplicity brought. He subscribed to the "mosaic picture" of the United States, Alan Ryan notes, as a way to combat the exclusionary "aspirations that nationalism fed on."[28] In a dictionary of philosophy and psychology published in 1901, Dewey was the first philosopher to codify pluralism; he noted the novelty of the term to English and recognized James's influence in defining this "theory that reality consists in a plurality or multiplicity of distinct beings."[29] Pluralist philosophy was strengthened by its promoters' shared feeling that it occupied a central place in an extraordinarily diverse American society. Dewey's own pluralism reflected not only his recognition of Americans' diversity of circumstances and beliefs but his desire to teach Americans to enrich themselves through it. His work as an educator at Chicago and Columbia was at the heart of the new pluralist movement. For Dewey, education should help individuals to appreciate alternative values by means of shared experience and know themselves better as a result of the encounter. In a pluralist society, education fosters mutual understanding and the search for personal enrichment through the discovery of other people's values.[30] Only through the participation of all citizens in the collective good could American democracy survive.

From this common philosophical position rejecting nineteenth-century absolutes, liberal reformers promoted two expressions of pluralism, one as politics and the other as culture. Political and cultural pluralism partially overlap; at the same time, they represent different currents of thought. With the first concept, based on politics and economics, a group of political scientists sought to guarantee the equitable distribution of power. As national impersonal interest groups superseded and redirected local, concrete, voluntary associations, they saw pluralism as a new possibility for political participation. The American Political Science Association, founded in 1904, insisted that political science build a science of politics.[31] It was at this time that Arthur Bentley formulated his theory of interest groups, which served as the founding principle of twentieth-century political pluralism: As "there is no group without its interest," intergroup competition is the central reality of politics.[32] With the sharp decline in the number of voters at the beginning of the century, political scientists would look to conflicting interest groups to maintain political balance. Group rivalry, according to them, remained the best guarantee of democracy.[33] The young Walter Lippmann, while still under James's spell at Harvard, articulated first and most acutely the need for countervailing powers in conflict resolution in 1914.[34] He understood the rise of "interest group" politics around him, coming from labor unions, consumers, women, and others, as part of a larger institutionalization of politics.

Political pluralists turned to the Founding Fathers for models of how to grapple with interest groups. They harkened back not to the nineteenth-century dualisms, which they rejected, or a localism that was no longer relevant, but to the Confederation that had imprinted a constellation on the Great Seal of the new nation.[35] Charles Beard revived James Madison's 1787 thesis (Tenth Federalist) that a state or government need not be feared so long as there were several groups competing for its benevolence, that a continental-sized republic would not become the instrument of a single concern if many groups were vying for its favors, and that no majority could "invade the right of other citizens" in a society broken into many "parties and interests."[36]

Although political pluralism posed the essential question of the relation between the center and the periphery, between the single and the many, between the whole and its parts, the reformulations of eighteenth-century political philosophy could not easily be translated into clear principles for an industrial society. The flagrant inequality and reappraisal of the principles of justice at the century's birth spelled trouble for the new theory. Defending the existence of multiple loyalties could not translate into the support of any one in particular. As a consequence, pluralism was rapidly outstripped by the search for justice for the oppressed. Charles Beard himself sought to demonstrate, in *An Economic Interpretation of the Constitution of the United States* (1913), that the founding fathers, aware of the material bases of political action, acted in accordance with their own economic interests. The thesis has long since been disproved. What is important, however, is that Beard claimed as his inspiration the new political pluralism. In fact, although his interpretation of the Constitution owes little explicitly to Marx, to whom he never refers directly, it nevertheless remained closer to popular dualism than to either Madisonian pluralism or Bentley's interest-group theories.[37] In the end, Beard chose justice over complexity, dualism over pluralism.

Modern political pluralism was born an abstraction and stubbornly remained one. Supporting multiple loyalties resulted in ambiguity toward all. Unlike nineteenth-century local voluntary associations, twentieth-century national interest groups were distant from their members. Even the more practical applications of pluralism, like organizing lobbies or oiling machine politics, could never match the daily face-to-face relationships of voluntarism. Voluntarism was constantly put to the test of human interaction. Pluralism, however, had trouble with realities. Theoreticians of pluralism struggled with that problem. Among them was Hungarian-British scholar Harold Laski, who spent the World War I years at Harvard.[38] Laski imagined a decentralized federalist political system in which the formal structures of representation would share power with informal groups. As he wrote to his dear Justice Holmes, "Your skepticism comes, I venture, from a further doubt as to the worth of life; my pluralism comes from a certainty—you have yet to meet my wife—of its richness. And I see that richness so largely evolved out of the multiplicity of groups which are trying to think out some way of life. . . . I want my variety validated in its freedom to make itself felt. I hope I am clear."[39]

The second pluralistic concept was more social and cultural in nature. At the turn of the century, large-scale immigration gave a sense of urgency to the pluralist debate. Cultural pluralists understood the American nation as a plurality of groups defined by skin color, religion, language, nationality, and culture and felt the urge to give them voice. Another of William James's former students, Horace Kallen, posed in 1915 the question of "Democracy versus the Melting Pot?" He would later coin the expression "cultural pluralism."[40] Kallen's final position was to conceive of America as a de facto federation of ethnic groups—an idea that at least on the surface ran counter to the American assimilationist tradition. Kallen was Jewish, and he believed that the biggest threat faced by the diaspora in the United States was not anti-Semitism but assimilation. Kallen's pluralism, however, owes much more to James's influence than to his Jewish upbringing and belongs to a much wider trend toward cosmopolitanism and a new transnational culture, as shown by the work of several of his contemporaries such as Randolph Bourne, Van Wyck Brooks, and H. L. Mencken.[41] Ultimately, such a culture fostered assimilation.

Cultural pluralism could not be conceived independent of assimilation. In the United States, where ethnic life has never been parked in large territorial federations, it has proven difficult to isolate the parts from the whole. Most American intellectuals who are read as theoreticians of pluralism also promoted assimilation. They were caught between their conflicting desires to respect ethnic cleavages and to help immigrants conform to commonly accepted norms. Although nobody was more interested in the ethnic diversity of American urban life than the founders of urban sociology at the University of Chicago—Robert Park, Ernest Burgess, and their students, as well as the social workers who, in the tradition of Jane Addams, gravitated around them—they too let the ambiguities between majority and minorities stand. While questioning the notion of cultural homogeneity, they supported the ideology of assimilation for ethnic enclaves. Pluralism in their hands was also fast becoming an attribute of the center and a framework for assimilation.[42]

The new pluralism, political or cultural, promoted autonomy while emphasizing the many links among diverse groups. Pluralists advocated diversity as an asset, not a threat. Ethnic groups in America could erect boundaries, but each group was also free to adapt to the norms of the community. As most did both, political and cultural pluralism merged into a systematic right to difference as we can see in Supreme Court Justice Louis Brandeis's public stands. FDR called Brandeis the prophet Isaiah but the judge liked to think of himself as the "people's lawyer." Historian Thomas McCraw showed he was rather a small entrepreneurs' lawyer.[43] I think of Brandeis as a perfect illustration of pluralism's travails. Precisely because this talented jurist sat on the Supreme Court, he illustrates the ties between the center and the peripheries in the making of modern pluralism. Brandeis also displayed a unique mixture of both political and cultural pluralism.

Born into a family of small businessmen from Louisville, Kentucky, Brandeis reacted against big business's tendency toward homogenization. With the rise of the great capitalist corporations, Brandeis was a major voice in antitrust battles. He persuaded the Interstate Commerce Commission to reject the railroads' request for increased fares, even though they were needed. As defender of the small against the mighty, Brandeis was no doubt more interested in preserving the independence of small business than in understanding the needs of an integrated economy. To him, keeping parts separate meant resisting economic activities that unify and flatten out differences.

Brandeis's work in the social and economic domains—he led the fight against overconcentration and in defense of local autonomy—would be sufficient reason to classify him among political pluralists. But in addition, the future Supreme Court justice adopted a form of cultural pluralism that was revolutionary for someone of his standing. After shunning for many years his Jewish origins, he became the leader of the Zionist movement within the American Jewish community. Having opposed a transformation of America into a centralized, hierarchical society, dominated by the rich, Brandeis later realized that his Jewishness was as important for his identity as his Americanism.[44] It was possible to be Jewish as well as American. Thus diversity, the right to individual difference and to group identity, were becoming the pluralistic requirements for democracy.

TOWARD RELIGIOUS PLURALISM

To gain credence at the grassroots level, the new pluralism had to be adopted by the multiple religious units of voluntarism. The resulting tensions in the religious sphere provide a telling illustration of the ways in which Americans coped with a new appreciation for the extraordinary range of their society and put pluralism to work. Modern pluralism eventually gained credence as the arrival of millions of Catholic and Jewish immigrants led to reweaving the social fabric. The national religion's hegemony collapsed as Catholics and Jews made themselves heard and freed the idea of tolerance from its Protestant straitjacket. But the process entailed much tension between individual and group commitments, spiritual and sociological influences, and the conflicting demands of moral absolutes and tolerance. Religious life proved to be an important medium for the traumatic shift from voluntarism, which emphasized the search for truth at the expense of tolerance, to pluralism, which valued tolerance over the search for truth.

By the end of the nineteenth century, the numbers still seemed to be on the side of the Protestant majority, according to the people who made it their business to count. In his 1893 census of religion, Henry K. Carroll reported 150 Protestant denominations in 42 families. He counted 111,036 ministers in 165,297 reporting congregations for a population generously estimated at 49,630,000 Protestants. That left only 7,360,000 Catholics and 5,630,000 Jews and other non-Christians, "leaving only 5 million belonging to the non-religious and antireligious classes, including freethinkers, secularists, and infidels."[45] The year that census was taken, the Protestant ministers, who met in Chicago at the Parliament of Religion held in conjunction with the World's Columbian Exposition, were exposed to the cultures of other faiths in distant parts of the world.[46] But their newfound tolerance was still unknown in most parishes. Despite the reassuring census numbers, a mounting wave of xenophobia confronting ethnic groups at the end of the nineteenth century took place as the "new immigrants," in John Higham's words, "had the very bad luck to arrive in America en masse when nativism was already running at full tilt."[47] Under these circumstances, the encounter that national unification was provoking between the hegemonic culture of a white Anglo-American Protestant nation and the many communities of the minorities was more likely to spell disaster than an ideology of respect for difference.

And yet pluralism ultimately prevailed. Through a good deal of turmoil, American religious tolerance was ultimately enlarged to make room for non-Protestant faiths. To begin with, Protestant missionaries faced serious obstacles in turning immigrants into Protestants. Middle-class Protestants, who invested heavily in the Social Gospel, saw good works as a way to meet spiritual goals. The movement's promoters, however, quickly realized that the practical approach was to include immigrants into a broadly redefined religious pluralism rather than convert them against their will into full-fledged Protestant Americans.[48] As a result, the many Protestants involved with one form or another of good works, such as settlement house work or friendly visiting, were compelled in the face of the sheer numbers of immigrants to differentiate between the tasks of assimilation and conversion. Avoiding immigrants as in the nineteenth-century fragmented polity was an option viable only in wealthy enclaves.[49]

Although the Social Gospel's drive to assimilate newcomers drew members of many origins (Walter Rauschenbusch was Baptist), the Methodists played a leading role. Their activities were instructive of the ways in which immigrant religious practices were ultimately left intact while other cultural differences were drastically narrowed. To Methodists, the Social Gospel became a statement of their commitment to worldly reform. Whether urbanites or still living on the family farm, Methodists had become, by the early twentieth century, primarily middle-class Americans, and ultimately their class affiliation prevailed over their religious one. As middle-class, native-born Americans, descendants of older immigrants, Methodists were sympathetic to the fate of poor immigrants and embattled workers. At first, they stressed individual regeneration. But inequality strengthened their involvement in the larger Progressive movement. Methodists emphasized equal rights, worker protection, abolition of child labor, a living wage, and a more equitable distribution of wealth. Although the southern church was much less concerned with the plight of labor than the northern congregations, their efforts to create a better society culminated in 1908 with the development of the famous Social Creed of Methodism, adopted four years later almost verbatim by the newly formed Federal Council of Churches of twenty-eight denominations.[50]

Even though these worldly concerns were expressed all in the name of God, they led "social gospelers" to redirect their efforts and to assimilate newcomers to middle-class America rather than to Protestant America. The Social Gospel, as exemplified by the peculiar Methodist blend of theology and social vision, then stood as the symbol of a new Protestant campaign meant not to exclude but to assimilate outsiders by bringing them to the center of American life, regardless of their religious affiliation. The Social Gospel ultimately downplayed religion among the many factors to take into account in the assimilation process. Assimilating religious outsiders meant bringing them into the fold of a benign pluralism with a dwindling religious content. It was no longer a matter of merely extending the voluntary principle to immigrant communities. Rather, it was a question of extending the application of tolerance beyond Protestantism and of turning pluralism into a national value. The principle was to grant to all Americans the right to be different without forcing them to hide in the recesses of local autonomy.

CONSERVATIVE REACTION

Pluralistic tolerance provoked a conservative reaction. Thus in the 1920s, although the massive wave of immigration had begun to subside under the quota system, many perceived a renewed threat to the Protestant world from immigrants who were assimilating without converting. In the name of national purity, several million people joined a resurgent Invisible Empire in the 1920s and promoted 100 percent Americanism, by which they meant white

Protestantism. The version of Protestant unity motivating the resurgence of the Klan was largely a lower middle-class, blue-collar, urban phenomenon, no longer confined to the South.[51]

That Protestantism was no longer so sure of its unchallenged dominance of America became even clearer in the harsh, dualistic, antipluralist election campaign that pitted Herbert Hoover, the voice of mainstream Protestant America, against Al Smith, the voice of immigrant Catholicism. The battle between Hoover and Smith in 1928 was about religion only after the term had been stripped of much of its meaning. It was about the identity crisis that pitted "us" against "them."

The fierceness of that battle took Smith by surprise. It came as news to the street-smart, Irish-American governor of New York, a state with a large Catholic population, that, if elected to the presidency, he would play into the hands of a subservient-to-Rome Catholic hierarchy. Not much of a thinker, Smith was at a loss to answer the charge that his presidency could threaten the integrity of American politics. As he said, "I never heard of these bulls and encyclicals and books."[52] In contrast, Hoover knew how to appeal to the Protestant evangelical tradition. He praised "the divine in each human being" and suggested "devotion to the Sermon on the Mount" as a way to remedy those abuses and injustices brought about by intense competition.[53] He situated himself squarely in the tradition of a more familiar Protestantism at once individualistic and sectarian.

The resurgence of these dualisms only highlighted the threat of the new pluralism. So did the virulent attack Richard Niebuhr launched against tolerance in the 1930s. To Niebuhr, who was losing what little faith he once held in the reforming power of religious voluntarism, the growing acceptance of a diversity of churches was another sign of American spiritual decline. In *The Kingdom of God in America,* published in 1937, Niebuhr rejected what he considered the reductionist sociological approach of his previous work. He invested new hopes for spiritual life not in the medium of institutions, which he blamed for the watered-down religious commitments of modern liberalism, but in individual spirituality. Finding a fresh inspiration in Henri Bergson's "great study of static and dynamic faith," and in Karl Barth's theology, he abandoned "institutions" for "movement" and "law" for "gospel."[54]

Twentieth-century Americans, Niebuhr felt, had lost spiritual depth; they had turned the "Kingdom of God" into the "kingdom on earth." Niebuhr saw his fellow Americans engaged in an insipid dialogue with "a God without wrath" who "brought men without sin into a kingdom without judgment through the ministrations of a Christ without a cross."[55] To Max Weber, secularization was the process by which religion becomes a separate and limited activity in modern societies. To Niebuhr, however, secularization meant stripping religion of its essence, that is, taking the spiritual out of religious experience. That kind of secularization was the direct result of modern pluralism. While voluntarism had at least occasionally generated the hope of purity, pluralism was killing it.[56] At bottom, Niebuhr saw the appreciation of diversity as a major obstacle to true religious communion and pluralism as a regrettable invention of the "kingdom on earth," which could in no way be reflective of the "kingdom of God." Unfortunately, the many reformulations of the same argument have only served to justify bigotry in the name of purity.

Whether their intensity declined or not, Americans have persisted in their religious commitments. As William James had asserted in his famous lectures, "we and God have business with each other."[57] Although the Great Depression was the first serious economic downturn not to have provoked an evangelical revival and the New Deal the first totally secularized great social program, a multifaceted religious practice has kept steady in the United States, in contrast to the rest of the Western world.[58] Numerous surveys have shown Americans unfailing in church attendance despite the decline of voluntary associations in other domains. In 1950, 55 percent of all Americans were registered as dutiful church members; in 1959, the figure reached an all-time high of 69 percent.[59] Choice of congregation has remained one of the few options twentieth-century Americans have fully exercised to maintain a sense of elective character in an otherwise homogenizing society. Religious bonds have helped Americans to negotiate and maintain many differences in identity, outlook, and politics. Moreover, if we think of secularization as the removal of religion from the public sphere, it is difficult to speak of American secularization. Robert Bellah is correct in pointing out that twentieth-century public life has remained impregnated with religious symbols.[60] The famous wall that Jefferson had imagined would separate religion from the state was never solidly built.

Religious pluralism was the touchstone for ethnic pluralism. While nineteenth-century voluntarism served primarily the interest of a narrowly defined national religion, early twentieth-century religious diversity became the foundation for a broader pluralistic-assimilationist outlook. By the 1940s, sociologists could take as evidence the growing rate of intermarriage among coreligionists regardless of their national origins and point to a "triple melting pot," one among Protestants, one among Catholics, and one among Jews.[61] With this major simplification of the old ethno-religious mosaic, even the harshest fight among the major faiths were beginning to take on a new tone. When

Congregationalist-turned-Unitarian minister Paul Blanshard vocally charged at mid-century that Catholicism and Communism were equivalent threats to American democracy, he actually took pains to differentiate between ordinary American Catholics "who fight and die for the same concept of freedom as do other true Americans" and their priests.[62] As he knew, some Catholics and Protestants joined in McCarthyism; others, however, united in tolerance.[63]

There were groups not included in this broader outlook. Pluralism, sadly but unsurprisingly, failed to welcome African Americans into its fold. Accordingly blacks, counting only on themselves, invested the longest in the principle of voluntarism. Throughout most of the twentieth century, the clergy in the mainstream white denominations remained subservient to white middle-class prejudices in excluding African-American parishioners. Thus Methodism, the denomination only second to the Baptists in number of black congregants, remained split into between northern and southern branches. Slavery originated the divorce in 1844. When the branches finally reunited in 1939, they did so only by segregating black churches in a separate jurisdiction within the Methodist Church. The same basic racial division held true of other denominations. Only in 1946 did the Federal Council of Churches renounce segregation. In Edwin Gaustad's accurate assessment of Protestantism in the first half of the century, "resolutions were passed, lynching was denounced, integrated meetings—with some tentativeness—were held, and commissions on race relations were appointed. Little of all this filtered down to the parish level, however, with any genuine effectiveness, or with any radical reversal of traditional patterns of voting, schooling, worshiping, dining, dating, and thinking."[64] Catholics fared no better.[65] Pluralism was not benign when it came to race. At mid-century, white churches had fared as poorly as the market in extending membership across the color line.

A benign pluralism, however, had entered the mainstream of American life. It was a way for most Americans to preserve multiple identities by leaving the relationship among them undefined. Turning the art of equivocation into a national ideology was no easy task. At first, pluralism demanded much self-confidence, as Lippmann had pointed out.[66] But as Americans became good at tolerating conflicting loyalties, there came the frequent complaints that strife among "interest groups" was paralyzing public authority, maintaining the status quo, and perpetuating injustices.[67] No matter the limitations, pluralism gained enough status so that sectarianism lost much of its old rigor.[68] Dwight Eisenhower confidently declared at mid-century that every American should practice a religion, no matter which one. That was the new middle way.[69] Pluralism has played a significant part in the lives of twentieth-century Americans as a guide, no matter how amorphous, that has allowed us to manage our right to.be "different." It has been an act of accommodation, born of necessity, with admittedly shallow philosophical roots and limits to its application. Under such circumstances, one can only be startled by the resilience of pluralism in sustaining this country's respect for difference at home and fight against totalitarianism abroad. At the same time, one cannot be surprised that the cracks in the system would soon widen.

CHAPTER SEVEN

ENLARGING THE POLITY

Let us therefore begin by setting aside all the facts, for they do not affect the question. The researches which can be undertaken concerning this subject must not be taken for historical truths, but only for hypothetical and conditional reasonings, better suited to clarify the nature of things than to show their true origin.

JEAN-JACQUES ROUSSEAU[1]

While pluralism engendered mutual understanding among participants in the polity, its rhetoric of tolerance masked persistent exclusionary practices *and* fueled nationalist propaganda. John Dewey failed to recognize these problems as he reflected on "the rights of nationalities" still "troubling the Old World" in the aftermath of the Great War. Dewey offered a uniquely "radical" and "American contribution" to the European quandary. In the United States, Dewey explained, "the very peoples and races who are taught in the Old World that they have an instinctive and ineradicable antipathy to one another live here side by side in comity, often in hearty amity." The reason is simple enough, he concluded. Within the United States, we have completely separated "nationality from citizenship." "Not only have we separated the church from the state," but we have depoliticized culture by isolating "language, cultural traditions, all that is called *race,* from the state—that is, from problems of political organization and power." (Like most members of his generation, Dewey thought of white immigrants as belonging to different "races.") The American solution, he explained, was that "language, literature, creed, group ways, national culture, are social rather than political, human rather than national interests. Let this idea fly abroad: it bears healing in its wings."[2]

Dewey's statement was not all fantasy. The Civil War had saved a union, not a confederation of distinct nationalities such as existed in the Austro-Hungarian Empire. And pluralism among white Americans was a legitimate way to enlarge the national community. So powerful in his mind was the pluralistic side of America he wanted to highlight that Dewey ignored large episodes of American history that stubbornly defied his theory of separation between politics and culture. By optimistically integrating race within a larger anthropological framework of culture, he seems to have forgotten that if the Civil War had ended slavery, Reconstruction had failed to check racial exclusion. And for all his involvement with key transformations of his time, Dewey also bypassed the problems of discrimination on the basis of class and gender.

The very idea of exclusion was hard to assert in an age and continent that did not want to recognize group discrimination and implement mechanisms of redress. Yet the extensive success of pluralism eventually led to the embattled claims for group rights that divide Americans today. The people excluded from full participation in the many advantages to be gained from membership in the pluralistic polity fought back by proposing alternative solutions. Industrial workers, African Americans, and women waged well-known struggles. Although not the only victims in American society, their effort to enlarge the polity is informative. These groups fought for justice and equality in the context of the larger shift from nineteenth-century voluntarism to twentieth-

century pluralism. Because they were partly or completely excluded from pluralism, they clung to voluntarism, where the benefits of community life
blunted the harshness of inequality. But as twentieth-century social engineering limited the effectiveness of voluntarism, exclusion became less and
less tolerable, and the fight against it intensified.

WORKERS WITHOUT COLLECTIVE BARGAINING

White male workers were full participants in American politics. They were
avid voters, a propensity reenforced by the Democratic machines in large
cities, which naturalized large numbers of recently arrived immigrants at election time. While socialists were occasionally threatened by shrewdly worded
local ordinances aimed at disfranchising them, most nineteenth-century white
males exercised their vote.[3] But despite their political power, workers had no
voice at the workplace and little protection against the vagaries of labor markets. Workers therefore pushed in their meetings for the legal endorsement
of collective bargaining. Employers, however, refused to recognize labor
unions as a legitimate extension of working-class voluntarism. Even while acknowledging workers' First Amendment right to assemble peacefully, employers knew how to denounce as coercive the programs that emerged at
trade-union meetings. They saw union rule not as the "embodiment," in
Christopher Tomlins's words, of the "aggregated free will" of their members
as they should have in a voluntary society but as criminal conspiracy. Labor
voluntarism, therefore, led not to the acceptance of collective bargaining but
to recurrent charges of restraint of trade.[4]

The judicial conservatism that helped undermine working-class claims
emerged directly from the pressures industrialists applied to judges. With the
courts increasingly called upon to regulate economic matters, judges were
asked by business interests to curb what they took to be "unreasonable" regulatory legislation passed by state and local governments. Responding favor-
ably, judges relied increasingly on the due process clause of the Fourteenth
Amendment in their defense of property rights and liberty of contract to out-
law workers' otherwise legitimate efforts at collective bargaining. As a result,
the labor movement was considerably weakened. To give only one illustration,
between 1880 and 1931, the courts issued more than 1,800 injunctions
against strikes.[5]

With the judicial branch constantly challenging labor activism, workers'
progress in controlling their worklife rested on two distinct strategies. The
first was working-class solidarity. In order to achieve this goal, job and status-

conscious skilled workers had to open their restricted craft unions to less fortunate sections of the working class. Thus the Knights of Labor made their mark
in the 1880s by their ability momentarily to blur lines of both race and skill
by asserting the common interests of all productive workers against the "un-
productive" class of capitalists and financiers. But this was an exceptional moment. Most often, craft unions remained exclusive, pushing away African-
American and unskilled workers from the labor movement. As Richard
Oestreicher sums it up, "union success was possible because of class consciousness, yet unions defined themselves in ways which prevented the development
of class consciousness."[6]

The second and more successful strategy was for groups of workers to
sway public opinion in their favor by gaining the high moral ground. Late
nineteenth-century workers turned the tide of legal action in their favor by
sharing common ground with small entrepreneurs also threatened by the
expansion of the corporate system and by enlisting the support of reform-
minded politicians and professionals.[7] By the end of the nineteenth century,
labor had risen sufficiently in the public esteem for Henry Carter Adams to
note in his 1896 presidential address to the American Economic Association
that labor unions were "no longer universally condemned," strikes "no longer
considered universally illegal," and "the law of conspiracy" progressively
"confined within its legitimate sphere."[8] Collective exploitation was more
likely to be exposed not by a section of the labor movement alone but by a
broader coalition, especially when it was more a matter of the human right
of safety than the group right of collective bargaining. But such cooperation
was hard to achieve. Labor economists and other reformers who concentrated
on the issue of industrial safety walked a difficult line. They worked with employers' organizations, which felt little obligation to protect workers, and
AFL-affiliated unions of skilled workers, which were reluctant to revisit the
high wages and labor provisions of bread-and-butter unionism they had successfully negotiated and were afraid of losing in front of conservative judges.
It was in collaborating with the conservative National Association of Manufacturers, not with labor unions, that the reformist American Association for
Labor Legislation succeeded in promoting some state safety regulations and
passing worker's compensation laws in thirty-seven states by 1917.[9]

Early in the century, even conservative judges inclined to side with capital
were ruling more often in favor of labor. In his famous dissent in *Lochner* v.
New York (1905), Oliver Wendell Holmes argued that the State of New York
had the prerogative to interfere with the liberty of contract to prevent bakers

from overworking their employees. Against the other justices, he saw no constitutional basis for reversing the state's decision. Holmes was an impassioned defender of local autonomy. Although his social philosophy was Spencerian, he was tolerant and disturbed by formalistic abuses of the law. He called for judicial realism and felt free to side with victims, not because of empathy for the groups to which they belonged, but because he was capable of questioning the assumptions of the majority. Not supporting the overworked workers reflected, in his words, "an economic theory which a large part of the country does not entertain." As he put it pithily, "the Fourteenth Amendment does not enact Mr. Herbert Spencer's social statics."[10] That was enough to make him a hero for the coming Progressive generation. It may have been convenient, as robber barons would have liked, to justify "the crowding out of the weak" by natural selection, but fewer and fewer observers of industrial life accepted the view.[11] Enough did, however, to postpone any real breakthrough in favor of collective action for another generation.

Meanwhile, as long as the ethnic community continued to provide a framework for security, working-class families escaped much of the inhospitable work environment by turning to their own voluntary institutions for mutual help. With ethnic voluntarism as cushion, the voluntary culture of the nineteenth century persisted into the new mass society. Overlap between ethnic and labor voluntarism produced a complex behavioral pattern where working-class consciousness was both freely expressed and negated in local institutions—at once reinforced in the socialist lodge or the men's saloons where the socialist press circulated, but vanishing at church and the many church-sponsored institutions of education and mutual help. Split consciousness generated divided energies and uncertain allegiances.[12] But despite the importance of ethnic voluntarism, the once-thriving numerous ethnic enclaves that dotted American industrial cities became increasingly anachronistic in the interwar years. The combined effects of World War I and immigration law of the 1920s restricted the flow of new arrivals.[13] As their more successful members moved away, these communities lost some of their cross-class vitality to become more restricted working-class mill villages.[14] National economic reorganization made them less autonomous. Large insurance companies and credit union networks, which had sometimes originated from within the ethnic community but had outgrown it, took more and more business away from local institutions. So did the spread of mass consumption and the ultimate victory of mass unionism one generation after the adoption of mass production and mass distribution.[15]

GHETTOIZED BLACKS

If the pattern for white ethnic voluntarism partly vindicated Dewey's notion
that "group ways" could be at least temporarily removed from national politics, the pattern for black voluntarism entirely contradicted it. Black voluntarism was not a matter of choice, and race was never severed from national
politics in the United States. Moreover, the amorphous quality of group consciousness that was possible among white ethnic groups proved highly unreal-
istic between whites and blacks. As African Americans emerged from slavery,
it seemed for a while that, in the great constitutional sweep of Radical Reconstruction, they would become participants in an enlarged political and social
order. Reconstruction implemented drastic measures to integrate the
freedmen into the polity and instilled hope that every black man would be
able to live both as an "American" and a "Negro."[16] Its constitutional amend-
ments and related civil rights legislation were the first significant effort to guarantee that nobody could be excluded from basic civil rights on the basis of
race. The program created a key reference for the future, and its demise initiated a sense of moral outrage that long outlived it.

As we know, the freedman's prospects dimmed quickly. If passage of the
Fourteenth Amendment marked, in abolitionist Wendell Phillips's words, the
"Negro's hour," the program of emancipation of such congressional members
as Thaddeus Stevens, Charles Sumner, Zachariah Chandler, George W. Julian,
as well as of many emerging African American leaders across the South was
undermined almost as soon as it was implemented.[17] New laws could not
change deeply ingrained habits of white supremacy. And the laws, if passed,
were easily repealed. There was little African Americans could do when in
1883 the Supreme Court declared the 1875 Civil Rights Act, guaranteeing
full access to inns, theaters, restaurants and other places of public conveyances,
unconstitutional on the grounds that the Fourteenth Amendment did not
prohibit private discrimination. Local black leader Henry McNeal Turner in
Louisville, Kentucky, could call the repeal of the civil rights legislation "barba-
rous" and suggest that American blacks should recreate their nation in Africa,
but neither he nor other black leaders in the South could halt the trend toward
disenfranchisement.[18]

In responding to the many challenges to Radical Reconstruction that
reached the Supreme Court, the justices used their power of legal interpretation to undo the congressional program.[19] In pursuing this course, they merely
realigned the constitutional framework, only momentarily disturbed, with social practice. By claiming legislation "powerless to eradicate" those "racial

instincts" enforcing the separation of the races, they would inspire William Graham Sumner's theory that laws cannot change folkways.[20] They also questioned the propriety of any law singling out any group, effectively voiding the constitutional innovations before they could possibly have any effect. In the end, northerners valued social peace among whites more than racial justice, and southern whites tenaciously resisted change in race hierarchy. This left African Americans without allies to fight a losing battle for justice while feeling the full force of renewed racial hostility. As W. E. B. Du Bois wrote, "in well-nigh the whole rural South the black farmers are peons, bound by law and freedom to an economic slavery, for which the only escape is death or the penitentiary."[21]

But tragic as the failure of Reconstruction was, some seeds of racial justice were planted. Justice John Marshall Harlan—the lone dissenter on issues of race—spoke in terms that prefigured those of the Warren court seventy-five years later, displaying the kind of principled anger that twentieth-century counterparts would turn into an activist view of the law.[22] A former slave owner, Harlan had repudiated the prosegregation views of his youth during his unsuccessful gubernatorial campaign in Kentucky in 1871. As Harlan emerged as a power in Republican politics, Rutherford Hayes appointed him to the court in 1876. From the very same inkstand that Judge Taney had used to write *Dred Scott,* Harlan wrote his dissent in the 1883 Civil Rights Cases. Arguing that state and private action should be judged by the same standard, Harlan insisted that "the national legislature" should do as much "for human liberty" as it had done in the past "for the protection of slavery." Harlan also insisted that victims, once recognized, should be protected for a long time. He dismissed summarily the majority argument that a freedman who had hardly had the time to assume his new status was automatically ready to "take the rank of a mere citizen."[23] Harlan would go even further in his lone dissent in *Plessy* v. *Ferguson* (1896), when the Court institutionalized the separation of the races by upholding segregated public accommodations. Rejecting the prevailing notion that segregation was compatible with equality, Harlan argued that "there is in this country no superior, dominant, ruling class of citizens. There is no caste here."[24] Just like Du Bois, Harlan was prescient in arguing that "the destinies of the two races" were instead "indissolubly linked."[25] But the alliance of conservatives and progressive reformers who believed in the scientific basis of racial differences prevailed.

One solution for African Americans was to move away from the South toward more hospitable shores just as immigrants had pushed the frontier westward. Millions of African Americans moved North, gradually at first, and then en masse during the Great Migration of the First World War. In the North, they crowded in the ghetto. Because the ghetto housed a rich urban culture as well as a differentiated economy within which there were opportunities for positions of wealth and leadership, it was a significant improvement over sharecropping. For some observers, this migration and urban resettlement promised to lead to inclusion into the polity, much the way other voluntary communities of immigrants functioned simultaneously as a cultural shelter and a port of entry into the main pluralistic society. The liberating possibilities of this hegira were the basis for Chicago sociologist Robert Park's tempered optimism. The former secretary to Booker T. Washington advanced the theory that blacks in the Northern ghetto would follow a pattern of settlement similar to that of immigrants, eventually freeing themselves from initial segregation. That idea implied that the ghetto was at least partly the result of voluntary clustering, "a natural area," as Park put it, and that blacks, like white immigrants before them, would eventually be welcome elsewhere.[26]

The ghetto, however, turned out to be a closed and restrictive environment in which blacks became trapped. The only option available to its residents was to bend together to make it livable. No matter their intention, inhabitants of communities defined by race could not leave their initial area of settlement. As the right to choose was denied to blacks, an enduring northern ghetto was maintained through violence and hostility. Although the Court outlawed public zoning as a means of racial exclusion, private covenants among white neighbors could easily achieve the same purpose, and the terrorism of local race riots completed the task.[27] Furthermore, blacks who had migrated from the South to work in northern factories during World War I did not keep their industrial jobs when the war emergency was over. They were the first ones to be fired in the postwar recession, and they would not reenter industrial jobs in large numbers until the next world war. The message they heard from the white labor unions was that they were not welcome. Under these circumstances, their segregation into growing ghettos completed their isolation from the rest of society. No matter the efforts advocated by race leaders to accommodate and/or resist white prejudice, the "color line" only hardened with time.

It is therefore not surprising that African-American elites made the best of old-style voluntarism. Black ministers took the lead. Other black elites turned inward in the 1920s to escape the harshness of segregation and retain a sense of agency, dignity, and culture. They even enjoyed a cultural renaissance in the ghetto before the Depression put an end to it. The New Negro put his talent to the service of only his or her community: black doctors and nurses healing black patients in black hospitals, black lawyers representing black defendants before black judges, black educators preparing black students for black colleges.[28] Thus African Americans were torn between the need to protect themselves by creating alternative channels of opportunity and the desire to achieve equal rights and justice. Although they retained a degree of control of their lives by making the ghetto livable, the overriding reality of their lives was the near impossibility of escaping discrimination from an exclusionary white society that believed in white supremacy.

THE WOMEN'S BREAKTHROUGH

White male supremacy amounted to a powerful justification for ignoring the problem of others by blaming the others' fate on their assumed shortcomings. Women were best positioned for fighting this view because their pretended weaknesses led them to be confined only to a separate sphere rather than a ghetto. Furthermore, groups of middle-class women had gained considerable organizational skills in transforming their voluntary associations, mostly devoted to charitable causes, into influential alternative forms of public life under their own control.[29] Their political experience led them to a major innovation in denouncing their treatment. They effectively turned the reasons invoked for their exclusion into arguments for recognition. Unlike African Americans, women were able to use the biological determinism that served as justification for excluding them from much professional and public life to secure both inclusion and special treatment. While blacks could not effectively combat racism by endorsing racist stereotypes, women reformulated sexist images of women into a strategic advantage. They reconceived gender differences as part of a larger approach toward gaining justice and turned their alleged inferiority into a weapon. Their strategy was a genuine discovery in combating inequality.

Women abolitionists had initially emphasized that suffrage should be open to all human beings without distinction of sex any more than of race. When the feminist and abolitionist movements were linked, women feminists argued that race and sex were "'two accidents of the body' unworthy of constitutional recognition."[30] The failure to include women in the Fifteenth Amendment, however, created an irreparable split between the freedmen and advocates of women's rights. The Equal Rights Association, which had fought for voting rights for both women and blacks, splintered. Although Frederick Douglass had been quick to point out that civil rights were a matter of life and death for members of his race and therefore deserved priority, he failed to persuade

Elizabeth Cady Stanton and the other leading feminists of the association, who believed educated women deserved the vote more than newly freed and illiterate Negroes.

As a result, women activists rethought their strategies. They set aside the view of gender as a mere accident and stressed difference between the sexes as a reason for extending suffrage. In other words, they endorsed the prevalent male view as a way to bring a "feminine element" into the government.[31] Fighting for the vote, women sought to enlarge the polity by diversifying it. A women's vote was an experiment in feminism. Promoting oneself as the weaker sex deserving protective legislation was another. Protecting women gained even more force when it was linked to protecting children.[32]

Male workers of different skill levels, who had every incentive to unite, could not bring themselves to do so or to build durable alliances with middle-class reformers who envisioned a larger agenda for the labor movement. Middle-class women who had every reason to ignore women workers spoke in the name of all women to demand a new treatment. Educated, organized middle-class women intent on smoothing the worst effects of industrialization on their working-class sisters built a successful coalition with middle-class male reformers to secure judicial review of women's rights in the workplace. Job safety for men was hard to achieve. And workers were worried it might cost them money. It became a right for women because legislation specifically took into account women's physical characteristics and alleged inferiority.

As Theda Skocpol correctly points out, "the justices of the Supreme Court, who unanimously decided in 1908 to treat women workers as a special class deserving public protection, were strongly affected by contemporary public understandings of gender differences." In *Muller* v. *Oregon* (1908), the justices, who upheld Oregon's law limiting the work day for women to ten hours, saw "not individuals whose rights were being infringed, but mothers who needed protection."[33] They felt that biological differences and the realities of childbearing justified creating a special category of legislation for women. Louis Brandeis and Josephine Goldmark wrote a brief illustrating with a mountain of facts and figures that women deserved special consideration from the court. And Brandeis argued that "the well-being of the race" amply justified "legislation to protect her from the greed as well as the passion of man."[34] It was by accepting their alleged limitations that women began the move beyond "Mr. Spencer's social statics." As Lester Ward, himself a Spencerian and the exponent of a new sociology influenced by evolutionary biology, explained it: "The survival of the fittest is simply the survival of the strong, which implies, and might as well be called, the destruction of the weak. And if nature progresses through the destruction of the weak, man progresses through the *protection* of the weak."[35]

Protective legislation, once passed, led to a protracted, still ongoing debate between protectionists and egalitarians within the women's movement and the population at large. Coming as they did from the charity organization movement or the settlement movement and active in such progressive organizations as the Congress of Mothers or the Federation of Women's Clubs, middle-class feminists, among them Florence Kelley, Jane Addams, and Julia Lathrop, knew intimately the conditions of the poor but held firm to ingrained middle-class values. By making sure women assumed their proper place, they built winning coalitions with male politicians and reformers but also accepted much of their own ascribed inferiority. As they campaigned effectively for state and local legislative initiatives to protect women, they were also determined, as Linda Gordon has pointed out, to stress family hierarchy and not make it "too easy" for female welfare recipients. Thus Julia Lathrop, who first headed the U.S. Children's Bureau was concerned about "its pauperizing tendencies."[36] The measures these women supported, invariably including not only means testing but also proof of moral rectitude, have never been fully removed from U.S. legislation.

Egalitarians, however, wanted full equality. Alice Paul's creation of the National Woman's Party in 1919 created a deep split within the women's movement. As ratification of the Nineteenth Amendment in 1920 highlighted the sexist assumptions that underlay women's gains, egalitarians put advocates of protective legislation on the defensive. The more radical feminists launched the pro–Equal Rights Amendment campaign in 1923. Also in 1923, the Supreme Court declared unconstitutional, in *Adkins* v. *Children's Hospital,* a Washington, D.C., law guaranteeing a minimum wage for women workers. Returning to the familiar freedom of contract line of argument, the court contended that "in view of the great—not to say revolutionary—changes which have taken place . . . in the contractual, political and civil status of women, culminating in the Nineteenth Amendment, it is not unreasonable to say that these differences have now come almost, if not quite, to the vanishing point." This opinion prompted Holmes quickly to retort: "I will need more than the Nineteenth Amendment to convince me that there are no differences between men and women, or that legislation cannot take those differences into account."[37]

By capitalizing on their special status, women established the principle of singling out a large group of Americans for the purpose of protecting them or granting them special rights. They created a legal space for group rights in a limited but significant way by arguing that it was impossible to protect women on a case-by-case basis when all women were potentially abused in the workplace. However small the wedge, and however restricted the means, gaining recognition as a group was a conceptual breakthrough. Singling out a group of Americans for the purpose of maintaining a prevailing discriminatory practice, as in *Plessy*, was being superseded by the opposite policy of protecting groups. Alleged inferiority for blacks, who attempted to change folkways, led to exclusion; alleged inferiority for women, who did not, to their protection and ultimately to their inclusion.

A PLURALISM OF WHITE MALES

From that point on, the interplay of race, class, and gender would not work in favor of women's rights any more than blacks'. Much of the early welfare legislation for women was weakened before falling onto hard times as a consequence of both judicial conservatism and the Great Depression.[38] The New Deal was the white worker's hour, postponing a significant second chance for blacks and women until the Second Reconstruction of civil rights in the 1960s.[39] By the end of the Depression, women's achievements seemed meager indeed. In 1930, no woman in any state could claim her part of family income unless she had earned it herself by working outside the home.[40] As more men were thrown out of work, married women in the workplace were accused of taking men's positions. Section 213 of the 1932 Federal Economy Act prohibited more than one family member from working in federal civil service. In half of the states, bills were proposed to prohibit the hiring of married women in any job. Among the married women in the labor force, an increasing number felt they had to keep their marriage a secret.[41] Furthermore, vocational experts pushed women toward jobs where they had little competition from men (family law, teaching, etc.), hence initiating a lasting cycle of job segregation.

As Linda Gordon declares, "New Deal political culture . . . glorified the breadwinner-male/domestic-female family."[42] That philosophy was clear in the 1935 Social Security Act, which benefited women primarily as dependents within a male-headed family. By and large, workmen's compensation, unemployment insurance, and old-age pension excluded jobs held by women (such as domestic workers). In line with previous protective legislation, women and their dependent children not subordinated to a man could get help only by submitting to stringent moral codes. By contrast, male-dominated conservative mass unionism became a full participant in the larger pluralism of interest-group politics in the 1940s. Its battles had become legitimate. At mid-century, political scientist David Truman saw unions as an integral part of "the government process" and credited them as instruments of stabilization in economic relationships. They also brought, in Truman's judgment, "equilibrium in the life of workers both within and outside the factory."[43]

Although women joined the labor force in massive numbers during the Second World War, feminism was at a nadir when peace and prosperity returned. Ironically, some of the ideas propounded by American feminism found their expressions in distant lands rather than at home. As I will explain in the next chapter, the American authorities in postwar Tokyo, who rewrote the Japanese constitution in 1946, magnanimously granted full equality to apolitical Japanese women that American feminists have consistently failed to this day to write into U.S. law.[44] At home, postwar policymakers promoted the ideal of the one wage-earner family, supported by a male-oriented G.I. bill that helped working-class families join an expansive middle class.[45] Vice President Richard Nixon hailed the merits of the American wife and mother fully occupied in her suburban "model" home, a case he made in his 1959 so-called kitchen debate with Secretary Khrushchev, which took place in a model ranch house on display at an American exhibition at the Sokolniki Park in Moscow.[46] But although one-wage-earner, working-class families were indeed joining the mainstream of American consumers, many observers, Nixon included, failed to take seriously the parallel trend that more and more women were working outside the home, questioning the limitations of separate spheres, and yearning for greater autonomy. These women felt the pressures of double consciousness that would lead to the feminist revolution of the 1960s.

The situation of African Americans remained precarious and ambiguous during the middle years of the century for other reasons. Before the war, blacks had only limited access to the industrial workforce. While the traditional barrier that separated skilled from unskilled workers had vanished in mass-production industries, no division among workers remained more blatant than that of race, as southern African Americans who migrated to find jobs in northern factories found themselves segregated not only at home but when working. Many factories had designated lunchrooms, bathrooms, and even workbenches.[47] As a result, as August Meier and Elliott Rudwick point out in their study of Detroit, even "during the period of the UAW's great organizing drives between 1937 and 1941, Detroit's blacks exhibited considerable resistance to unionization."[48] When employers looked for strikebreakers, many African Americans with no love of the unions signed up.

Despite the high-mindedness of most union leaders and pressures from the Fair Employment Practices Committee established in 1941 to prevent discrimination in defense-related work, the rank and file did not relent.[49] Typical was the attitude of UAW local 662 in Anderson, Indiana, which had a collective agreement with a subsidiary of GM. Of 312 job classifications, "Negro employment" was restricted to five. The local also excluded black members from social activities. Members refused to change the policy even for a banquet organized to show union support for the war effort in 1941.[50] In other industries, such as Chicago meatpacking, the unionization drive of African Americans was significantly more successful. But an urban riot designed to keep blacks in the ghetto was never far off. Some of the most violent race riots in American history erupted in Harlem and in Detroit in the summer of 1943.

This was the situation at mid century. White male workers' permanent victories were written into New Deal labor legislation and turned mass unionism into a legitimate part of pluralistic politics. Although women had had access to the ballot box for a generation and gained some labor protection, they had much to do to expose widespread gender-based discrimination. Blacks, disfranchised in the South and trapped in the northern ghetto, still could do little. It was unclear how, in these circumstances, women and blacks could join forces to seek justice. But it required convincing policymakers and judges alike that the discrimination they suffered was not the obvious consequence of their alleged natural inferiority but of oppression.

PLURALISM ON TRIAL

The key was to break free from a benign ineffectual pluralism to a policy of redress for groups that had suffered discrimination. As this strategy emerged only after World War II, I will conclude this chapter with a brief foray into the postwar period to take this story to its logical conclusion. In parts 1 and 2 of this book, the institutional matrix that supported the American knowledge organization and the policies that made the age of high mass consumption possible were fully developed and understood as American principles by the 1940s or early 1950s. The matrix remains with us, even though it is changing; consumption has become only more pervasive; but pluralism was a much more fragile achievement than the creation of a large institutional matrix of knowledge and the growth of a white middle-class society of consumers. Describing what happened to a now moribund pluralism is another way of highlighting its flaws.

Pluralism was about to break up at the very time middle-class Americans embraced it, for the blind hegemony of white-male, middle-class values gave it no room to expand. Thus, in the forties, Gunnar Myrdal called the discrepancy between creed and conduct in race relations that paralyzed Americans the America dilemma.[51] It was in attempting to resolve that disparity between beliefs and deeds that Americans turned pluralism into a controversial policy of affirmative action.

This new strategy initially came from African Americans. As the civil rights movement was making headway, NAACP lawyers and their social scientist allies finally succeeded in turning "inferiors," that is, those individuals "marked as inferior by the law," into victims living in a society of victimizers.[52] With Brown v. Board of Education (1954), the Supreme Court accepted much controversial evidence in acknowledging that blacks' mediocre educational achievements were in part the result of the psychological "damage" they had suffered by being segregated from white society. The social scientists and law-yers who had built the case knew how weak it was. How much and what kind of damage, the evidence could not really say.[53] But that was beside the point since the strategy paid off. Hard-won civil rights legislation, however, was seldom applied after the landmark Brown decision. Implementation of the mandate to desegregate the nations' schools would be excruciatingly slow.

Despite this legal victory that exposed the limits of the pluralistic consensus, liberal policymakers were still taking a gradual approach to the problem of racial discrimination in the face of much conservative resistance from estab-lished, primarily southern interests, until grassroots' pressures to create a truly "great society" including blacks and women erupted with a new force in the 1960s and 1970s. Recalling only two episodes of the Second Reconstruction will allow me to make more explicit the connection between historic discrimi-nation and redress and its ultimate consequences for redrawing the boundaries of identity away from the broad center of mass society.

The first incident took place in 1964 at a time when black and white activists who worked together in the more radical trenches of the civil rights movement experienced a heightened level of tension. Radical black civil rights leaders of SNCC were expelling white co-leaders and turning away white women mili-tants who resented their sexist attitude.[54] But unexpected help in forging a government-sponsored alliance between blacks and women came from the oddities of congressional log rolling. At issue was the need to make progress in enforcing civil rights legislation. In the wake of Kennedy's assassination, President Johnson picked up the civil rights banner. The second civil rights bill the Johnson administration presented to Congress in 1964 was partly designed to put an end to employment discrimination based on race, creed, color, and national origin. Its passage, it turned out, was the occasion for Congress to recognize both blacks and women as victims of historic discrimination.

The unexpected rapprochement was unwittingly orchestrated by Virginia congressman Howard Smith, a former circuit court judge and anti-civil rights conservative southern Democrat. Judge Smith was also the powerful chairman of the House Committee on Rules at the time of the debate on the second Civil Rights Act of 1964. With his delaying tactics, the Virginian was coordinating southern opposition to the bill. When stalling was no longer possible, Judge Smith resorted to a last minute proposal. Why not, he said, add a ban on sex discrimination to the bill? Smith had been a congressional sponsor of the Equal Rights Amendment starting in 1945. Having maintained ties with the National Women's Party, he had been influenced by southern women associates of Alice Paul who were no friends of civil rights for blacks. Smith was also attuned to the interests of small Virginia textile mill owners who preferred equal rights for women over the protective legislation that set limits on their prerogatives as employers and raised the price of labor. In this instance, by loading the bill with potentially offensive provisions, his intent was clearly to sink civil rights for blacks by adding a guarantee for women most had never envisaged and few took seriously. Indeed, the real purpose of this ostensibly friendly amendment was understood by Smith's fellow southerners.[55]

But to everybody's surprise, the amendment did not prove to be an obstacle to the passage of the bill. As a result, with the provision barring discrimination on the basis of sex written into title VII of the Civil Rights Act, the Equal Employment Opportunity Commission was created to enforce it. And blacks and women were thus reunited under the law. On the surface, it was merely a legislative accident. Deeper, however, the incident reflected the failure of pluralism and the coming to the fore of long-repressed feelings. It was a return to the days when blacks and women abolitionists had joined forces to gain the vote, before Frederick Douglass and Elizabeth Cady Stanton parted ways over the Fifteenth Amendment. They shared strategies again. Women, who had historically accepted "inferiority" to gain protection, now had a legal precedent for adopting the tactic of exposing their oppressors. They did it in increasing numbers. And the federal government, by backing the alliance, made it possible to move beyond the empty rhetoric of benign pluralism to focus on specific legislation. Enlarging pluralism meant writing into law the idea that discrimination against individuals was generally part of a pattern of prejudice against the group to which this individual belonged. It would then follow that the entire group deserved not only protection but also redress.

The second incident, some fourteen years later, is a sober reminder of how fragile the legal program of the Second Reconstruction really was, not unlike that of the First. In a revealing judicial concurrence in a widely discussed challenge to affirmative action, Justice Thurgood Marshall who, as a lawyer for the NAACP, had been among those who had helped shape the Brown decision, expressed his fears that the Second Reconstruction was already coming to an end. The landmark case involved a white applicant who had been passed over for admission to medical school and who successfully claimed that less qualified minority candidates had been unduly given priority over him. It was an instance of a white American successfully turning affirmative action into reverse discrimination. In *Regents of the University of California* v. *Bakke* (1978), the University of California Regents were forced to admit Alan Bakke, the white male victim, after the court decided that the medical school had discriminated against him by reserving sixteen of the one hundred openings exclusively for minority candidates.[56]

Marshall fully captured the difficulty of writing race consciousness into law. Well aware that it had taken half a century for the civil rights movement to establish grounds for victimization, Marshall's brief was based on historical analysis as well as legal precedent. To Marshall and other civil rights leaders, an aggressive strategy of legal redress was the only viable option for integrating blacks into the polity. That conviction had prompted the Reverend Martin Luther King to hail C. Vann Woodward's *The Strange Career of Jim Crow* (1955) as the "historical Bible of the civil-rights movement." King brandished the small volume of lectures on southern history that Woodward had given at the University of Virginia to a crowd of dedicated supporters assembled in front of the Alabama state capitol in 1965.[57] This is because the southern historian had so beautifully captured the conviction that it was in the power of the law to better society rather than reflect its prejudices. If legal action had produced segregation, it could also create integration. What law could do, law could undo.

It is in that spirit that Marshall thought it appropriate to refer to the great measures of Radical Reconstruction—the 1865 Thirteenth Amendment abolishing slavery, the Civil Rights Acts of 1866 bestowing citizenship upon the Negro and anticipating the Fourteenth Amendment, the equal protection clause of the Fourteenth Amendment, and the 1870 antidiscrimination clause in voting rights of the Fifteenth Amendment—as the "first affirmative action programs of the nation." As part of this affirmative action effort, Marshall also included the Freedmen's Bureau, created in 1865 to provide relief, rations, medical care, and schools for freed blacks, as well as protect their rights as laborers, and the Civil Rights Act of 1875.[58] Marshall's formulation was anachronistic, a projection onto the past. The post–Civil War programs were enforcement vehicles against a reluctant South, not affirmative action in the modern sense; they had no provisions for special compensations of victims of past discrimination.

Yet Marshall had reason to connect the Second Reconstruction to the First. His understanding of the spirit of Radical Reconstruction as that of affirmative action—the will to grant rights to groups for the express purpose of reversing past discrimination—was justified. Marshall was effectively engaging in a conversation with Harlan, who in his lone dissent to the 1883 reversal on civil rights had referred to the extension of citizenship that came with passage of the Fourteenth Amendment as an "affirmative grant" from the nation to the African-American people.[59] In their conversation across a century, Marshall and Harlan were sharing a conviction in the moral obligation to use the power of law to bring about social change. What Harlan had hoped for and what Marshall reaffirmed was the need to go beyond pluralism's ideological mode of functioning in order to break racial prejudice. Affirmative action was in effect a judgment on pluralism.

These two incidents revealed the enormous challenge of turning pluralism, a philosophical call for appreciating difference, into a national policy of compensatory treatment that enshrined differences in a legal code. The first difficulty was in deciding who should receive special treatment. It was the EEOC, together with the Office of Federal Contract Compliance, that led the way in designing affirmative action programs to help blacks and women but also identifying other minority groups as victims of past societal discrimination entitled to compensatory preference in employment. These two bureaucratic agencies initiated the controversial counting by race and gender to end discrimination. To assist the EEOC in that task, Betty Friedan and other middle-class women formed the National Organization for Women in 1966.[60]

Americans had much experience with the statistical management of society. They had invented the average American and refined many tools of market analysis and political surveys. But this time, the charge was not to draw representative samples or compute the mean of a bell-shaped normal distribution but to identify outliers and bring them in. As a method of enlarging the center, the new statistical particularism has limits. As David Hollinger correctly asks, what is the point of an "ethno-racial pentagon," this bizarre invention of American bureaucrats that divides the American population into mutually exclusive categories of African American, Asian American, Native American, Euro-American, and Hispanic American when most Americans, even members of minority groups, can legitimately claim multiple identities, or modify their identities as an act of will?[61] Designed to help victims of historic discrimination, compensatory treatment became theoretically available to all who found themselves in a situation where they could successfully claim a recognized generic attribute. The results are making Americans uneasy. The white majority has learned to some extent to acknowledge the existence of victims and its responsibility for victimization. The new statistical particularism, however, has proved no more satisfying than the previous generation's reliance on the average in establishing durable links between the parts and the whole.[62] Conceiving of the country simultaneously in the singular and in the plural remains a prerequisite for enlarging the polity.

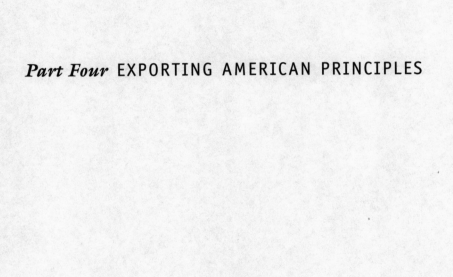

Part Four EXPORTING AMERICAN PRINCIPLES

CHAPTER EIGHT

INDIVIDUALISM AND MODERNIZATION

The American Experiment in Japan

_If the memories of the bestialities of the Japanese prison camps were not so fresh
in mind, one might have felt sorry for Shigemitsu as he hobbled on his wooden
leg toward the green baize covered table where the papers lay waiting. He
leaned heavily on his cane and had difficulty seating himself. The cane, which
he rested against the table, dropped to the deck of this battleship as he signed.
No word passed between him and General Douglas MacArthur._

HOMER BIGART[1]

At the end of World War II, the potential for a new realm of American experimentation was greatest in Japan and Germany, for much if not all had to be
rebuilt. Although the Allies had resolved to disarm both countries and to
curtail drastically their industrial might, they also felt the need to fashion a
new partnership with former enemies. As the only country to emerge from
the war with a strong economy, America led by redirecting the use of their
previous adversaries' local resources to "democratic" purposes. In this endeavor, the American influence is most readily apparent in Japan, where it
was also most deeply felt. It is less manifest in partitioned Germany, where
Americans had to compromise with the other Allied forces.[2] American lever-
age on the destiny of Europe is also less prominent. Although it may have
been a basic premise of the Marshall Plan to help create an "integrated Europe
looking like the United States of America— 'God's Own Country,' " as an
official of the British Treasury once put it, the European partners saw the
American plan more often as a way to avoid disastrous economic disruptions
than as an opportunity to rethink their vision of economy and society. The
Americans' assumption, growing out of their own economic experience, was
that "a large internal economy integrated by free-market forces" would lay
"the groundwork for a new era of economic growth and stability."[3] Europeans, however, adhered to their own national blueprints.[4]

Postwar Japan, by contrast, constitutes a unique case of unalloyed influence
from the United States. Not only did Americans occupy the entire country,
they had a free hand in determining policy even though the Japanese were
allowed to maintain a government of their own and to keep their emperor.
Truman's decision to drop the bomb had been motivated partly by Washington's desire to keep the Soviets away from postwar Japan.[5] The other Allies
did not interfere with American policy, and the Washington-based international Far East Commission (FEC) was American-dominated. The exclusivity
of the U.S. dialogue with Japan makes it possible to retrace the Americans'
image of their own culture as reflected in their agenda for the postwar order.

Between the Japanese surrender on August 15, 1945, and the end of the
American occupation on April 28, 1952, Japan became the site of an unprecedented political, social, and economic experiment in transplanting American
ideas in foreign soil. Douglas MacArthur, the supreme commander of the
American occupation of Japan and his large contingent of American personnel
attempted to transform Japan according to American principles. At first, it
was more urgent to avoid food riots than draw blueprints. But Americans
proceeded immediately with long-term plans for rebuilding.

Having themselves lived through a major organizational revolution in the half century preceding the occupation, it was normal for Americans to turn to their own recent history for guidance. The circumstances they faced in Asia made it difficult, however, to reconcile economic, political, and social matters as they understood them at home with their intended conduct of affairs abroad. Although victory gave them a renewed confidence in their own means of generating prosperity and individual freedom, they were not sure what to export of their own experiment to this devastated country. While the so-called postwar consensus was emerging at home, its fragility would be exposed as soon as Americans attempted to export their principles abroad. Policymaking in Japan would reflect the many fractures of the American system, and consequently the history of the occupation would be a replay of many of the old debates on organization and technology, class and consumption, pluralism and the search for self-realization that I have analyzed in the preceding chapters.

To understand what took place in Japan and, beyond that, to discern the norms Americans hoped to export abroad requires moving away from the attractive but all-too-abstract theory of American hegemony and settle for the messy facts and unexpected turns of the Pax Americana. As rulers in Japan, Americans faced the challenge of defining objectives rapidly as well as designing legal, economic, and social policies to follow in occupation and rebuilding. We need therefore to pay close attention to misunderstandings, contradictions in policy, changing circumstances, and unexpected outcomes. Only then will Americanization become a heuristic concept, not a foregone conclusion of global power or an exercise in wishful thinking.

PRECONDITIONS IN THE UNITED STATES AND IN JAPAN

To restate the American case briefly, at mid-century, Herbert Croly's 1909 program of applying "Hamiltonian means" to achieve "Jeffersonian ends" had become a daily part of American life. Not only had Americans come to terms with formidable industrial organizations but they had given the state the power to regulate the economy. The sources of wealth had shifted from exploitation of natural resources and easy access to cheap farm land to a system of industrial production dominated by large center firms, relying heavily on technology and research and geared toward mass consumption by an expanding white middle class. While early twentieth-century Americans had feared the impact of big corporations, big labor, big government, and big science and had been ambivalent about what role, if any, America could play in the world, mid twentieth-century Americans, on the surface, downplayed such worries. Prosecuting the war had decisively pulled them out of what was left of the Great Depression. Winning it consolidated their faith in a tight connection between the economics of bigness and the pursuit of individual self-realization. It confirmed their belief in the institutional matrix, in the average American, and in the pluralist vision. Strengthened by collective action, American workers were bargaining the high wages and low prices that made possible conservative mass unionism and the consumer society.

Croly had defined the "substance" of the American "national promise" in economic terms. He had seen it as a tireless "vision of a better future" in which "an improving popular economic condition," guaranteed by "democratic political institutions," produces "moral and social amelioration."[6] He had insisted that economic prosperity, democratic politics, and individual well-being could only reinforce each other. At the time of the occupation, mid twentieth-century Americans were still theorizing on the mutual reinforcement of prosperity and freedom. They were labeling a modified version of Croly's ideas "modernization" and trusted their ability to generate the necessary abundance to make the system work.

Facing the wealthy and victorious Americans were the exhausted Japanese, who had seemingly severed their connection with the West in prosecuting their imperialist ambitions in Asia and in the war. Few Americans were willing to remember at the time of the occupation that the Japanese had met the West before, or that the Japanese understood the lessons to be learned from this encounter. Their past engagement with the West, however, would prove critical in giving the Japanese an alternative past to which they could turn.[7]

Numerous witnesses of the Meiji Restoration have reported on Japan's early attempt to begin anew. Thus Erwin Baelz, a German doctor who was a keen observer of late nineteenth-century Japan, entitled his diary "Awakening Japan." Baelz depicted the 1870s as a period when the Japanese "felt a contempt for their own history, their own religion, their own art."[8] Among a generation of educators nourished with Western philosophies, Yukichi Fukuzawa, who founded Keio University in 1868, wrote his own version of the American Declaration of Independence in the opening sentence of his most famous book on education: "It is said that Heaven does not create one man above or below another man. This means that when men are born from Heaven they are all equal. There is no innate distinction between high and low." Published in 1872, the book had by some estimates sold about 3,400,000 copies by the time of the author's death in 1901.[9]

The early Meiji even saw the rise of a Japanese bourgeoisie, especially in the countryside, that exhibited individual entrepreneurship by controlling the agricultural surplus in the villages.[10] The popular vogue of Western-style success stories attests to a serious Japanese encounter with individualism. Japan was fertile ground for British best-selling author Samuel Smiles, whose *Self-Help* was a best seller in the early Meiji. If the translator experienced difficulty finding words equivalent to individualism and individuality, he nonetheless conveyed Smiles's message that "national progress" was "the sum of individual industry, energy, and uprightness." Translations of Smiles's stories as well as those of Horatio Alger continued to be popular and found their way into school textbooks, where they were read well into the twentieth century.[11]

Although Japan's emerging Western-style bourgeoisie did not last long, the dialogue with the West continued as Japan industrialized. The Japanese had considerably Americanized their business systems by the 1920s. Some of the larger concerns had been looking for models of industrialization in Germany, England, and the United States. They were especially attracted by the American model of welfare capitalism, with its insistence on loyalty to the firm, that some of the biggest American companies were promoting and that American officials, like Commerce Secretary Herbert Hoover, were also championing.[12]

Many Japanese industrialists, however, fought the idea of workers' rights in the name of efficient competition with the West, and economic individualism remained elusive.[13] Never to be suspected of ethnocentrism, American economist Thorstein Veblen remarked in 1915 that Japan might actually be better off without Westernization. He underscored "Japan's opportunity" to graft imported modern technology on domestic feudal values so as to avoid the traumas and social cost of industrialization.[14] Although a small labor movement had emerged in Japan, Veblen suggested that "personal ties" and "vertical relations of loyalty" might permit a smoother industrialization than the Western blend of collective bargaining and economic individualism. While Veblen praised obedience, philosopher John Dewey, who visited Japan in 1919, felt estranged from a society where he could find no trace of participatory democracy.[15]

Others, like political scientist Charles Beard, proved more tolerant and also optimistic that the Japanese might eventually tie modernization and democratization together—American style. Called upon by Count Gotō, then mayor of Tokyo, to help rebuild the Japanese capital after the disastrous 1923 earthquake, Beard was keenly aware that Japanese society was far from democratic. Although at the time of the earthquake, Tokyo was engaged in "a program of modernization," including building dams, paving streets, installing sewerage, and making harbor improvements as well as erecting hospitals and playgrounds, the city remained a collection of villages, where people, crowded in small wooden buildings along narrow streets, barely participated in the political process. Despite an expansion of the municipal electorate in 1922, universal suffrage was resisted. And Tokyo, in Beard's words, was "progressing" only slowly toward democracy.[16]

Under such circumstances, Beard forcefully argued that it was more important to work with the Japanese on problems of urban engineering, sanitation, and municipal reform than to inculcate in them the values of the Declaration of Independence and the Constitution, which offered them no skills in dealing with the problems they faced. The technical methods of social intelligence, not high-minded but empty rhetoric, would have a lasting effect and would lead the Japanese to democracy.

By the time of the occupation, however, Americans had little sense they could renew a genuine dialogue with the Japanese. Impressed by the recent Japanese history of repression at home, brutal empire building in Asia, and relentless prosecution of the war, most Americans argued that they could not have landed on a shore more foreign to their ideas than Japan.[17] Japan was an unlikely place for American-style economic management, the creation of new political institutions on the American model, or American ideas about social change. It was this great conceptual distance separating the two countries that gave MacArthur the feeling that he had indeed a lofty mission to accomplish.[18]

During World War II, the American Army's Office of War Information had turned to anthropologist Ruth Benedict to understand the bases of Japanese militarism. To fulfill her assignment, Benedict produced a book that has since become a classic, *The Chrysanthemum and the Sword: Patterns of Japanese Culture* (1946). Benedict's interpretation became, directly or indirectly, the accepted wisdom among those American policymakers and Army personnel whose charge it was to reform a part of the world that seemed so alien to their own habits.[19] In developing what would become the dominant postwar American interpretation of Japan, Benedict did not recognize the West in the experiment of the Meiji Restoration. She speculated instead about the ways Japan's new ruling class during the Meiji Restoration, unlike its counterparts in democratic nations, had kept alive what Alexis de Tocqueville called the aristocratic chain, a device that linked generations by keeping everyone at a "proper station."[20] Although an oversimplification, she saw Japanese society as having remained largely feudal.

By this, Benedict meant that the Japanese ordered all aspects of their world hierarchically. "In the family and in personal relations," she wrote, "age, generation, sex, and class dictate proper behavior. In government, religion, the Army, and industry, areas are carefully separated into hierarchies where neither the higher nor the lower may without penalty overstep their prerogatives. As long as 'proper station' is maintained, the Japanese carry on without protest. They feel safe. They are of course often not 'safe' in the sense that their best good is protected but they are 'safe' because they have accepted hierarchy as legitimate." Stressing opposites, Benedict concluded that the Japanese's reliance on hierarchy is "as characteristic of their judgment on life as trust in equality and free enterprise is of the American way of life."[21]

These were the years when American social scientists constructed global schemes of national character. Ruth Benedict, who selected as working title for her report "Japanese Character," was no exception; she presented Japan as the opposite of the United States Louis Hartz would depict later in his classic *The Liberal Tradition in America* (1955). Louis Hartz, who was also influenced by Marx, extended Tocqueville's thoughts by contending that the absence of a feudal past had simply prevented the dialectic of class from being initiated in America and was the key to American exceptionalism. Hartz's America—a Jeffersonian country of small independent landowners—had never experienced feudal systems or aristocratic structures. It was a country that never knew Tocqueville's aristocratic chain, whereas Japan, according to Benedict, who overstated her case, never had to contend with a bourgeoisie even during the modern era.[22] Benedict's study was a tour de force made all the more remarkable by the fact that the author did not know Japanese and had never visited Japan. But as an American, she was the most brilliant among the neophytes. Although there were a few Japan specialists, like Edwin O. Reischauer, in both the State Department and occupation staff at the Supreme Command for Allied Powers (SCAP), most Americans were ignorant of anything Japanese. For the more than 3,000 American government personnel stationed in Tokyo, only American questions were worth asking and American concepts worth using.

The initial mandate of the occupation was entirely consistent with the unquestioned interpretation of Japanese society as modern feudalism and its corollary that a militarism of the magnitude the Japanese had displayed could take hold only in a deeply stratified and hierarchical society. This situation called for immediate dismantling not only of the powerful military organization but also of Japan's large industrial corporations, which had made it possible for the military to prosecute the war so relentlessly (that is, the *zaibatsu*, literally "money cliques"—groups of "diversified businesses" originally "owned exclusively by a single family or an extended family" that had over the years evolved into increasingly complex managerial structures).[23] In that endeavor, MacArthur was to follow guidelines he had received from the Joint Chiefs of Staff and the joint State, War, and Navy Coordinating Committee. The drafting of these guidelines had been influenced by the State Department China lobby's punitive stance toward Japan, by "radical" New Dealers in Washington who were against big business, and by the Morgenthau plan to turn Germany into a big farm, a plan Lt. Colonel Charles Kades, one of MacArthur's close associates at SCAP, had helped draft.[24]

The guidelines combined demilitarization with industrial deconcentration, specifying the principle of reparations and the relocation of key Japanese industries in Asian countries formerly dominated by Japan. The directives outlined a reorganization of labor, industry, and agriculture on a "democratic basis," favoring a "wide distribution of income and of the ownership of the means of production and trade" to be achieved by removing business leaders who had not directed the country to peaceful purposes, and by dissolving large industrial combines.[25] The charge was therefore to destroy the bases of Japanese militarism—and that meant dismantling not only the military hierarchy but also the industrial corporations and bureaucratic structures that had supported the military. While victorious Americans accepted unquestionably the close relationship at home between big business and the military, as occupiers, they punished the first for its collaboration with the second. While Americans naturally credited their own industrial-military complex for serving democracy, they felt they had to destroy the corresponding Japanese organization for having served fascism.

The schematic conviction that dismantling the *zaibatsu* was the first step in preventing future Japanese aggression limited Americans' options for the economic rebuilding of the country. Furthermore, turning home for recent models of development could provide only partial guidance. For replicating recent American history would mean supporting the very elements of Japanese society most responsible for the disaster. Democratization required instead ousting the parties in the war contract and rebuilding Japan without them on principles significantly closer to those of nineteenth-century than of twentieth-century America. By identifying Japanese big organizations as the culprit, Americans rendered useless much of their own recent past for rebuilding Japan. Herein lies the first built-in paradox of the American occupation: the desire to create an American political and economic culture when conditions made it virtually impossible to duplicate modern America. While Americans were celebrating bigness at home, they had to destroy it in Japan to create the foundations for freedom and democracy. And they had to do it with great speed to implement the directives received from the Joint Chiefs of Staff in Washington.

Despite Washington's policy guidelines, the supreme commander had much leeway in actual implementation, especially in the first two years of the occupation.[26] MacArthur, however, had not lived in the United States for many years. Hesitant about economic matters, he clung to an older vision of America based more on traditional Emersonian self-reliance than on Lippmann's mastery. This may be why Perry Miller, the well-known historian of American puritanism who visited MacArthur while on an educational mission in Tokyo, quipped that all MacArthur could think of was to create in Japan an Asian version of the American Midwest.[27]

AN UNPRECEDENTED REFORM EFFORT

Despite MacArthur's uncertainty, the American reform program and the scope of Americanization during the postwar occupation were unprecedented. As the Americans made their plans known, it became clear that they amounted to an entirely new framework for life in Japan. A new constitution implemented American pluralism: the separation of church and state, new independence for local governments, the formulation of civil rights, and other major social changes. American efforts also included major land reform and industrial restructuring designed to rebuild the class structure along the American model. There was also broad educational reform. All this was pursued with deliberate speed. Four weeks were sufficient for investigating and reporting on education, but that seemed long compared to the record seven days assigned for drafting the new constitution.[28] The Japanese government acted as a buffer zone between American ideology and Japanese culture but was in no position to argue.[29] Each item on the reform agenda—constitutional revision, educational measures, land redistribution, industrial restructuring, transformation of labor relations—if taken separately, makes for an extraordinary story; when combined, they add up to a singular experiment in Americanization that is most remarkable for its inevitable contradictions. My intent is not to review the entire effort but to highlight the difficulty of exporting the American system.

U.S. objectives demanded the creation of a new civil society supported by an economy free of the grip of those industrial giants who had prosecuted the war. Industrial dismantlement as punishment, however, posed a major policymaking dilemma: By dismantling industrial combines in the name of democracy, Americans left unresolved the question of lifting the defeated and exhausted country out of poverty. They had no idea how smaller businesses could generate wealth anew in Japan. To make matters worse, by pushing the countervailing powers of labor against a seriously weakened managerial structure, they produced only chaos. In the midst of these conflicting strategies, the planned land reform, as we will see, offered at best a modest hope. For Americans at home, the pursuit of national prosperity and individual welfare were inseparable, as Croly had suggested. In Japan, the two goals seemed contradictory; the collective rebuilding effort was so demanding that individual benefits had to be postponed. Furthermore, there was a significant mismatch between American rulings designed to restructure the Japanese economy and measures aimed at promoting civil rights.

The new Japanese constitution, which was drafted by SCAP officials in just one week in February 1946 to implement "limited monarchy, renunciation of war, and abolition of feudalism," was Americans' best effort to export pluralism.[30] Save for a ceremonial emperor who had forsaken his divine origins, it was an American document where one could retrace distinct periods of American jurisprudence. It was the constitution's third chapter, "Rights and Duties of the People," which provided a framework for the workings of a pluralistic civil society in Japan. In line with American ideology, "rights and duties" were designed to help the Japanese realize their individual potential. Thus the constitution made education more accessible, emancipated individual household members from established hierarchies, abolished domestic forms of spying, protected the rights of the accused in a court of law, guaranteed basic civil liberties. It also ended discrimination on the basis of race, religion, ethnicity, class, or gender, and required the separation of church and state. The constitution incorporated not only traditional American concepts of individual free speech and free action, but those group rights of collective action that had been written into the American polity by New Deal reforms. Thus article 28 of Chapter 3 guaranteed "the right of workers to organize, and to bargain and act collectively." This clause, meant to support an American-style conservative labor movement, would prove of major significance for the reorganization of postwar Japan.

Women's rights were also included. Among the Americans who drafted the constitution, there was, almost by accident, a young woman by the name of Beate Sirota who had just returned from college in the United States, where she had been sent before the war by Austrian-Jewish parents who had settled in Tokyo. Visiting with her family for Christmas 1945, Sirota was hired at SCAP and assigned to assist the American lawyers with the drafting effort. She did not need legal training, however, to realize that the American male lawyers had forgotten women.[31] She scurried around to find wording and inserted the "women's rights" provision at the last minute. Her wording giving unqualified equal rights to women was actually significantly more radical than its American counterpart. In the end, the Japanese were left to grapple as best they could with ideas about individual self-realization, civil rights, and pluralism that would have seemed for the most part quite natural only to white male Americans.

While the Meiji Constitution had proceeded from German originals Japanized by the Itō commission, this one was primarily American. American legal concepts were used with little or no concern for equivalent terms in the Japanese language. This shortcut left Japanese officials with the opportunity to find endless subtleties and insert planned ambiguities in translation, adjusting the American document to Japanese practice to the extent that was feasible with the hope that custom would take precedence over law in Japanese life. Thus opened a new chapter in the history of Japanese civil society, where "stateways" and "folkways" would for a while pull in different directions. Japanese and Americans had to work out compromises to manage the misunderstandings that occurred subsequently. Thus the Japanese government continued to tax temples although it was a violation of the principle of separation of church and state as Americans understood it.[32] Japanese women may have been freed on paper, but it would take another generation for mutual consent actually to become the basis of marriage and for domestic hierarchical relations slowly to loosen. In the multitude of adjustments that needed to be worked out to reconcile stateways and folkways, the Japanese government helped American policymakers along by maintaining the fiction, widely believed in the countryside where American occupants were rarely in sight, that it had initiated the reforms. The American origins of much policy would not be known until after the occupation, as late as 1955.[33]

Whether the implementation of individual and group rights would achieve their intended results in promoting an American-style civil society depended, in large part, on how the Japanese would use their newly recreated economic instruments. Of these, land exploitation was first on the agenda. MacArthur had a personal stake in the success of land reform. Reading history as a student, he had concluded that the decline of the Roman Empire was inevitable, brought about even before the birth of the empire, when wealthy slave owners of the Roman Republic had destroyed the family farm by assassinating Tiberius Gracchus. He had witnessed his father's inability, as military governor of the Philippines, to free the Filipino peasants from oppression by the landed elite. His turn had come to do for the Japanese what even Radical Reconstruction had failed to do for the American freedmen, that is, turning exploited tenants into independent, small-scale democratic capitalists.[34]

MacArthur felt "that any man who farmed the land should, by law, be entitled to his crops."[35] By the time he was done in December 1949, 89 percent of the land was farmed by its owners, up from 54 percent in 1945.[36] This transformation, he would claim, demonstrated the Japanese's ability to "handle the tools of democracy."[37] As usual, MacArthur's accomplishments were not as impressive as he would have liked us to believe. Japanese officials were ready for land reform. As historian Ronald Dore has concluded, "war or no war, American occupation or no American occupation, it is unlikely that the tenancy system . . . would have lasted for long." Prime Minister Shigeru Yoshida assisted the reform because he recognized that rural conditions were so bad that the landlords might be overthrown in a blood-bath of insurrection.[38]

Stunningly ignorant of the previous seventy years of American history and discounting the misfortunes of the American family farm, MacArthur claimed that "every farmer" in Japan "was now a capitalist in his own right."[39] The subdivided plots, however, were too small for efficient farming. The ultimate success of the land reform depended therefore on industrial policy and on the post-occupation farm-to-city movement. Only when farmers left to work in rebuilt factories, would farms grow in size making them viable again. In Croly's language, the land reform would eventually initiate a lasting connection between political democracy and economic life. It is still credited for much political stability in postwar Japan. MacArthur, however, had not used the "Hamiltonian means" at his disposal to achieve "Jeffersonian ends" in the modern sense that Croly had intended, that is, of galvanizing individual energies "by a sense of joint responsibility" to the larger community.[40] He had instead created a Japanese version of an old-fashioned Jeffersonian democracy, and it suffered much the same fate.

If land reform was intended to render a makeshift vision of early nineteenth-century America in Japan, industrial reform made the conditions for recreating modern managerial capitalism impossible. In industrial matters, MacArthur was unsure about what to do. American policy in Japan was in the hands of radical, that is, Brandeisian "New Dealers" such as Edwin Martin in the State Department, and in the occupation staff.[41] Their first order of business was to dismantle the *zaibatsu*. These large concerns were uniformly held responsible for Japan's aggressive militarism. Closer to the truth was the view that a belligerent new group of *zaibatsu*, especially invested in heavy industries, but weaker in international trade, had been most closely allied to the military bureaucracy.[42] In late 1945, the State and Justice departments sent Corwin Edwards, an antitrust expert from Northwestern University, to Japan. The Edwards report further strengthened the deconcentration program. Edwards's description of the *zaibatsu* relationship between labor and management as "semifeudal" was not original and his claim that feudalism impaired the rise of the middle class was tautological.[43] Unproven was the report's proposition that wholesale *zaibatsu* dissolution was a precondition for changing the Japanese class structure. Nonetheless, FEC-230 directive, an explicit outcome of the Edwards report, served as a guide for the sustained deconcentration efforts and for MacArthur's appointment, in August 1946, of the Holding Company Liquidation Commission (HCLC) to break up the great cartels and to remove the old *zaibatsu* families from both ownership and control.[44]

Japanese resistance and the durability of the informal personal networks among big businesses and their small suppliers and contractors made for very slow progress until January 1947, when MacArthur launched the purge of Japanese business leaders, resulting in 2,200 leaders being ousted by mid-1947. HCLC then proceeded with stock redistribution. For the young staff members of SCAP's labor division who yearned for a version of the New Deal now forgotten in America and for State Department officials who had a say in implementing the initial policy directives of breaking up industrial combines, this policy promised to serve two purposes. By dismantling concentrations of wealth, they would render powerless those most responsible for the military might of Japan. They would also achieve the extensive antitrust agenda and ambitious program of industrial regulation that had failed at home. Thus Theodore Cohen, one of the few occupation personnel who knew something about Japanese history (having written a master's thesis on the Japanese labor movement of the interwar years) and who, as head of SCAP's labor division, worked hard for the creation of a noncommunist labor movement, characteristically entitled his insider's account of the period, *The American Occupation as New Deal*.[45] The postwar export of an older antitrust agenda weakening center firms was, however, clearly out of synch with the massive promotion at home of mass consumption that had been New Deal policy since at least 1937 and the postwar support of that policy by a labor movement generally turned conservative.

Much of the vast American reform program, only a part of which I have reviewed here, was therefore based on an outdated vision of American history, a strange mix of nineteenth-century Jeffersonian agrarian ideals and New Deal labor radicalism. More often than not, the first wave of American policy in

Japan was a rendition of an America that no longer existed. It was a vision of individualism, social justice, and democratization closer to Progressive yearnings than to the postwar neo-Keynesianism that was fast becoming the hallmark of policy made for home consumption. It is not surprising, with such disparity of viewpoints, that American actions could produce outcomes quite inimical to American intentions. The rapid rise of communism in postwar Japan is a case in point. Even though occupation forces wanted a conservative labor movement, local forces played otherwise, and it seemed for a while that a reborn communist leadership might be in a position to decide the future of Japanese industry. Communists enjoyed a brief period of intense moral authority in the immediate postwar period, for they were the only group in Japanese society who had consistently opposed the war. They had the aura of having been persecuted, gagged, jailed, and forced to seek refuge in exile.[46] The military regime had left nothing to chance: even books that had a Marxist leaning had been shelved off limits in university libraries.[47] Now that communists emerged unscathed as untainted opponents of militarism, they used their new moral authority to promote their vision of social justice. So careful were they not to tarnish their pacifist image among Japanese workers that they would not openly let returned Japanese soldiers who had adopted communism in Chinese war camps enter positions of union leadership.[48]

Americans, who supported the creation of a conservative labor movement along the policy lines of the Wagner Act at home, unwittingly boosted the Japanese communists' image and fostered their ascent. What better publicity stunt for First Amendment rights than freeing jailed communist leaders? But what stranger scene than seeing communist leaders officially thanking MacArthur for their newly discovered freedom and recognition?[49] Communist popularity was further enhanced by big business weakness, largely due to American policy. The managers of large companies, who did not know what to expect in the face of huge imposed but unfinished structural reforms, became easy target for labor organizers.

Although most American labor advisers who joined SCAP from the AFL and the CIO were staunchly anticommunist and proponents of American-style bread-and-butter unionism, the Japanese context (as well as FEC's directives) led this occupation personnel, for the most part, to support a larger political role for labor unions. SCAP's labor division was tolerant of the Japanese Communist Party's effort to organize workers as part of a larger "open-ended" social reform.[50] Unhappy, Prime Minister Yoshida could call SCAP labor advisers "the idealists," but there was little he could do. Meanwhile communists gained great influence in factories, in the countryside, and in schools all around the country. In turn, the Japanese communist leaders had good reasons to mistake the young staffers of the labor division as pro-communists. For much of what these Americans and their SCAP colleagues were busy doing—*zaibatsu* dismantlement, labor reform, land reform—seemed to further the communist goal. In the name of antimilitarism was thus created, to borrow William James's phrase, an "organization of misunderstandings."[51]

The newly created, communist-controlled Japanese Congress of Industrial Organizations (Sanbetsu) gained membership very rapidly, reaching an estimated 1,500,000 adherents in June 1948, thus dominating the politically affiliated labor movement. By contrast, the Japan General Federation of Labor (Sōdōmei), controlled by socialists, counted only 900,000 members. Independent unions made up the bulk of the newly unionized workforce or 4,000,000.[52] By 1947–48, all unionized workers had reached their all-time postwar high of 55 percent of the labor force (compared to 34 percent in 1975 and 24 percent in the 1990s).[53]

Arming communist leaders with new civil rights while unleashing them on weak industries proved ruinous to the economy. Communist and other labor organizers brought fearful managers to kangaroo courts, food riots erupted, and the black market dominated economic transactions. Many, in Japan as well as in the United States, were wondering what if anything would ever give Japanese managers and workers the sense of a common national purpose. Could unity be found again in peace and rebuilding? Without waiting for an answer and under new political pressures from Washington in the face of such increasing unrest, SCAP put a stop to communist influence—officially prohibiting the February 1, 1947, strike aimed at toppling the conservative Yoshida cabinet—and reversed its conciliatory stance toward labor. This was a prelude to the massive 1949 red purge, this time in line with anticommunist measures taken at home after the passage of Taft-Hartley. By June 1951, after the creation of Sōhyō (General Council of Trade Unions), only 47,000 members were left in Sanbetsu.[54] The communist honeymoon with SCAP was definitely over, although something of its spirit would outlive it.

REVERSING THE COURSE

Cracking down on communism was not the only sign of a new policy in Japan. By 1948 came the famous reverse-course policy of industrial rebuilding. Although motivated by Cold War imperatives, the reverse course was very much desired, even pushed, by the Yoshida government and supported by Japan specialists regaining influence over the China lobby in the State Department.[55] Yoshida had seen no merit in the American theory that Japanese militarism was deeply rooted in its industrial structure. He argued that Japanese industrialists had merely stumbled.[56] Now he was to receive a big boost from U.S. businessmen and architects of containment alike who felt that too radical a deconcentration of Japanese business would facilitate the spread of communism in Asia. The radical New Dealers who had been instrumental in making Japan policy in the State Department were replaced by influential corporate managers who worried about communism. The first had promoted industrial deconcentration; the second pushed for industrial reconstruction. As a result, the old conflict over bigness which had evolved during a half century of American history, from the Progressive era to the New Deal, was replayed in occupied Japan. It was a high-speed rerun.

A major turning point came when James L. Kauffman, who had been a Tokyo lawyer in prewar days representing virtually every major American corporation there, reported to Washington that FEC-230 was creating chaotic conditions in Japan. When *Newsweek* made the Kauffman report public in December 1947, it underscored his contention that radicals in the occupation staff were imposing "an economic theory . . . far to the left of anything tolerated in this country."[57] Both Secretary of the Army William Draper and Secretary of Defense James Forrestal (previously of the Wall Street firm of Dillon, Read & Co., whom Kauffman represented), along with George Kennan, were impressed by Kauffman's criticisms of the anti-*zaibatsu* program and helped initiate the "reverse course." Kennan traveled to Japan in March 1948 and told MacArthur to stop the purge of business leaders and the deconcentration. By October 1948, occupation policy was taken over by the National Security Council, who wanted a recovered Japan as part of an eastern crescent of regional economic strength against communism and to lighten Japan's heavy drain on U.S. resources.[58]

With deconcentration halted and the purges at an end, it was relatively simple to rehire experts to fill key jobs. Banks, which had not been targeted in the dissolution, played a pivotal role in rebuilding the large firms, although they did so under new managerial principles. Americanization was not abandoned, but it took a new course. American ideas on pluralism which had served the demilitarization/defeudalization program were now replaced by American managerial principles. It would be a mistake to think that reverse-course erased the radical New Dealers' measures. What emerged was an amalgam of the initial deconcentration program with the new goals of economic rebuilding. The result of this unlikely encounter was to create in Japan the

conditions for the emergence of a new managerial capitalism, this time compatible with American management and with an American-style conservative
labor movement.[59]

The new policy served also to revive existing Japanese managerial dynamics
that American policymakers had previously ignored despite their influence on
the inner workings of the *zaibatsu*. The new occupation reforms reestablished
a process started decades earlier, for the old *zaibatsu* families had begun to
cede control to professional managers in the 1920s. This is a key interpretive
point in Chalmers Johnson's landmark book, *MITI and the Japanese Miracle*.
Other historians date the transition even earlier.[60] Although there was a variety
of patterns of family-management-government relationships, a new managerial capitalism functioned in earnest in Japan in the 1920s, promoted by such
personalities as Harvard-educated Seihin Ikeda, appointed by the Mitsui families to run their affairs. Ikeda would become Minister of Commerce and Industry in 1938. Chalmers Johnson persuasively argues that postwar industrial
policy was rooted in prewar institutional innovation and that this historical
continuity with the Japanese institutional matrix is a more important reason
for the postwar success than features of Japanese culture like group commitments over individual ones.[61]

With the war had come not only a major shift from light to heavy industry
(from 35 percent of all manufacturing in 1930 to 63 percent by 1940), but
also an intense rivalry for control of the economy among the civilian bureaucracy, the military bureaucracy, and *zaibatsu* management.[62] Occupation policies mattered most in putting this rivalry finally to rest and making it possible
for the Japanese government and businesses to cooperate again. The consequences of SCAP's dissolution of the *zaibatsu* families was to put financial
control of industry into the hands of banks and strengthen management control. SCAP also dramatically increased the power of the Japanese civilian bureaucracy while eliminating the rival military bureaucracy. Under SCAP, the
civilian bureaucracy, which had been working since before the war on blueprints for a new, export-based Japanese economy, was at the height of its
powers.[63] The prewar Ministry of Commerce and Industry, replaced during
the war by the Ministry of Munitions, reformed into MCI in 1945, was reorganized as the Ministry of International Trade and Industry (MITI) in 1949 to
perform coordination functions among big firms and facilitate production for
export.

After 1949, the civilian bureaucracy sought a cooperative relationship with
industrial managers. To do so, MITI relied increasingly on "administrative
guidance" (backed by its power over foreign exchange budgets) to monitor

the guidelines on management and production that it created cooperatively through its Industrial Rationalization Council. Thus emerged from this multi-faceted U.S.–Japan encounter the celebrated model of Japanese strategic capitalism as industrial managers and state bureaucrats were left to work together. It was a new type of mixed economy, distinct from the American model, with both government direction and free market aspects, shaped by the cumulative impact of established cultural and institutional characteristics and occupation reforms as well as the resurgence of business confidence and the development of MITI's administrative guidance. Was it more Japanese than American? Did it reflect continuity rather than change? This endless debate over antecedents is a major theme in the historiography of modern Japan just as it is a staple of discussions of other dominated areas (such as the American New South). We can expect occupation policies, whether of the first or second wave, to have worked best when they added to an existing pattern rather than contradicted it. More to the point, the policy of returning Japanese managers to center stage without abandoning bread-and-butter unionism promoted a version of Americanization much closer to operating principles at home than its previous incarnation.

To many observers who liked the initial democratization impulse with its emphasis on individual liberty, the reverse course seemed like a huge contradiction on the part of Americans, and in some ways it was. Many historians see this reversal of policy, forced on Japan by American Cold War imperatives, as the end of democratization.[64] The same Americans who had liberated communists from prison were now forcing them out of their jobs and underground again. They had prompted democratization only to stop it. From the standpoint of mid twentieth-century American policymakers, however, the unhappy episodes of red scare paranoia aside, reverse course really was not such a contradiction. Americans had been pondering the respective merits of economic concentration and deconcentration over a half century of heated public debates on regulation. Now, instead of projecting an older image of themselves, they were merely aligning their Japan policy with current American practice. They were applying abroad the tools best known at home to generate prosperity. Nobody, however, was predicting an economic miracle at the time. This is why Detroit banker Joseph Dodge, who was sent to Japan with the mission of putting an end to the economic chaos, signaled the reverse course by fighting poverty and unrest with tough anti-inflation measures. The Dodge line, however, put even more pressure on small businesses while favoring the reemergence of center firms better equipped to withstand the anti-inflationary program.[65]

In order to allow the big industrial firms to expand and become the core of the new economic rebuilding, the Americans effectively shielded them economically, agreed to an exceptionally favorable exchange rate, accepted Japanese protectionism, and signed a security treaty in San Francisco in 1951 guaranteeing Japan's borders. Not all decisions favored the Japanese economy (the China market was off limits) but the Korean War procurement contracts initiated an irreversible trend toward recovery.[66] By putting their money and power behind reconstruction, Americans sided not just with management against labor but with the growing national will, including even workers, who had often aborted strike plans to rebuild the country. Reverse course was far more than mere Cold War politics. It may have appeared as a brake on democracy—but the new policy was in line with what Americans called modernization.

Where Americans misled the Japanese, however, was in failing to emphasize development and democracy equally. This is amazing considering the fact that Americans at home had worked hard for half a century, following Herbert Croly's lead, to reconcile the twentieth-century organizational revolution with nineteenth-century individualism. In prosecuting the Pax Americana in Asia, however, they separated them. Here is the second great contradiction of the occupation: While phase one had promoted freedom at the expense of industrial modernization, phase two put a narrow definition of modernization ahead of individual liberties. At home, McCarthy's crusade against communism was at least challenged; in Japan, it was unhampered. The Japanese were left to figure out their own synthesis between modernization and democracy.

Americans needed only to reflect on the interwar years, when their influence overseas had been felt through expanding market networks and the spread of new economic "systems" significantly more than through political and diplomatic channels, to realize the ambiguities of modernization. In the 1920s and 1930s, American modernizing techniques such as Taylorism and Fordism had become basic ingredients of the Soviet five-year plan. The Ford experiment had been critical in the development of Citroën in France and of Volkswagen in Germany. Taylorism had also attracted the Japanese long before W. Edwards Deming's quality control became the rage of postwar industrial technology.[67] But American corporate capitalism was singular in using these techniques to foster an increased standard of living at home.

That brand of modernization could easily be divorced from democratic politics elsewhere. The Soviets had not raised workers' wages for a long time or produced affordable consumer durables. The Nazis had adopted American-made IBM tabulating machines to track the population's racial characteristics.

It was abundantly clear that there could be no guarantee that American systems would be put to the use that confident modernizers assigned them. But American postwar modernizers continued to assume that the connection Croly had sought in the American context among the new means of economic efficiency, prosperity, and democratic politics would be replicated quite naturally in any context. Convinced that modernization at home reinforced rather than weakened democracy, American policymakers insisted on making modernization an integral part of a new international economic and political order reconstructed under their leadership. In their new role on the world scene, they promoted modernization as a theory of social improvement and political freedom meant to expand the opportunity structure and materially benefit an increasingly large portion of the world population. It is not surprising that Walt W. Rostow, widely regarded as the preeminent postwar American theoretician of modernization, took his inspiration directly from Croly, that is, in thinking of modernization not simply as "the rationality of means and ends" but as the connection between the mechanics of economic prosperity and the institutions of democracy. In contrast with Croly, however, but in tune with the new bases of wealth, Rostow turned away from bucolic Jeffersonian America and concentrated on industrial England as the first example of "take-off." Focusing on the link between "economic and non-economic behavior" that Karl Marx had left unresolved, Rostow saw in American modernization not just a replay of British history but rather the American "promise" of universal abundance in a democratic mass society.[68]

Like many mid twentieth-century intellectuals and policymakers, Rostow celebrated American history. To Croly's eyes in the early years of the century and to our eyes today, Rostow might have been thinking of another civilization when he wrote: "Looking back over our national history since the Civil War, it is not too much to say that the United States has come near to solving many of the great issues of its domestic life." While Croly was capable of seeing that "American history contains much matter for pride and congratulation, and much matter for regret and humiliation," Rostow felt we had arrived at a happy ending.[69] By turning modernization into a "non-communist manifesto" for the Cold War, Rostow made it in many ways the mirror image of Marxism. Both theories of economic and social development outlined historical stages and explained the transition from one to the other. Both showed little respect for the richness of diverse cultures and local contexts. Both believed in universal progress. For Marxists, the working class was the agent of progress; for modernizers, it was an expanding middle class. For Marxists, progress meant a "classless society" and "the end of alienation"; for modernizers, progress entailed, in Christopher Lasch's words, the "democratization of affluence."[70] The theoretical outcome of modernization was managerial capitalism orchestrating a mass consumption economy and promoting acquisitive individualism.

For the time being, however, Japan had to recover from the war, and reverse course merely gave new life to the community of misunderstandings. The end of the American occupation gave Japanese policymakers the first opportunity to redefine their economic priorities in ways that led them to pursue the creation of a leading industrial sector while at the same time rejecting individualism that Americans had promoted at first. The hard reality is easy to see. As the American troops left, the Japanese were still poor and pessimistic, but intent on rebuilding. It was hard for them to imagine prosperity. Turning the economic system to the service of individualism was a luxury they simply could not afford or even consider. And the magnitude of the task they set out to achieve—such as making technologically complex products they could export—returned them to traditional forms of collectivism on which they had historically relied.

The Americans had failed to appreciate the extent to which their vision of the intimate connections between modernization and their particular system of generating prosperity rested on their investment in the average consumer.[71] The Japanese system of producing wealth would yield a different set of connections. In contrast to the United States, where policymakers promoted mass consumption as the mechanism that kept the economy running and turned Americans into satisfied customers, the Japanese mix of managers and bureaucrats now making policy delayed gratification and favored savings that could be reinvested for the future collective good. To achieve their goals of rebuilding an industrial economy, they opted for a fiscal policy that gave tax breaks for savings, which banks then turned into industrial investments.[72] Even though some industrial leaders envisioned the growth of the domestic market as early as the mid 1950s, the postoccupation Japanese policy generally moved away from American-style objectives and policy.[73] The Japanese put Hamiltonian means not to the service of the individual but to the service of the nation. If the Japanese were to modernize, they would do it their own way, motivated as they were to regain their rank among major nations by replacing military might with economic might and by creating an alternative capitalist sphere that would ultimately challenge Americans and Europeans. The growing divergence between U.S. and Japanese policies was immediately echoed in the 1960s scholarly debate on modernization. One school (including Marius Jansen, Kennedy's ambassador to Tokyo Edwin Reischauer, and John Hall) sided with the Japanese; they designated Japan as a most successful "late modern-izer" and reminded their audiences of the difficulty of translating such con-cepts as free enterprise and individualism in the Japanese language.[74] In other words, they attempted to separate "modernization" from "democratization"; their critics (John Dower, Rober Bellah) denounced them as immoral and hiding behind " 'value free' scholarship."[75] Aside from the fact that both camps exchanged charges of ethnocentrism, their conflict was yet another re-play of the prewar domestic confrontation over bigness and individualism.

Meanwhile, the initial occupation strategy of freeing the labor movement on a weak economy began to pay off in the most unsuspected way as another silent, but major, transformation took shape in the Japanese workplace. Blue-and white-collar workers were breaking old hierarchical rules and for the first time joining forces.[76] That alliance would move Japanese society one step closer to American-style conservative unionism. While in prewar Japan, white-collar employees, not unlike their German counterparts, had insisted on main-taining a strict status boundary between themselves and skilled and semiskilled laborers, that crucial divide became increasingly irrelevant in the postwar labor negotiations that led to the creation of thousands of company unions. As white-collar workers realized how insecure their own jobs had become, they joined forces—with much apprehension and friction but also ultimate suc-cess—with blue-collar workers. The process involved a great deal of haggling between shopfloor and office. In the end, however, it worked, and white-and blue-collar workers often came together in the rebuilding of the labor movement and the eventual turn into bread-and-butter unionism that Ameri-cans favored.

When the Korean War provided a timely boost to the struggling Japanese economy and the economic "miracle," or "take-off" followed, the general rise in the standard of living only added meaning to this unexpected rap-prochement. Labor disputes continued sporadically throughout the 1950s, to climax in the eight-month strike of the Mitsui coal miners at Miike in 1960. But wages improved dramatically at the annual so-called Spring offensive of labor negotiations for twenty-five straight years (Japanese workers received annual increases of 30 percent from 1968 to 1974). So did levels of domestic consumption (by 7.51 percent per year between 1955 and 1973), together with the highest household savings rate of the industrial world (23.2 percent by 1976), and greatly expanded outlays for welfare programs and housing, as well as expansion of the lifetime employment system.[77] No doubt, as in America, cooperation eventually replaced conflict in the Japanese labor move-ment.

With the decline of the agricultural sector and simultaneous rapid rise of both white- and blue-collar sectors with middle-class aspirations, the Japanese began planning their well-known "income-doubling" policies and the creation of their own style of consumer society.[78] The meritocratic reforms of a rapidly expanding educational system also helped blur the distinction between blue-collar and white-collar by fostering intergenerational mobility. American-style modernization just would not go away. Could Ruth Benedict have ever fathomed that we would be debating today the status of a Japanese "middle-class" society of consumers in terms comparable to those used to describe twentieth-century Americans, replete with references to "middlebrow" culture, meritocracy, mass society, and the like?[79]

The postwar U.S.–Japan experience provides us with a rare opportunity to reflect on the meaning of "Americanization." When Americans occupied Japan, they felt especially confident in making a strong connection between their ways of producing wealth and of expanding the opportunity structure under democratic principles. Half a century has now passed. The American economic system has been challenged by a rebuilt Europe, a rebuilt Japan, and economic globalization. Even though winning the Cold War brought a degree of satisfaction, Americans are no longer so sure of the robustness of their formulas for connecting national wealth and individual well-being. They are thinking anew the managing of democratic mass society. Today's uncertainty brings them back closer to the intellectual premises Croly was struggling with in the early twentieth century, than to Rostow's unnecessarily mechanical certainties at mid-century.

Japan has not only rebuilt; it has achieved a system of development that was the envy of the world in the 1980s.[80] But Japan shares also in the problems of a mature economy—that is, the challenge of maintaining prosperity under stiff competition and recovering from unexpected major setbacks and/or excesses. Many issues of self-fulfillment and individualism, initially promoted by Americans but shoved aside in the face of rebuilding priorities, are very much on the agenda. As a result, there is a sense of insecurity in Japan today. The challenge is no longer to catch up with the West but to maintain gains and to expand the opportunity structure. Like Americans, and like Europeans, the Japanese are now searching for their own ways of putting more of their national wealth to the service of individual well-being while relying on consumerism to foster their economy.[81] That, in the end, may be the most telling sign of Americanization.

Americanization—keeping in mind the variety of contexts and contradictory processes that have been the lot of U.S.–Japan relations—is a matter of

conceptual change. Americans did not succeed in imposing a new social contract on Japan, but they have influenced the terms that the Japanese, and
others, now use to debate the social contract. Americans may have intended
for all people to become like them but that could not happen, no matter
how hard they tried. Rather, Americans made a difference abroad, somewhat
unwittingly, by altering the visions of political economy. More than other
people, they have put on the world agenda their understanding of the relationship among national wealth, individual freedom, and personal well-being.
That various parts of the industrialized world, including Asia, compete nowa-
days partly on American terms, each region with its own history and plan, is
a direct outcome of the story I have told. Americans may have been contradictory, naïve, even selfish, and hegemonic. They may have acted time and again
against their own agenda, motivated as they were to counter the Soviets. The
outcome, however, is more important than the motivation or the mishap. For,
whether in approval, ambiguity, or contempt, not only Americans but a large
part of the world now wrestle with the "American promise."

CHAPTER NINE

THE POWER OF UNCERTAINTY

A road is not an invitation to leave it elsewhere than at its end.

OLIVER WENDELL HOLMES, JR.[1]

Among the Americans who helped formulate a model for the twentieth century and export it abroad, few were as consistent as Beardsley Ruml. An ardent believer in social engineering, Ruml trained in applied psychology and participated in the World War I Army experiment in intelligence testing. Soon thereafter, Ruml masterminded the Rockefeller Foundation's backing of the social sciences. As a philanthropist and dean of social sciences at the University of Chicago, he worked to enlarge our vision of mass society and develop tools for managing it democratically. By leaving academia for business in the late 1920s, Ruml recognized the significance of mass consumption as the engine of economic growth and led the New Deal toward the Keynesian path. As a member of FDR's braintrust, he initiated such fiscal reforms as automatic payroll deduction for income tax withholding to increase the government's revenues as well as its ability to intervene in the economy. Always an important broker in the institutional matrix, Ruml was instrumental on behalf of the Carnegie Corporation in selecting Swedish economist Gunnar Myrdal for *An American Dilemma*, when it appeared that only by calling in a foreigner could Americans hope to have an unbiased study of the race problem in the United States.[2] As a policymaker behind the scenes, away from public eyes, Ruml helped engineer the emerging American century. He operated within several of the contexts that I draw on in the preceding chapters: the institutional matrix of knowledge, the large middle-class of consumers, and the elites concerned for pluralistic consensus.

Other figures did not fully endorse the changes that made the American century. Carter G. Glass, who, as Virginia's senator, helped create the Federal Reserve System in 1913 and subsequently revamped investment banking during the Depression, worked hard for national prosperity, but he was determined to "eliminate the darky as a political factor."[3] As a white southerner, his vision of a cohesive national community did not require the entitlement of all.

And then there were the plain nay-sayers. Reformulating early twentieth-century anxieties in the context of the rise of totalitarian regimes, economist Joseph Schumpeter entitled a lecture he gave in January 1936 at the U.S. Department of Agriculture "Can Capitalism Survive?" The former finance minister of Austria, turned Harvard professor, although he opposed New Deal policies, was not really concerned about the lingering effects of the Great Depression on the American economy. What made him so gloomy, as a theoretician of entrepreneurship, was the culture of bigness that the New Deal had reaffirmed. Schumpeter indicted the excessive rationalization of industrial life and feared that capitalism might collapse under the attacks of "Bolshevism,

Hitlerism, or socialism"—not because the economy was weak but because of issues of individual fulfillment. He deplored the debilitating effects of rationalization on "habits of thought." Schumpeter believed that totalitarian ideologies might win out because of the moral deficiencies of capitalism, "just as Christianity presented itself at a time in the Roman world when nobody could have foretold [its decline] from its economic process."[4]

The Second World War and its immediate aftermath stood as an impressive collective denial of Schumpeter's worries and sanction of Luce's predictions of the coming of an "American century." Large-scale organizations successfully engineered America's victory in the war, the return to peacetime prosperity, and subsequent globalization. As Americans assumed their new world responsibilities, they increasingly conflated the concepts of the "American century" and of the "Pax Americana." Those who still insisted on keeping the two ideas separate in order to preserve America's independence, as Herbert Hoover did after World War II, were perceived as reactionaries. Hoover, when leading the relief effort in Belgium during World War I and when hiring social scientists to advise him at the Commerce Department and the White House, had been at the forefront of the American century's drive toward social intelligence; he was also more an internationalist than FDR in the early years of the New Deal.[5] But by turning against the Pax Americana, the aging Quaker was "out of tune with the world," as biographer Joan Hoff Wilson put it. Hoover resented the open-ended use of American economic and military power to keep other countries afloat and shield them from communism. He wanted instead strict limits on the Marshall Plan and the display of American troops.[6]

For most policymakers, however, the "American century" and the new world order were becoming one and the same, for American prosperity would continue to expand only if Americans looked outward. Moreover, the time had come to applaud the American blend of democratic institutions and managerial capitalism and to credit them for victory. It was an auspicious moment to contrast the American system to the Fascist regimes and the dangerous Soviet Union, and to act on that understanding. In a little-remembered episode of World War II, the American military made many of the 400,000 mostly German POWs distributed in camps throughout the United States read Wendell Willkie's 1943 best-selling plea for internationalism, *One World*, as part of their indoctrination. Twenty-three thousand German inmates in a Virginia camp were given a six-day course on the book in 1945, just before being sent home.[7] They learned what America could do for the world that "neither Hitler nor Mussolini nor Hirohito" could have hoped to achieve. Willkie's text combined modernization with the glorification of everything

American. "The people in every land, whether industrial or not," Roosevelt's Republican opponent of 1940 wrote, "admire the aspirations and accomplishments of American labor, which they have heard about, and which they long to emulate. Also they are impressed by American methods of agriculture, business and industry. In nearly every country I went to," Willkie continued, "there is some great dam or irrigation project, some harbor or factory, which has been built by Americans. People like our works, I found, not only because they help to make life easier and richer; but also because we have shown that American business enterprise does not necessarily lead to attempts at political control."[8] Postwar internationalism under American auspices prompted economists and sociologists to perfect their own varieties of modernization theory for a new world order under American auspices. That the quest for national security and prosperity and the ability to change the world could at best match most imperfectly, as was abundantly clear when General MacArthur and his occupation staff left Tokyo in April 1952, was somewhat beside the point. Their theoretical overlap justified the "Pax Americana."

As Americans embraced new world responsibilities in the postwar era, the enlarged scale of their operations did change life at home. Nowhere was it more visible than in the institutional matrix of knowledge, where the military became the prominent player. When the Manhattan project was launched, it was an exceptional effort in the collaboration among engineers, officers, and professors under extraordinary circumstances, but its history pointed to an inescapable trend that would embody the new America: industrial science as a lasting intermediary between a consumer and a military society.[9] As chemist and Harvard president James Conant put it, "The military are no longer the conservatives . . . at times they seem to be fanatics in their belief of what the scientists and the technologists can do."[10]

To create a new generation of scientists, postwar America invested in higher education. The same Conant, who was committed to the democratization of universities, fully backed the Educational Testing Service at Princeton to counter the power of the moneyed elite in controlling access to the best institutions of higher education. Designing some of the tests that would be used nationwide, psychologist Carl Brigham, a key figure in the early twentieth-century movement to measure intelligence, publicly denounced his own racist writings of the twenties. To him as to Conant, refined tools of applied psychology were the most neutral method of opening access to knowledge, jobs, and goods, and giving equality of opportunity to a greater portion of the population.[11] Meanwhile Vannevar Bush, FDR's wartime director of the Office of Scientific Research and Development and leading authority behind the establishment in 1950 of the National Science Foundation, popularized the term "basic research" and posited "science" as "the endless frontier."[12]

The effects of mass consumption became everywhere more visible. As numerous social and economic surveys of the 1950s and 1960s have shown, white workers joined the mainstream of American consumers with middle-class aspirations. Once there, it became more and more difficult to distinguish them within the midst of an ever expanding middle class. By 1960, Walt W. Rostow described "the age of high mass consumption" as the last of his stages of economic growth, which all countries would eventually reach.[13] Economists, who were now advisers to presidents, entertained the hope of permanent prosperity. "When the cost of fulfilling a people's aspirations can be met out of a growing horn of plenty—instead of robbing Peter to pay Paul—ideological roadblocks melt away, and consensus replaces conflict," declared Walter Heller, who headed Kennedy's Council of Economic Advisors.[14]

Even American pluralism took on global dimensions now that Jews and Catholics were full participants in it. It is an *American* Jesuit, John Courtney Murray, who led Pope John XXIII's Second Vatican Council to adopt the concept of religious liberty. In so doing, Murray described the United States as the "civilization of the pluralist society" and the American consensus as the recognition of our differences and acceptance of confusion.[15] But as Murray expressed these views in 1960, the pluralistic consensus was about to break apart for failing to address the issues of racial segregation. Despite the widespread feeling in the first two decades of the postwar era that we had solved most of the problems Herbert Croly had diagnosed at the dawn of the century, the misgivings of John Marshall Harlan and W. E. B. Du Bois resurfaced with great force. Women added their concerns for equal opportunity. And the traumatic episodes of Vietnam would soon undermine Americans' faith in managerial expertise. The pluralistic consensus was fragile indeed.

Unlike historians and social scientists of the 1950s, I have not focused on timeless American traits to explain and praise the American model.[16] I have instead shown the challenges American elites faced in establishing the model over a course of a long half-century. To recover a sense of what issues they faced, I have reconstructed some of their debates without taking postwar celebratory formulations at face value. Nor have I, unlike more recent critics, systematically condemned past elites for their myopic vision, for our vision, though different, is no better. And I believe we can learn much for our times by understanding how the histories of knowledge, class, and pluralism intersected to create a strong center capable of major achievements at home and abroad. At the same time, we must know why scientists, professionals, policymakers, and so-called public intellectuals created major obstacles for themselves and their country by mistaking success for understanding, abstractions for realities, and ideology for ideas.

Some of the anxieties Americans faced early in the twentieth century while they formulated strategies for modern times have reappeared with a force that could not have been anticipated at mid-century and have come into sharp focus only in the last fifteen years. If a new Henry Luce were to write an "American Century" editorial today, that person could not be blind to the loss of aura of expert knowledge and cracks in the once seemingly unassailable managerial paradigm. Doubts about the corrosive effects of excessive rationality flourish. And so do religious intolerance and other forms of bigotry no longer contained by pluralism. Americans as a people are no longer so sure of the connection between their ability to generate prosperity and the quality they call happiness.

Even though there are few political restraints left on exporting our ideas, new European and Asian worlds challenge them even as they adapt some of them for their purpose. In turn, we as Americans are having serious second thoughts about what these ideas are and about claiming the wholesale relevance of American solutions for the rest of the world. Now that adversary regimes have collapsed, the ideological certainties of a clear model are no longer relevant to our self-image and the time has come for reassessing the domestic and international orders simultaneously. In so doing, we are confronting anew the questions that Americans asked at the dawn of the century about mastery and irresolution, abundance and indigence, and homogeneity and diversity.

ACKNOWLEDGMENTS

If this is a long acknowledgment for a short volume, it is because each part of this book originated in a distinct community of inquiry.

I began working on Part 1, "Making the Century American," when the late Jacques Roger convinced me that the intellectual history of Darwinism, which he was studying, was closely related to some of the social and organizational changes that I had just described in *Making America Corporate* (University of Chicago Press, 1990). Sadly Jacques died before he could attend the meetings of the two-part conference on modernism he, Dorothy Ross, Peter Weingart, and I organized at the Rockefeller Foundation's Bellagio Study and Conference Center and the Center for Interdisciplinary Studies at the University of Bielefeld in 1990 and 1991. I published a preliminary version of chapter 1 in the resulting volume of proceedings, *Modernist Impulses in the Human Sciences,* ed. D. Ross (Johns Hopkins University Press, 1994). A continuing dialogue with several conference participants, especially James T. Kloppenberg, David Hollinger, and Richard Rorty, considerably sharpened my understanding of the history of knowledge. David eventually gave me an extremely helpful assessment of my entire book manuscript. I want also to mention the important contribution to Part 1 of my friend the late Donald E. Stokes, who generously shared with me his manuscript on the relationship between basic and applied science, now available as *Pasteur's Quadrant: Basic Science and Technological Innovation* (Brookings Institution Press, 1997).

Conceptualizing Part 2, "The Social Contract of the Market," was partly triggered by Stanley I. Kutler's request in 1992 that I formalize my thoughts on the American class structure for a background essay in his *Encyclopedia of the United States in the Twentieth Century* (Charles Scribner's Sons, 1996). Writing sections of Part 2 while a scholar in residence at the Russell Sage Foundation in the Summer of 1993, I benefited from regular conversations with Robert K. Merton, Richard Swedberg, and Eric Wanner. In New York, my friend Jeffrey Kroessler helped me explore the Rockefeller Foundation archives in Poncantico Hills, Tarrytown.

"Embattled Identities" originated when Lucette Valensi asked me in the mid 1980s to prepare an essay for a special issue of the French *Annales: Économies, Sociétés, Civilisations* on "les sociétés plurielles," (Mars–Avril 1987). The article, translated as "Genesis of American Pluralism" in *The Tocqueville Review/La Revue Tocqueville* (1987–88) led me to a sustained dialogue on the topic with David Riesman, and with Ira Katznelson among other friends; it served as a springboard for the book's third part.

"Exporting American Principles" or Part 4 is the result of a fortunate encounter with Japanese civilization. My interest in Japan was awakened when John Mollenkopf, who chaired the Social Science Research Council's committee on New York City of which I was a member, organized systematic comparisons among global metropolises. These comparisons took me to Tokyo in 1990 and 1991. Shortly thereafter, my friend Akira Iriye asked me to prepare an essay on the importance of social change for understanding U.S.–Japan relations for a workshop at the Japanese National Institute for Research Advancement in Tokyo in 1993. The resulting essay, "Exporting American Individualism," published in *NIRA Research Output* (1, 1994) and *The Tocqueville Review /La Revue Tocqueville* (2, 1995) was the seed for this book's last section. I thank my Japanese friends who welcomed me again in 1996 and helped me wrap up my work on this section, especially Tadashi Aruga, Kiyoko Ishikawa, Akira Kojima, and Fumiko Nishizaki. At their request, I published a preliminary version of chapter 8 in Seikei University's *Review of Asian and Pacific Studies* (1997).

I was greatly helped in the task of assembling the four parts by my French colleagues who have asked me to present my work in progress every year at the American history seminar of the École des Hautes Études en Sciences Sociales. Jean Heffer and François Weil, loyal friends and wonderful hosts at the École, have been outstanding critics. I have floated just about every idea that has made it into the book first in their seminar, and much of my essay "Recentrer l'histoire américaine," written for their *Chantiers d'histoire américaine* (Belin, 1994), served as a first formulation for the introduction. In addition, I have immensely benefited from the invitation to give a public

lecture series at the Collège de France on the theme of the American century
in the spring of 1997, where Emmanuel Le Roy Ladurie and Marie-Jeanne
Tits-Dieuaide have extended me a warm welcome. Paris would not be quite
the same without the regular hospitality of Maurice Aymard at the Maison
des Sciences de l'Homme and of Jean-Luc Lory at the Maison Suger, and
without the editorial meetings of *The Tocqueville Review/La Revue Tocqueville,* so carefully orchestrated by Laurence Duboys-Fresney, Françoise Mé-
lonio, and Henri Mendras.

In addition to the preliminary essays mentioned above, I have published
in French small excerpts of chapter 1 in *Rigueur et Passion. Hommage à Annie
Kriegel* (Cerf/L'Âge d'Homme, 1994), of chapter 6 in *L'Histoire grande
ouverte. Hommages à Emmanuel Le Roy Ladurie* (Librairie Arthème Fayard,
1997), and of chapter 8 in *La France démocratique. Mélanges en l'honneur
de Maurice Agulhon* (Publications de la Sorbonne, 1998) as a token of appreciation for my mentors. Sadly Annie died before this book was finished. So
did François Furet, who was unfailing in his support of my various endeavors.

I could not have completed this work without release time for research and
writing, which was generously granted by the Hagley Museum and Library,
the Russell Sage Foundation, the University of Virginia's Bankard Fund for
the Study of Political Economy, the University of Virginia's Edgar F. Shan-
non, Jr., Center for Advanced Studies, and the Virginia Foundation for the
Humanities. At Virginia, our former dean of Arts and Sciences Raymond Nelson and the past two chairmen of the history department, Melvyn P. Leffler
and Peter Onuf, have gone out of their way many times to make it easier for
me to work on this book. Mel and Peter have also shared many insights with
me and suggested ways in which I could improve my argument.

Other friends have helped with broad-ranging conversations, regular corre-
spondence, and pointed comments on my draft manuscripts. It is a pleasure
to thank Joyce Appleby, Brian Balogh, Lenard Berlanstein, David D. Bien,
Paul Boyer, André Burguière, Alain Catta, W. Bernard Carlson, Kathleen
Neils Conzen, François Crouzet, Vincent Descombes, Elisabeth Glaser-
Schmidt, Claude Fohlen, Patrick Fridenson, Richard Wightman Fox, Paul M.
Gaston, Jon Gjerde, Nancy Green, Ran Halévi, William H. Harbaugh, John
Higham, Janet Horne, Michael Holt, Marius Jansen, Richard L. Kagan, Jo-
seph F. Kett, Jürgen Kocka, Maurice Kriegel, the late Bernard Lepetit, Hervé
Le Bras, Nelson Lichtenstein, Edward Lurie, Allan Megill, Jacques Revel, Ste-
phen Schuker, James Turner, David Ward, G. Edward White, and Joseph C.
Zengerle for their many astute suggestions and their supportive friendship.

The list would be very incomplete if I did not mention the constant revitalization I have received from the talented graduate students, past and present, whose time at Virginia has coincided with the preparation of this book. In sharing their thoughts with me, they have learned over the years to subject my work to the same rigorous criticism I was subjecting theirs. I want to thank especially Nicolas Barreyre, Cornelius Bynum, Lyman Bruce Coffey, Jr., Meg Jacobs, Andrew J. F. Morris, Amy Murrell, Shelley Nickles, David Vandermeulen, and C. Harwell Wells. Alan Berolzheimer and Keith Revell have been involved in every stage of the project, and Maire A. Murphy has taken a very active role in its completion. I have also benefited from the able research assistance of Laura Belmonte, Colleen Doody, Robert Guffin, Abigail Schweber (from Harvard), and the precious daily secretarial help of Kathleen Miller.

Four friends displayed unusual patience during the final one-year push for drafting the manuscript. When inflicted with constant requests for feedback, Robert D. Cross, Charles Feigenoff, Pap Ndiaye, and Stephen Innes responded with a wonderful blend of affectionate humor and tough criticism. Whatever clarity exists in this book owes much to their special intellectual companionship, especially Charlie's, even if I have managed to escape some of his best advice under the spurious pretense that history could not be so clear after all.

This is the third book that I have published with University of Chicago Press senior editor *extraordinaire* Douglas C. Mitchell and the third that has been reviewed in minute detail by manuscript editor Jean Eckenfels. It is hard to imagine more supportive allies. Other people at the press who have helped turn this manuscript into a book are designer Jill Shimabukuro and promotions manager Barbara Fillon.

My children—Emmanuel and Sophie, and Emmanuel's wife Patricia— have sustained me daily with their affection and artistic and professional achievements, while their mother, Christine, gently demands everyday that I try my best, whatever the task at hand may be.

Despite this heavy load of accumulated debts, I am solely responsible for the deficiencies that undoubtedly remain in the book that you have just read.

NOTES

PREFACE

1. *Congressional Record,* 56th Cong., 1st sess., 1900, 33, pt. 1:710.

2. "The American Century," *Life,* February 17, 1941, 61–65; on Luce's career, see James L. Baughman, *Henry R. Luce and the Rise of the American News Media* (Boston: Twayne Publishers, 1987); Wolcott Gibbs wrote an amusing parody of Luce's own ascent, "Time . . . Fortune . . . Life . . . Luce" for *The New Yorker,* November 28, 1936, reprinted in *Parodies: An Anthology from Chaucer to Beerbohm—and After,* ed. Dwight Macdonald (New York: Random House, 1960), 338–51.

3. Frederick Winslow Taylor, *Principles of Scientific Management* (1911; New York: W. W. Norton, 1967), 7; see also Robert Kanigel, *The One Best Way: Frederick Winslow Taylor and the Enigma of Efficiency* (New York: Viking, 1997).

4. Woodrow Wilson, *The New Freedom: A Call for the Emancipation of the Generous Energies of a People* (Garden City: Doubleday, Page & Co., 1913), 7.

5. André Siegfried, trans. H. H. Hemming and Doris Hemming, *America Comes of Age: A French Analysis* (New York: Harcourt, Brace & Co., 1927); the passage quoted exists only in the preface to the French edition, *Les États-Unis d'aujourd'hui* (Paris: Librairie Armand Colin, 1927), 2, a study commissioned by the French Musée Social.

6. Walter E. Weyl and Walter Lippmann were the other two editors. On the 1914 founding of *The New Republic,* see the notice by Robert B. Westbrook in *A Companion to American Thought,* ed. Richard W. Fox and James Kloppenberg (Cambridge, Mass.: Blackwell Publishers, 1995), 490–92.

7. Herbert D. Croly, *The Promise of American Life* (1909; New Brunswick: Transaction Publishers, 1993), 12.

8. For a concise and lucid treatment of America's changing position in the world, see Akira Iriye, *The Globalizing of America, 1913–1945*, vol. 3 of *The Cambridge History of American Foreign Relations* (New York: Cambridge University Press, 1993).

9. William Appleman Williams has been the leading voice behind the theory of "the legend of isolationism"; in the latest revised edition of his 1959 essay, *The Tragedy of American Diplomacy* (New York: Dell Publishing Co., 1972), 31, 177, 238, Williams integrated the work of his former students, especially Walter LaFeber's *The New Empire: An Interpretation of American Expansion, 1860–1898* (Ithaca: Cornell University Press, 1963), Lloyd C. Gardner's *Architects of Illusion* (Chicago: Quadrangle Books, 1970), and Thomas J. McCormick's *China Market: America's Quest for Informal Empire, 1893–1901* (Chicago: Quadrangle Books, 1967); further refinements of Williams's approach—seeing American diplomacy primarily as the outcome of domestic economic interests—has led historians to formulate a sophisticated "corporatist" model for interpreting American foreign policy; see Thomas J. McCormick, "Drift or Mastery: A Corporatist Synthesis for American Diplomatic History," *Reviews in American History* 10 (December 1982): 318–30; and Michael J. Hogan, "Corporatism," in *Explaining the History of American Foreign Relations*, ed. Michael J. Hogan and Thomas G. Paterson (New York: Cambridge University Press, 1991), 226–36.

10. Thus completing a task I began in *Making America Corporate, 1870–1920* (Chicago: University of Chicago Press, 1990).

11. A condition which prompted a national debate on individual and group identity; see, as a prominent example, David Riesman, in collaboration with Reuel Denney and Nathan Glazer, *The Lonely Crowd: A Study of the Changing American Character* (New Haven: Yale University Press, 1950).

12. James T. Kloppenberg, *Uncertain Victory: Social Democracy and Progressivism in European and American Thought, 1870–1920* (New York: Oxford University Press, 1986), 145–46, 241; Alan Brinkley, *The End of Reform: New Deal Liberalism in Recession and War* (New York: Alfred A. Knopf, 1995), 8–9.

13. Roland T. Rotunda, "The 'Liberal' Label: Roosevelt's Capture of a Symbol," *Public Policy* 17 (1968), ed. John D. Montgomery and Albert O. Hirschman: 384–85; see also Gary Gerstle, "The Protean Character of American Liberalism," *American Historical Review* 99 (October 1994), 1043–73.

14. C. Wright Mills, *The Power Elite* (New York: Oxford University Press, 1956); David Halberstram, *The Best and the Brightest* (New York: Random House, 1972).

15. Dorothy Ross, "Liberalism," in *Encyclopedia of American Political History: Studies of the Principal Movements and Ideas*, ed. Jack P. Greene (New York: Charles Scribner's Sons, 1984), 3:757.

16. On Henry Steele Commager, *The American Mind: An Interpretation of American Thought and Character since the 1880s* (New Haven: Yale University Press, 1950) and on Louis Hartz, *The Liberal Tradition in America: An Interpretation of American*

Political Thought Since the Revolution (New York: Harcourt, Brace, 1955), see David A. Hollinger, "The Problem of Pragmatism in American History," in *In the American Province: Studies in the History and Historiography of Ideas* (Bloomington: Indiana University Press, 1985), 23–43, 191–96; and Dorothy Ross, "The Liberal Tradition Revisited and the Republican Tradition Addressed," in *New Directions in American Intellectual History,* ed. John Higham and Paul K. Conkin (Baltimore: Johns Hopkins University Press, 1979), 116–31.

17. Arthur M. Schlesinger, *The Vital Center: The Politics of Freedom* (Boston: Houghton Mifflin Co., 1949); idem, "Liberalism in America: A Note for Europeans" (1956), in *The Politics of Hope* (Boston: The Riverside Press Cambridge and Houghton Mifflin Co., 1963), 67–68, 71; for a good discussion of the liberal project and the consensus school, see Larry G. Gerber, *The Limits of Liberalism: Josephus Daniels, Henry Stimson, Bernard Baruch, Donald Richberg, Felix Frankfurter and the Development of the Modern American Political Economy* (New York: New York University Press, 1983), 1–12.

18. Carole Pateman, "The Fraternal Social Contract," in *Civil Society and the State,* ed. John Keane (London: Verso, 1988), 101–28.

19. The social history of right-wing movements is more recent; see Leonard J. Moore, "Good Old-Fashioned New Social History and the Twentieth-Century American Right," *Reviews in American History* 24 (December 1996): 555–73.

20. See my essay, "The Synthesis of Social Change: Reflections on American Social History," in *Reliving the Past: The Worlds of Social History,* ed. Olivier Zunz (Chapel Hill: University of North Carolina Press, 1985), 53–114; and for a more skeptical appraisal of the now old new social history, John Higham, *History: Professional Scholarship in America,* updated paperback edition (Baltimore: Johns Hopkins University Press, 1989), 235–71.

21. Clifford Geertz, in his preface to the French edition of *Bali* (Paris: Gallimard, 1983), 9.

22. François Furet, *Le passé d'une illusion. Essai sur l'idée communiste au XXe siècle* (Paris: Robert Laffont and Calmann-Lévy, 1995), 12.

CHAPTER ONE

1. "Les observations sont l'histoire de la physique et les systèmes en sont la fable"; Montesquieu, *Mes Pensées* 4: "Science et Industrie"; 2: "Sciences physiques et naturelles," posthumously published first in 1899 and 1901; reprinted in *Œuvres complètes* (Paris: Gallimard, bibliothèque de la Pléïade, 1985), 1:1182.

2. Frank Jewett, "The Origins of the Industrial Research Directors Group," Hagley Museum and Library (HML), Acc. 1851, Box 1; on the National Bureau of Standards, and on research in England, France, and Germany, see Box 1, vol 2: 1929–1942.

3. A. P. M. Fleming, *Industrial Research in the United States of America* (New

York: Arno Press, 1972), 48–56; Donald E. Stokes, *Pasteur's Quadrant: Basic Science and Technological Innovation* (Washington, D.C.: Brookings Institution Press, 1997), 35; Eric Ashby, "Education for an Age of Technology," in *A History of Technology: The Late Nineteenth Century, c. 1850 to c. 1900,* ed. Charles Singer, E. J. Holmyard, A. R. Hall, and Trevor I. Williams (Oxford: Clarendon Press, 1958), 5:776–98; David C. Mowery and Nathan Rosenberg, *Technology and the Pursuit of Economic Growth* (New York: Cambridge University Press, 1989), 113, 115–17; Thomas S. Kuhn, *The Essential Tension: Selected Studies in Scientific Tradition and Change* (Chicago: University of Chicago Press, 1977), 64, 142–47, 150, 238; see also A. E. Musson and Eric Robinson, *Science and Technology in the Industrial Revolution* (Manchester: Manchester University Press, 1969).

4. Kuhn, *Essential Tension,* 143; see also Joseph Ben-David, "The Universities and the Growth of Science in Germany and the United States," *Minerva* 7 (Autumn–Winter 1968–69): 1–35; and Konrad H. Jarausch, "American Students in Germany, 1815–1914: The Structure of German and United States Matriculants at Göttingen University" and Kathryn M. Olesko, "German Models, American Ways: The 'New Movement' among American Physics Teachers, 1905–1909," in *German Influences on Education in the United States to 1917,* ed. Henry Geitz, Jürgen Heideking, Jürgen Herbst (Washington, D.C.: German Historical Institute; New York: Cambridge University Press, 1995), 129–36, 145–46, 197; and Fritz Ringer, "The German Academic Community," in *The Organization of Knowledge in Modern America, 1860–1920,* ed. Alexandra Oleson and John Voss (Baltimore: Johns Hopkins University Press, 1979), 409–29; Konrad H. Jarausch, ed., *The Transformation of Higher Learning, 1860–1930: Expansion, Diversification, Social Opening, and Professionalization in England, Germany, Russia, and the United States* (Chicago: University of Chicago Press, 1983).

5. Laurence Veysey, *The Emergence of the American University* (Chicago: University of Chicago Press, 1965), 125–33.

6. Kuhn, *Essential Tension,* 145–46.

7. Contrast Kuhn's *Essential Tension* with Thomas P. Hughes, *American Genesis: A Century of Invention and Technological Enthusiasm* (New York: Viking, 1989).

8. Claude Lévi-Strauss, *La pensée sauvage* (Paris: Librairie Plon, 1962), 33; although I am aware that some American historians of technology use tinkerers to describe only early nineteenth-century clockmakers, I use the term here in a broader acceptation; I do not imply that tinkerers were necessarily foreign to scientific approaches—see Edwin Layton, "Mirror-Image Twins: The Communities of Science and Technology in Nineteenth-Century America," *Technology and Culture* 12 (October 1971): 562–80.

9. Laurence Veysey, *The Emergence of the American University,* 5; for a more positive assessment of traditional colleges, see Julie A. Reuben, *The Making of the Modern University: Intellectual Transformation and the Marginalization of Morality* (Chicago: University of Chicago Press, 1996), 11–12; on engineering education, Monte Calvert, *The Mechanical Engineer in America, 1830–1910* (Baltimore: Johns Hopkins Univer-

sity Press, 1967), 43–62; see also David Noble, *America by Design: Science, Technology, and the Rise of Corporate Capitalism* (New York: Alfred A. Knopf, 1977), 22–23; Robert V. Bruce, *The Launching of American Science, 1846–1876* (Ithaca: Cornell University Press, 1987), 159–65; and John Hubbel Weiss, *The Making of Technological Man: The Social Origins of French Engineering Education* (Cambridge: MIT Press, 1982).

10. See David A. Hounshell, *From the American System to Mass Production, 1800–1932: The Development of Manufacturing Technology in the United States* (Baltimore: John Hopkins University Press, 1984); on learned societies, Bruce Sinclair, "Science, Technology, and the Franklin Institute," in *The Pursuit of Knowledge in the Early American Republic: American Scientific and Learned Societies from Colonial Times to the Civil War,* ed. Alexandra Oleson and Sanborn C. Brown (Baltimore: Johns Hopkins University Press, 1976), 194–207.

11. Alexander Gerschenkron would have said "latecomers" (*tarde venientibus*), see his *Economic Backwardness in Historical Perspective: A Book of Essays* (Cambridge: Harvard University Press, Belknap Press, 1962), 172–73.

12. In Richard Hofstadter and Wilson Smith, eds., *American Higher Education: A Documentary History* (Chicago: University of Chicago Press, 1961), 2:636.

13. Edward Lurie, "Alexander Agassiz and Private Science," n.d., unpublished paper.

14. Oleson and Voss, eds., *The Organization of Knowledge in Modern America,* xii; see also Roger L. Geiger, *To Advance Knowledge: The Growth of American Research Universities, 1900–1940* (New York: Oxford University Press, 1986), and Alfred D. Chandler, Jr., with the assistance of Takashi Hikino, *Scale and Scope: The Dynamics of Industrial Capitalism* (Cambridge: Harvard University Press, Belknap Press, 1990), 82; I am borrowing the figure of 245 national professional associations from David Montgomery, *The Fall of the House of Labor: The Workplace, the State, and American Labor Activism, 1865–1925* (New York: Cambridge University Press, 1987), 176; on tensions between traditional generalists and specialists, Thomas Haskell writes: "To redefine 'social science' as a university-based, research oriented enterprise with its own community of full-time practitioners was to make social science virtually irrelevant to the professional men who founded and sustained the American Social Science Association"; *The Emergence of Professional Social Science: The American Social Science Association and the Nineteenth-Century Crisis of Authority* (Urbana: University of Illinois Press, 1977), 166. There is a growing body of historical works on professional associations; see especially Samuel Haber, *The Quest for Authority and Honor in the American Professions, 1750–1900* (Chicago: University of Chicago Press, 1991).

15. See David A. Hounshell and John Kenly Smith's introduction to their *Science and Corporate Strategy: Du Pont R&D, 1902–1980* (New York: Cambridge University Press, 1988) for references to the standard works as well as recent scholarship on R&D, 1–9, 616–18; on AT&T, George D. Smith, *The Anatomy of a Business Strategy: Bell, Western Electric, and the Origins of the American Telephone Industry* (Baltimore:

Johns Hopkins University Press, 1985); on General Electric, Leonard S. Reich, *The Making of American Industrial Research: Science and Business at GE and Bell, 1876–1926* (New York: Cambridge University Press, 1985).

16. At GE, Steinmetz was chief *consultant* engineer; see Hughes, *American Genesis*, 161–62.

17. See "Industrial Research Laboratories in the United States, Including Consulting Research Laboratories," comp. by Alfred D. Flinn, rev. by Ruth Cobb, in the *Bulletin of the National Research Council*, no. 16 (December 1921); and the 7th edition, no. 104 (December 1940), comp. by Callie Hull. The original list was compiled using the responses of the labs to the questionnaire sent by the NRC. It was expanded and refined with the help of the Chemical Catalog Company, which did a survey of chemical companies circa 1920. Perhaps because of this, the categorization for research in chemistry is more precise than in other areas. Many companies did research in several areas and are included under several headings; the detail of each response varies considerably.

18. See the article by Howard Bartlett (from MIT), an author of the 1941 NRC volume, "The Development of Industrial Research in the United States," in *Research, A National Resource, Sec. II, Industrial Research*, Report of the National Research Council to the National Resources Planning Board (Washington, D.C.: GPO, 1941), 19–156, especially 25; Mowery and Rosenberg, *Technology and the Pursuit of Economic Growth*, 30; see also Thomas J. Misa, *A Nation of Steel: The Making of Modern America, 1865–1925* (Baltimore: Johns Hopkins University Press, 1995).

19. Chandler, *Scale and Scope*, 17–18.

20. W. Bernard Carlson, *Innovation as a Social Process: Elihu Thomson and the Rise of General Electric, 1870–1900* (New York: Cambridge University Press, 1991), 347–49; Olivier Zunz, *Making America Corporate, 1870–1920* (Chicago: University of Chicago Press, 1990), 69–79.

21. Joel Mokyr, *The Lever of Riches: Technological Creativity and Economic Progress* (New York: Oxford University Press, 1990), 143–44.

22. Hughes, *American Genesis*, 156–57; Carlson, *Innovation as a Social Process*, 347; Leonard S. Reich, "Irving Langmuir and the Pursuit of Science and Technology in the Corporate Environment," *Technology and Culture* 24 (April 1983): 199–221; idem, *The Making of American Industrial Research*, 126; Carlson, "Building Thomas Edison's Laboratory at West Orange, New Jersey: A Case Study in Using Craft Knowledge for Technological Invention, 1886–1888," *History of Technology* 13 (1991): 150–67.

23. See Hounshell and Smith, *Science and Corporate Strategy*, 228–29; Wallace Carothers, who would make a major breakthrough with his research on polymers, was only a young instructor at Harvard when hired. The company had been turned down by all the prima donnas in the field.

24. *Congressional Record*, 49th Cong., 2d sess., 1887, 18, pt. I:720–31, pt. II: 1038–46, 1076–83; Alan I. Marcus, *Agricultural Science and the Quest for Legitimacy: Farmers, Agricultural Colleges, and Experiment Stations, 1870–1890* (Ames: Iowa

State University Press, 1985), 188–216; Carnegie Foundation for the Advancement of Teaching, *Fourth Annual Report of the President and Treasurer* (New York, 1909), 97; U.S. Department of Agriculture, *Annual Report of the Office of Experimental Stations for the Year Ended June 30, 1903* (Washington, D.C.: GPO, 1904); see also A. Hunter Dupree, *Science in the Federal Government: A History of Policies and Activities* (Baltimore: Johns Hopkins University Press, 1986), 149–83; Charles E. Rosenberg, *No Other Gods: On Science and American Social Thought* (Baltimore: Johns Hopkins University Press, 1976), 133–209; Mowery and Rosenberg, *Technology and the Pursuit of Economic Growth*, 94, 95; and Joseph Ben-David, *The Scientist's Role in Society* (Englewood Cliffs: Prentice Hall, 1971), 147–52.

25. Deborah Fitzgerald, *The Business of Breeding: Hybrid Corn in Illinois, 1890–1940* (Ithaca: Cornell University Press, 1990), 42; on scientists developing a social and intellectual climate receptive to their questions, see Rosenberg, *No Other Gods,* 168.

26. Oleson and Voss, eds., *The Organization of Knowledge,* xii.

27. David A. Hounshell, "Industrial Research and Manufacturing Technology," in *Encyclopedia of the United States in the Twentieth Century,* ed. Stanley I. Kutler (New York: Charles Scribner's Sons, 1996), 2:831–57; Mokyr, *The Lever of Riches,* 143–44; see also Robert V. Bruce, *Bell: Alexander Graham Bell and the Conquest of Solitude* (Ithaca: Cornell University Press, 1973), and John W. Servos, *Physical Chemistry from Ostwald to Pauling: The Making of a Science in America* (Princeton: Princeton University Press, 1990).

28. Russell H. Chittenden, *History of the Sheffield Scientific School of Yale University, 1846–1922* (New Haven: Yale University Press, 1922), 21–24, 26–30, 405. See also Rosenberg, *No Other Gods,* 136 and 245, n. 5. Benjamin Silliman, Jr., assisted his father at Yale and also became a professor; Daniel Boorstin refers to the son in *The Americans: The Democratic Experience* (New York: Vintage Books, 1974), 44, as the chemist testing oil for Pennsylvania investors in 1855.

29. On the number of Ph.D.s awarded in the United States, see National Research Council, *A Century of Doctorates: Data Analysis of Growth and Change* (Washington, D.C.: National Academy of Sciences, 1978), 7, 12–13; *Historical Statistics of the United States, Colonial Times to 1970,* (Washington, D.C.: GPO, 1975), 1:386; *Memorial Volume Commemorative of the Life and Life-Work of Charles Benjamin Dudley, Ph.D.* (Philadelphia: American Society for Testing Materials, 1910); HML, Pennsylvania Railroad archives, Acc. 1810, Boxes 458, 459, 488, 609, 714.

30. On Wells, see Chittenden, *History of the Sheffield Scientific School,* 263–65.

31. Elihu Thomson began lecturing in MIT's Electrical Engineering Department in 1894; see Carlson, *Innovation as a Social Process,* 342; on education at MIT, see Thomas P. Hughes, *Networks of Power: Electrification in Western Society, 1880–1930* (Baltimore: Johns Hopkins University Press, 1983), 151–53.

32. The case is convenient to analyze because of Thomas Hughes's excellent biography, *Elmer Sperry: Inventor and Engineer* (Baltimore: Johns Hopkins University Press,

1971), which I supplemented by an exploration into Sperry's papers at the Hagley Museum and Library, Acc. 1893, especially box 5.

33. Hughes, *American Genesis,* 128.

34. Hughes, *Elmer Sperry,* 293; HML, Acc. 1893, Box 5; Daniel J. Kevles, *The Physicists: The History of a Scientific Community in Modern America,* rev. ed. (Cambridge: Harvard University Press, 1987), 155–56.

35. It is only in the last few years that a handful of historical studies on the work of specific foundations (Rockefeller, Carnegie) have appeared. Much more remains to be done to assess the foundations' role within the larger institutional matrix and prevailing paradigms. Most historians agree that the fear of a permanent income tax in the Progressive Era did not play a major role in the creation of foundations. In a seminal article on foundations as a group, Barry Karl and Stanley Katz deny the common charge that foundations were "hegemonic"; see their "Foundations and Ruling Class Elites," *Daedalus* 116 (1987): 1–40. As foundations matured, they acted increasingly as "idea brokers"; see James Allen Smith, *The Idea Brokers: Think Tanks and the Rise of the New Policy Elite* (New York: Free Press, 1991), and Gerald Jonas, *The Circuit Riders: Rockefeller Money and the Rise of Modern Science* (New York: W. W. Norton, 1989); for more in-depth treatments, see Ellen Condliffe Lagemann, *The Politics of Knowledge: The Carnegie Corporation, Philanthropy, and Public Policy* (Middletown: Wesleyan University Press, 1989) and Robert E. Kohler, *Partners in Science: Foundations and Natural Scientists, 1900–1945* (Chicago: University of Chicago Press, 1991); it took at least fifteen years for newly created foundations to have an impact on the natural sciences.

36. Daniel Kevles argues that this made them turn conservative in *The Physicists,* 170–84.

37. Susan J. Douglas, *Inventing American Broadcasting, 1899–1922* (Baltimore: Johns Hopkins University Press, 1987), 268–91; Margaret B. W. Graham, *RCA and the VideoDisc: The Business of Research* (New York: Cambridge University Press, 1986), 30–47; see also Daniel Kevles, "Physics and National Power, 1870–1930," in *The Michelson Era in American Science 1870–1930,* ed. Stanley Goldberg and Roger H. Stuewer (New York: American Institute of Physics, 1988), 252–57.

38. "Industrial Research Laboratories in the United States, Including Consulting Research Laboratories," comp. by Alfred D. Flinn, 20.

39. Alexis de Tocqueville, *Democracy in America,* vol. 1, 1835, vol. 2, 1840, trans. Henry Reeve, revised by Francis Bowen and further revised by Phillips Bradley, with an introduction by Daniel J. Boorstin (New York: Vintage Books, 1990), 1:27; 2:v, vi, 41–47, 54; on the Lazzaroni, see Mark Beach, "Was There a Scientific Lazzaroni?" in *Nineteenth-Century American Science: A Reappraisal,* ed. George H. Daniels (Evanston: Northwestern University Press, 1972), 115–32 and Lillian B. Miller et al., *The Lazzaroni: Science and Scientists in Mid-Nineteenth Century America* (Washington, D.C.: Smithsonian Institution Press, 1972).

40. Sperry to Smith, December 20, 1927, HML, Acc. 1893, box 5. For a traditional

NOTES TO PAGES 19-20

view of practicality, see Daniel Boorstin, *The Americans,* 597, 542. Daniel Calhoun focuses on the simpler American designs for bridges in *The Intelligence of a People* (Princeton: Princeton University Press, 1973), 291–322. David Hollinger, however, describes pragmatism as "the radical academicization of philosophy by superprofessionals" in his *In the American Province: Studies in the History and Historiography of Ideas* (Bloomington: Indiana University Press, 1985), 24, 27. For a discerning compromise between these seemingly contradictory definitions, see John Higham, "Rediscovering the Pragmatic American," in *Pragmatism as a Way of Life,* a symposium on American pragmatism held in Seoul, Korea, 1986, printed in the conference proceedings. Higham stresses the symbiosis between practicality and idealism (George Santayana described the American as an "idealist working on matter"), 216, and James T. Kloppenberg, "Pragmatism: An Old Name for Some New Ways of Thinking?" *Journal of American History* 83 (June 1996): 100–38.

41. In the words of Leonard Bacon, a minister close to the New Haven scholars; see Louise L. Stevenson, *Scholarly Means to Evangelical Ends: The New Haven Scholars and the Transformation of Higher Learning in America, 1830–1890* (Baltimore: Johns Hopkins University Press, 1986), 3.

42. Henry Adams, *The Education of Henry Adams: An Autobiography* (1918), Library of America (New York: Viking, 1983), 1067, 1070, 1136.

43. See James T. Kloppenberg, *Uncertain Victory: Social Democracy and Progressivism in European and American Thought, 1870–1920* (New York: Oxford University Press, 1986), 100, 352; Reuben, *The Making of the Modern University,* 3, 9; and Dorothy Ross, "Modernism Reconsidered," in *Modernist Impulses in the Human Sciences, 1870–1930,* ed. Dorothy Ross (Baltimore: Johns Hopkins University Press, 1994), 1–25, 309–11.

44. Charles Riborg Mann, *A Study of Engineering Education Prepared for the Joint Committee on Engineering Education of the National Engineering Societies,* Bulletin no. 11 (New York: Carnegie Foundation for the Advancement of Teaching, 1918), 129–30.

45. John Dewey, *How We Think* (Boston: D. C. Heath, 1910), 3, 62; also quoted in Robert Westbrook, *John Dewey and American Democracy* (Ithaca: Cornell University Press, 1991), 141–42. See also Dewey's essay, "The Experimental Theory of Knowledge," (1910), in *The Philosophy of John Dewey,* ed. John McDermott (Chicago: University of Chicago Press, 1973), 175–93. In *Logic: The Theory of Inquiry* (New York: Henry Holt, 1938), Dewey defined inquiry as "the controlled or directed transformation of an indeterminate situation . . . into a unified whole"; Bertrand Russell would take him to task on this very point; see notes 55 and 56 below.

46. Not just the young Walter Lippmann, but also Max Otto, Thomas Vernor Smith, Joseph Ratner among other philosophers; I thank David Hollinger for pointing me to their work; see Darnell Rucker, *The Chicago Pragmatists* (Minneapolis: University of Minnesota Press, 1969).

47. This formulation owes much to Richard Rorty's; as Rorty puts it, "American

pragmatism has, in the course of a hundred years, swung back and forth between an attempt to raise the rest of culture to the epistemological level of the natural sciences and an attempt to level down the natural sciences to an epistemological par with art, religion, and politics"; see his *Objectivity, Relativism, and Truth* (New York: Cambridge University Press, 1991), 1:63. See also Arthur Lovejoy, *The Thirteen Pragmatisms and Other Essays* (Baltimore: Johns Hopkins University Press, 1977). On Tocqueville and Einstein making distinctions among levels of knowledge, see Gerald Holton, *The Advancement of Science and its Burdens* (New York: Cambridge University Press, 1986), 13.

48. Horace Kallen, "John Dewey and the Spirit of Pragmatism," in *John Dewey: Philosopher of Science and Freedom*, ed. Sidney Hook (New York: Dial Press, 1950), 3–46.

49. David Hollinger, *In the American Province*, 24; and Kloppenberg, "Pragmatism: An Old Name for Some New Ways of Thinking?" 101.

50. Charles A. Beard, ed., *Toward Civilization* (New York: Longmans, Green & Co., 1930); John Dewey, "Philosophy," in *Whither Mankind: A Panorama of Modern Civilization*, ed. Charles A. Beard (New York: Longmans, Green & Co., 1928), 314.

51. Philip Pauly suggests that "Loeb was the single most important live model for Dewey's image of the scientific inquirer in the 1870s" in *Controlling Life: Jacques Loeb and the Engineering Ideal in Biology* (New York: Oxford University Press, 1987), 68.

52. Pauly, *Controlling Life*, 193; see also Charles Rosenberg, "The Scientist as Hero," in *Twentieth Century Interpretations of Arrowsmith*, ed. Robert Griffin (Englewood Cliffs: Prentice Hall, 1968), 47–56, and Pauly, "Modernist Practice in American Biology," in *Modernist Impulses*, ed. Ross, 272–89, 360–64, which seeks to explain the ways in which institutions influence knowledge.

53. Ronald Tobey, *The American Ideology of National Science, 1919–1930* (Pittsburgh: University of Pittsburgh Press, 1971), 124.

54. Westbrook, *Dewey and American Democracy*, 356.

55. Kloppenberg quotes James's advice in "Pragmatism: An Old Name for Some New Ways of Thinking?" 107. Hollinger refers to the Dewey-Russell episode in his *In The American Province*, 35–36. Westbrook takes Dewey's side in *Dewey and American Democracy*, 496.

56. Bertrand Russell, "Dewey's New Logic" in *The Philosophy of John Dewey*, ed. Paul Arthur Schilp (New York: Tudor Publishing Co., 1939, 1951), 143–56. Russell targeted Dewey's latest book, *Logic, The Theory of Inquiry* (1938). Dewey had synthesized his views on the history of philosophy of science in an earlier book, *Quest for Certainty: A Study of the Relation of Knowledge and Action* (New York: Minton, Balch, 1929), splendidly analyzed by Westbrook in *Dewey and American Democracy*, 347–61.

57. See Robert Seidel, "The Origins of the Lawrence Berkeley Laboratory," in *Big Science: The Growth of Large-Scale Research*, ed. Peter Galison and Bruce Hevly (Stanford: Stanford University Press, 1992), 21–45; see also Pauly, *Controlling Life*, 193–

94; and Pap Ndiaye, "Du nylon et des bombes. Du Pont de Nemours, l'État américain et le nucléaire, 1930–1960," *Annales: Histoire, Sciences Sociales* 50 (Janvier–Février 1995): 53–73.

CHAPTER TWO

1. "Les formes originales de pensée s'introduisent elles-mêmes: leur histoire est la seule forme d'exégèse qu'elles supportent, et leur destin, la seule forme de critique"; in Michel Foucault's introduction to the French edition of *Le Rêve et l'Existence* by L. Binswanger (1954), reprinted in *Dits et écrits, 1954–1988*, vol. 1, *1954–1969*, ed. Daniel Defert and François Ewald (Paris: Gallimard, 1994), 65.

2. "The American Century," *Life*, February 17, 1941, 61–65. On the disparity between creed and conduct, I am borrowing Gunnar Myrdal's well-known formulation in *An American Dilemma: The Negro Problem and Modern Democracy* (New York: Harper & Brothers, 1944); see Walter Jackson, *Gunnar Myrdal and America's Conscience: Social Engineering and Racial Liberalism, 1938–1987* (Chapel Hill: University of North Carolina Press, 1990), 186–271.

3. Thomas Haskell, *The Emergence of Professional Social Science: The American Social Science Association and the Nineteenth-Century Crisis of Authority* (Urbana: University of Illinois Press, 1977), 166; John Higham, "The Matrix of Specialization," in *The Organization of Knowledge in Modern America, 1860–1920*, ed. Alexandra Oleson and John Voss (Baltimore: Johns Hopkins University Press, 1979), 3–18; Robert C. Bannister, *Sociology and Scientism: The American Quest for Objectivity, 1880–1940* (Chapel Hill: University of North Carolina Press, 1987), 6; Theodore M. Porter, *The Rise of Statistical Thinking, 1820–1900* (Princeton: Princeton University Press, 1986); and idem, *Trust in Numbers: The Pursuit of Objectivity in Science and Public Life* (Princeton: Princeton University Press, 1995). On the relationship between Auguste Comte and John Stuart Mill, see Wolf Lepenies, *Between Literature and Science: The Rise of Sociology*, trans. R. J. Hollingdale (New York: Cambridge University Press, 1988), 107.

4. Edward Shils, "Social Science and Social Policy," in his *The Calling of Sociology and Other Essays on the Pursuit of Learning* (Chicago: University of Chicago Press, 1980), 259–88. On the relationship between scientism and American exceptionalism, see Dorothy Ross, *The Origins of American Social Science* (New York: Cambridge University Press, 1991). On the conflict between science and reform, see Mary O. Furner, *Advocacy and Objectivity: A Crisis in the Professionalization of American Social Science, 1865–1905* (Lexington: University of Kentucky Press, 1975) and Mark C. Smith, *Social Science in the Crucible: The American Debate over Objectivity and Purpose, 1918–1941* (Durham: Duke University Press, 1994).

5. Henry F. May, *Protestant Churches and Industrial America* (New York: Harper & Bros., 1949), 163–263; Paul Boyer, *Urban Masses and Moral Order in*

America, 1820–1920 (Cambridge: Harvard University Press, 1978), especially 162–74; Stephen Wise, *Challenging Years: The Autobiography of Stephen Wise* (New York: G. P. Putnam's Sons, 1949); Egal Feldman, "The Social Gospel and the Jews," *American Jewish Historical Quarterly* 58 (March 1969): 308–22; Benny Kraut, *From Reform Judaism to Ethical Culture: The Religious Evolution of Felix Adler* (Cincinnati: Hebrew Union College Press, 1979); John A. Ryan, *Social Doctrine in Action: A Personal History* (New York: Harper & Bros., 1941); Joseph M. McShane, S.J., *"Sufficiently Radical": Catholicism, Progressivism, and the Bishop's Program of 1919* (Washington, D.C.: Catholic University of America Press, 1986).

6. For example, John Dewey at Hull-House in Chicago, E. R. A. Seligman at Greenwich house in New York.

7. Sidney Fine, *Laissez Faire and the General-Welfare State: A Study of Conflict in American Thought, 1865–1901* (Ann Arbor: University of Michigan Press, 1956), 377; Arthur J. Vidich and Stanford M. Lyman, *American Sociology: Worldly Rejections of Religion and Their Directions* (New Haven: Yale University Press, 1985), 154.

8. Walter Rauschenbusch, *Christianity and the Social Crisis* (New York: Macmillan, 1913), 209. Rauschenbusch brought together "the nineteenth century tradition of evangelical reform and the twentieth century commitment to scientific reform"; see *A Companion to American Thought,* ed. Richard W. Fox and James Kloppenberg (Cambridge, Mass.: Blackwell Publishers, 1995), 569; see also Paul M. Minus, *Walter Rauschenbusch: American Reformer* (New York: Macmillan, 1988); and on Dwight Moody in Chicago, James Gilbert, *Perfect Cities: Chicago's Utopias of 1893* (Chicago: University of Chicago Press, 1991), 203–5.

9. Benjamin G. Rader, *The Academic Mind and Reform: The Influence of Richard T. Ely in American Life* (Lexington: University of Kentucky Press, 1966), 60–61; Richard T. Ely, *Ground under Our Feet: An Autobiography* (New York: Macmillan, 1938), 74.

10. Merle Curti and Vernon Carstensen, *The University of Wisconsin: A History, 1848–1925* (Madison: University of Wisconsin Press, 1949), 1:288–89, 502, 508; Ely, *Ground under Our Feet,* 174–81, 186–87, 190, 214. On Bascom, see Laurence R. Veysey, *The Emergence of the American University* (Chicago: University of Chicago Press, 1965) 217–20. Dorothy Ross argues that the "religious ties" of the likes of Bascom "placed distinct limits on the degree of innovation they could tolerate and left it to the more secular gentry to break the antebellum model," but she never said what those limits were; see *Origins of American Social Science,* 63, n. 16.

11. On the episode surrounding Ely, contrast Curti's and Carstensen's treatment in *University of Wisconsin,* 1:508–27, with Ross's in "Socialism and American Liberalism: Academic Social Thought in the 1880's," *Perspectives in American History* 11 (1977–1978): 48–52, 54–55, 64, and Kathryn Kish Sklar's in *Florence Kelley and Women's Political Culture* (New Haven: Yale University Press, 1995), 294–95. See also John R. Commons, *Myself* (New York: Macmillan, 1934), 8, 58, 92, 95. Thorstein Veblen would echo similar feelings when denouncing the congruence between the "captain

of erudition" and the "captain of industry"; see Edward Lurie, "An Interpretation of Science in the Nineteenth Century: A Study in History and Historiography," *Journal of World History* 8 (1965): 701; and Clyde W. Barrow, *Universities and the Capitalist State: Corporate Liberalism and the Reconstruction of American Higher Education, 1894–1928* (Madison: University of Wisconsin Press, 1990).

12. John R. Commons, et al., *History of Labor in the United States,* 4 vols. (New York: Macmillan, 1918–1935). Commons's best student, Selig Perlman, made the case for bread-and-butter unionism most forcefully in *A Theory of the Labor Movement* (New York: Macmillan, 1928). See Jack Barbash, "John R. Commons: Pioneer of Labor Economics," *Monthly Labor Review* 112 (May 1989): 44–49; Lafayette G. Harter, Jr., *John R. Commons: His Assault on Laissez-Faire,* foreword by Wayne Morse (Corvallis: Oregon State University Press, 1962); and Gerald G. Somers, ed., *Labor, Management, and Social Policy: Essays in the John R. Commons Tradition* (Madison: University of Wisconsin Press, 1963). Commons's skilled workers were mostly "old immigrants" and native-white Americans, but Commons was significantly less progressive toward unskilled "new immigrants"; see his *Races and Immigrants in America* (New York: Macmillan, 1907).

13. Theda Skocpol, *Protecting Soldiers and Mothers: The Political Origins of Social Policy in the United States* (Cambridge: Harvard University Press, Belknap Press, 1992), 194–203, 254–61; Charles McCurdy, "The Knight Sugar Decision of 1895 and the Modernization of American Corporation Law, 1869–1903," *Business History Review* 53 (Autumn 1979): 304–42, and idem, "Justice Field and the Jurisprudence of Government-Business Relations: Some Parameters of Laissez-Faire Constitutionalism, 1863–1897," *Journal of American History* 61 (March 1975): 970–1005. See also Barry D. Karl and Stanley N. Katz, "Foundations and Ruling Class Elites," *Daedalus* 116 (1987): 17–18, on Rockefeller and Carnegie deflecting Easley's overture for being too conservative.

14. I thank Richard Rorty for loaning me his uncle and aunt's autobiographical manuscript, Paul A. Raushenbush and Elizabeth Brandeis Raushenbush, "Our 'U. C.' Story: 1930–1967" (Typescript, 1968), 24; "U. C." stands for unemployment compensation. On the Rauschenbusch family dropping the *c*'s, personal communication from Richard Rorty. On Elizabeth's special policymaking role, see Linda Gordon, *Pitied but Not Entitled: Single Mothers and the History of Welfare, 1890–1935* (New York: Free Press, 1994), 144, 202.

15. In Morton Keller's informed judgment, early twentieth-century state regulation was still akin to "a dog that did not bark"; see his *Regulating a New Society: Public Policy and Social Change in America, 1900–1933* (Cambridge: Harvard University Press, 1994), 179.

16. Merle Curti, Judith Green, and Roderick Nash, "The Anatomy of Giving: Millionaires in the Late Nineteenth Century," *American Quarterly* 15 (Fall 1963): 425.

17. Donald Fisher, "The Role of Philanthropic Foundations in the Reproduction and Production of Hegemony: The Rockefeller Foundations and the Social Science,"

Journal of the British Sociological Association 17 (May 1983): 206-33; Martin Bulmer, "Philanthropic Foundations and the Development of the Social Sciences in the Early Twentieth Century: A Reply to Donald Fisher," *Sociology* 18 (November 1984): 572-79. The most important work has been done on the impact of foundations on science and medicine, as in Robert E. Kohler, *Partners in Science: Foundations and Natural Scientists, 1900-1945* (Chicago: University of Chicago Press, 1991).

18. Karl and Katz, "Foundations and Ruling Class Elites," *Daedalus* 116 (1987): 34.

19. Quoted in Paul Krause, *The Battle for Homestead, 1880-1892: Politics, Culture, and Steel* (Pittsburgh: University of Pittsburgh Press, 1992), 351; see also Nelson Lichtenstein, *The Most Dangerous Man in Detroit: Walter Reuther and the Fate of American Labor* (New York: Basic Books, 1995), 1-3.

20. David M. Grossman, "American Foundations and the Support of Economic Research, 1913-29," *Minerva* 20 (Spring-Summer 1982): 59-82; Fisher, "The Role of Philanthropic Foundations," 209; see also Andrew J. F. Morris, "A Characteristically American Entreprise: The General Education Board and the Farm Demonstration Program, 1906-1914" (Seminar paper, University of Virginia, 1996).

21. Joseph Frazier Wall, *Andrew Carnegie* (New York: Oxford University Press, 1970), 898.

22. Ely, *Ground under Our Feet*, 148; see also Commons, *Myself*, 97.

23. Warren Weaver, *U.S. Philanthropic Foundations: Their History, Structure, Management, and Record* (New York: Harper & Row, 1967), 26; James Allen Smith, *The Idea Brokers: Think Tanks and the Rise of the New Policy Elite* (New York: Free Press, 1991), 39-45; Barbara Howe, "The Emergence of Scientific Philanthropy, 1900-1920: Origins, Issues, and Outcomes," in *Philanthropy and Cultural Imperialism: The Foundations at Home and Abroad*, ed. Robert F. Arnove (Boston: G. K. Hall & Co., 1980), 38-39; David C. Hammack and Stanton Wheeler, *Social Science in the Making: Essays on the Russell Sage Foundation, 1907-1972* (New York: Russell Sage Foundation, 1994), vi; see also John M. Glenn, Lilian Brandt and F. Emerson Andrews, *Russell Sage Foundation, 1907-1946*, 2 vols. (New York: Russell Sage Foundation, 1947); for a view from the natural sciences, Daniel J. Kevles, "Foundations, Universities, and Trends in Support for the Physical and Biological Sciences, 1900-1992," *Daedalus* 121 (1992): 195-235.

24. Wolfgang J. Mommsen, *Max Weber and German Politics, 1890-1920*, trans. Michael S. Steinberg (Chicago: University of Chicago Press, 1984), 396; and Janet Horne, *A Social Laboratory for Modern France: The Musée Social and the Rise of the Welfare State* (Durham: Duke University Press, forthcoming).

25. On early efforts, see Haskell, *The Emergence of Professional Social Science*, 100-121; and Michael J. Lacey and Mary O. Furner, eds., *The State and Social Investigation in Britain and the United States* (Washington, D.C.: Woodrow Wilson Center Press; New York: Cambridge University Press, 1993); see also Robert DeForest and Laurence Veiller, *The Tenement House Problem* (1903; New York: Arno Press, 1970).

26. Russell Sage Foundation, *Confidential Bulletin 1: Constitution, Letters of Gifts, and Suggestions on the Scope of Work* (New York: Printed Privately for the Trustees, 1907), 121, 124, 138, 150; John M. Glenn, Lilian Brandt, and F. Emerson Andrews, *Russell Sage Foundation, 1907–1946* (New York: Russell Sage Foundation, 1947), 1: 16.

27. Paul Kellogg, "The Spread of the Survey Idea," *Proceedings of the Academy of Political Science* 2 (July 1912); (reprint, New York: Department of Surveys and Exhibits, Russell Sage Foundation, 1912), 6, 14. On the role of women reformers in the survey movement, see Gordon, *Pitied but Not Entitled*, 169–71.

28. See Martin Bulmer, Kevin Bales, and Kathryn Kish Sklar, eds., *The Social Survey in Historical Perspective, 1880–1940* (New York: Cambridge University Press, 1991); Mary Van Kleeck, *Wages in the Millinery Trade: To Be Incorporated in the Fourth Report of the New York State Factory Investigating Committee* (Albany: J. B. Lyon Co., 1914); Arthur H. Ham, *Credit Unions and Their Relation to Savings and Loan Associations,* an Address Delivered before the State League of Savings and Loan Associations, Port Jervis, N.Y., June 10, 1915 (New York: Division of Remedial Loans, Russell Sage Foundation, 1915); Earle Edward Eubank, "Loan Sharks and Loan Shark Legislation in Illinois," *The Journal of the American Institute of Criminal Law and Criminology* (Reprint, New York: Russell Sage Foundation, 1917).

29. Hastings H. Hart, *The Spiritual Dynamics of Social Work,* a Commencement Address Delivered at Wilberforce University, June 17, 1915 (New York: Russell Sage Foundation, 1916).

30. See Guy Alchon, *The Invisible Hand of Planning: Capitalism, Social Science, and the State in the 1920s* (Princeton: Princeton University Press, 1985); Donald T. Critchlow, *The Brookings Institution, 1916–1952: Expertise and the Public Interest in a Democratic Society* (DeKalb: Northern Illinois University Press, 1985); Smith, *Social Science in the American Crucible;* and especially Ellis W. Hawley, "Economic Inquiry and the State in New Era America: Antistatist Corporatism and Positive Statism in Uneasy Coexistence," in *The State and Economic Knowledge: The American and British Experiences,* ed. Mary O. Furner and Barry Supple (New York: Cambridge University Press; Washington, D.C.: Woodrow Wilson International Center for Scholars), 287–324.

31. Edmund Day, "Proposed Foundation Program in Economic Stabilization," September 14, 1931, Rockefeller Foundation (RF) archives, Poncantico Hills, Tarrytown, NY, Record group 3, series 910, box 2, folder 12.

32. Memorial Policy, Laura Spelman Rockefeller Memorial (LSRM), RF, Record group 3, series 910, box 2, folder 10; Martin and Joan Bulmer quote from the same text in "Philanthropy and Social Science in the 1920s: Beardsley Ruml and the Laura Spelman Rockefeller Memorial, 1922–29," *Minerva* 19 (Autumn 1981): 361–67, passim; see also Gerd Gigerenzer et al., *The Empire of Chance: How Probability Changed Science and Everyday Life* (New York: Cambridge University Press, 1989), 245.

33. LSRM, RF, Series 3, sub-series 6, box 63, folder 679.

34. LSRM, RF, Series 3, sub-series 6, box 63, folder 679 and Series 3, sub-series 6, box 58, folder 629.

35. On the merger, see Martin Bulmer and Joan Bulmer, "Philanthropy and Social Science in the 1920s," 148.

36. Day, "Proposed Foundation Program in Economic Stabilization," September 14, 1931.

37. LSRM, RF, Record group 3, series 910, box 10, folder 94.

38. Beardsley Ruml, "Recent Trends in Social Science," delivered at the dedication of the Social Science Research Building of the University of Chicago, December 17, 1929, LSRM, RF, Record group 3, series 910, box 2, folder 12. The same text was published in *The New Social Science,* ed. Leonard White (Chicago: University of Chicago Press, 1930), 99–111. This is *not* the consensus on science Ross describes in *Origins of American Social Science,* 400–407, or the objectivity Edward A. Purcell, Jr., sees in *The Crisis of Democratic Theory: Scientific Naturalism and the Problem of Value* (Lexington: University Press of Kentucky, 1973), 27–28.

39. John Dewey, *The Public and Its Problems* (New York: Henry Holt, 1927), 181; see Barry D. Karl, "Philanthropy, Policy Planning, and the Bureaucratization of the Democratic Ideal," *Daedalus* 105 (Fall 1976): 129–49.

40. Figures in "Register of Doctors of Philosophy of the University of Chicago, June 1893–June 1927," *University of Chicago Announcements* 28 (September 10, 1927). Historians have often missed the religious influence on the social sciences; for a counterpoint, see Julie A. Reuben, *The Making of the Modern University: Intellectual Transformation and the Marginalization of Morality* (Chicago: University of Chicago Press, 1996), 172.

41. Contrast Dorothy Ross's exclusive focus on Park's scientism in "An Historian's View of American Social Science," *Journal of the History of the Behavioral Sciences* 29 (April 1993): 99–112, with Winifred Raushenbush's sympathetic rendering of his views on religion in *Robert E. Park, Biography of a Sociologist* (Durham: Duke University Press, 1979), 168–72.

42. Charles A. Beard, "Government by Technologists," *The New Republic* 63 (June 18, 1930): 116; see also Thomas Bender, *Intellect and Public Life: Essays on the Social History of Academic Intellectuals in the United States* (Baltimore: Johns Hopkins University Press, 1993), 91–105, 164–66.

43. Beard, "Rebuilding in Japan," *Review of Reviews* 68 (October 1923): 382.

44. Beard, "A World Bureau of Municipal Research Being Considered by the League of Nations," *National Municipal Review* 14 (January 1925): 1–2.

45. Barry D. Karl, *Charles E. Merriam and the Study of Politics* (Chicago: University of Chicago Press, 1974), 217–18, and Reuben, *The Making of the Modern University,* 144.

46. Richard Wightman Fox, "Epitaph for Middletown: Robert S. Lynd and the

Analysis of Consumer Culture," in *The Culture of Consumption: Critical Essays in American History, 1880–1980,* ed. Richard Wightman Fox and T. J. Jackson Lears (New York: Pantheon Books, 1983), 101–41, 225–29.

47. Robert Fishman, "The Regional Plan and the Transformation of the Industrial Metropolis," in *The Landscape of Modernity: Essays on New York City, 1900–1940,* eds. David Ward and Olivier Zunz (New York: Russell Sage Foundation, 1992), 106–25.

48. Dewey, as quoted by Richard S. Kirkendall in *Social Scientists and Farm Politics in the Age of Roosevelt* (Columbia: University of Missouri Press, 1966), 2–3.

49. RF, Record group 3, series 910, box 2, folder, 13; see also Barry D. Karl, "Presidential Planning and Social Science Research: Mr. Hoover's Experts," *Perspectives in American History* 3 (1969): 359–60, 367–68, 376–77, 381–82; and William Tobin, "Studying Society: The Making of *Recent Social Trends in the United States, 1928–1933,*" in *Theory and Society: Renewal and Critique in Social Theory* 24 (August 1995), 537–65.

50. *Recent Social Trends in the United States: Report of the President's Research Committee on Social Trends,* with a foreword by Herbert Hoover (New York: McGraw-Hill, 1933), 1:lxx–lxxv.

51. Day, "Proposed Foundation Program in Economic Stabilization," September 14, 1931.

52. In *A Study of Rural Sociology: Its Organization and Changes,* ed. William F. Ogburn (Boston: Houghton Mifflin Co., 1935), John Harrison Kolb and Edmund de S. Brunner continued to wrestle with the problems they first confronted in *Recent Social Trends* of the relationship between recognizing trends and creating public policy, 601–11; see also Edmund de S. Brunner and Irving Lorge, *Rural Trends in Depression Years: A Survey of Village-centered Agricultural Communities, 1930–1936* (New York: Columbia University Press, 1937), 355, 371–72.

53. Rexford G. Tugwell, *The Industrial Discipline and the Governmental Arts* (New York: Columbia University Press, 1953), 18–21, 33, 84, 101–3, 107–8, 114–15, 129, 159–61, 189–219; see also David E. Hamilton, *From New Day to New Deal: American Farm Policy from Hoover to Roosevelt, 1928–1933* (Chapel Hill: University of North Carolina Press, 1991), 170–94, 216–36.

54. Jackson, *Gunnar Myrdal and America's Conscience,* 105.

55. John Harrison Kolb and Edmund de S. Brunner, *A Study of Rural Sociology: Its Organization and Changes,* ed. William F. Ogburn (Boston: Houghton Mifflin Co., 1935), 602.

56. Simon N. Patten, *The New Basis of Civilization* (New York: Macmillan, 1907), 69, 73, 77, 84–91; see also Alan Brinkley, *The End of Reform: New Deal Liberalism in Recession and War* (New York: Alfred A. Knopf, 1995), 67–68.

57. Daniel M. Fox, *The Discovery of Abundance: Simon N. Patten and the Transformation of Social Theory* (Ithaca: Cornell University Press, 1967), 69–70, 95.

CHAPTER THREE

1. As quoted by Joyce Appleby, "Jefferson and His Complex Legacy," in *Jeffersonian Legacies* ed. Peter Onuf (Charlottesville: University of Virginia Press, 1993), 13.

2. Horace Kallen, "Behaviorism," and Graham Wallas, "Jeremy Bentham," in *Encyclopedia of the Social Sciences,* ed. Edwin R. A. Seligman and Alvin Johnson (New York: Macmillan, 1930), 2:496, 518–19; Daniel T. Rodgers, *Contested Truths: Keywords in American Politics Since Independence* (New York: Basic Books, 1987), 17–44.

3. Stephen M. Stigler, *The History of Statistics: The Measurement of Uncertainty before 1900* (Cambridge: Harvard University Press, Belknap Press, 1986), 266; Theodore M. Porter, *The Rise of Statistical Thinking, 1820–1900* (Princeton: Princeton University Press, 1986), 296–314; see also Fred L. Bookstein, "Utopian Skeletons in the Biometric Closet," University of Michigan Institute for the Humanities Occasional Paper Number 2, May 1995, 13.

4. Gerd Gigerenzer et al., *The Empire of Chance: How Probability Changed Science and Everyday Life* (New York: Cambridge University Press, 1989), 42–43.

5. William James, "The Importance of Individuals," in *The Will to Believe and Other Essays in Popular Philosophy* (1897), *Writings, 1878–1899,* Library of America (New York: Viking, 1984), 648.

6. Ira Katznelson, *City Trenches: Urban Politics and the Patterning of Class in the United States* (New York: Pantheon Books, 1981), 207.

7. Dorothy Ross, *The Origins of American Social Science* (New York: Cambridge University Press, 1991), 230–53; see also Julie A. Reuben, *The Making of the Modern University: Intellectual Transformation and the Marginalization of Morality* (Chicago: University of Chicago Press, 1996), 156.

8. Quoted in Robert Westbrook, *John Dewey and American Democracy* (Ithaca: Cornell University Press, 1991), 54. On "statistical communities" and the "rise of the average man," see Daniel Boorstin, *The Americans: The Democratic Experience* (New York: Random House, 1973), 167–73.

9. Galton published *Inquiries into Human Faculty and Its Development* in 1883; see Florence L. Goodenough, *Mental Testing: Its History, Principles, and Applications* (New York: Rinehart & Co., 1949), 40, and Raymond E. Fancher, *The Intelligence Men: Makers of the IQ Controversy* (New York: W. W. Norton, 1985), 41–44.

10. Cattell, who worked with Galton after completing his dissertation in experimental psychology with Wilhelm Wundt at the University of Leipzig, also focused on speed as a measure of intelligence in 1886. In 1890 he published a series of tests in *Mind,* aimed at predicting success in college; Goodenough, *Mental Testing,* 40, 41; Fancher, *The Intelligence Men,* 44, 46–49.

11. Geneviève Paicheler, *L'invention de la psychologie moderne* (Paris: Éditions L'Harmattan, 1992), 12–15; Goodenough, *Mental Testing,* 43, 46–51, 65; Fancher, *The Intelligence Men,* 66–68, 71–72.

12. Clark University was a pioneering center of psychological research under the influence of G. Stanley Hall; see Dorothy Ross, *G. Stanley Hall: The Psychologist as Prophet* (Chicago: University of Chicago Press, 1972), 352–55.

13. Loren Baritz, *The Servants of Power: A History of the Use of Social Science in American Industry* (Middletown: Wesleyan University Press, 1960), 35–39, 44, 70; Matthew Hale, Jr., *Human Science and Social Order: Hugo Münsterberg and the Origins of Applied Psychology* (Philadelphia: Temple University Press, 1980), 154.

14. On Binet's influence, see Michael M. Sokal, ed., *Psychological Testing and American Society, 1890–1930* (New Brunswick: Rutgers University Press, 1987), 13, 47, 61–65, 146–47.

15. Raymond E. Fancher, *The Intelligence Men*, 80–82, 102–4, 153; Paula S. Fass, "The IQ: A Cultural and Historical Framework," *American Journal of Education* 89 (August 1980): 434.

16. Daniel J. Kevles, "Testing the Army's Intelligence: Psychologists and the Military in World War I," *Journal of American History* 55 (December 1968): 565–81.

17. One will find informative biographical sketches of Walter Van Dyke Bingham, Walter Dill Scott, Edward Kellog Strong, Jr., Edward Lee Thorndike, and Robert Mearns Yerkes in *Biographical Dictionary of Psychology*, ed. Leonard Zusne (Westport: Greenwood Press, 1984), 47–48, 387–88, 414, 426–27, 473–74.

18. Robert M. Yerkes, ed., *Psychological Examining in the United States Army, Memoirs of the National Academy of Sciences* (Washington, D.C.: GPO, 1921), 15: 299; see also Carl C. Brigham, *A Study of American Intelligence* (Princeton: Princeton University Press, 1923).

19. Yerkes, *Psychological Examining*, 327; see also John Carson, "Army Alpha, Army Brass, and the Search for Army Intelligence," *Isis* 84 (1983): 294–96.

20. Yerkes, *Psychological Examining*, 785; see also David M. Kennedy, *Over Here: The First World War and American Society* (New York: Oxford University Press, 1980), 188, n. 118.

21. Yerkes, *Psychological Examining*, 425.

22. Carson, "Army Alpha," 299, 294; Yerkes, *Psychological Examining*, 497.

23. "The Lippmann-Terman Debate: The Mental Age of Americans (1922)," in *The IQ Controversy: Critical Readings*, ed. N. J. Block and Gerald Dworkin (New York: Pantheon Books, 1976), 4–38.

24. Yerkes, *Psychological Testing*, 425.

25. Nicholas Lemann, "The Structure of Success in America," *Atlantic Monthly* (August 1995): 48; and Stephen Jay Gould, *The Mismeasure of Man* (New York: W. W. Norton, 1981), 195.

26. John William Ward, "The Meaning of Lindbergh's Flight," in *Red, White, and Blue: Men, Books, and Ideas in American Culture* (New York: Oxford University Press, 1969), 21–37.

27. Herbert Hoover, *American Individualism* (Garden City: Doubleday, Page & Co., 1922), 24–25.

28. John Dewey, *The Public and Its Problems* (New York: Henry Holt, 1927), 181; idem, *Individualism Old and New* (New York: Minton, Balch & Co., 1930), 24.

29. André Siegfried, *America Comes of Age: A French Analysis,* trans. H. H. Hemming and Doris Hemming (New York: Harcourt, Brace & Co., 1927), 174.

30. Nicholas Lemann, "The Great Sorting," *Atlantic Monthly* (September 1995): 84–100.

31. Horace Kallen, "Behaviorism," in *Encyclopedia of the Social Sciences,* 495–98.

32. His relationship to the Army was rocky; see Kerry W. Buckley, *Mechanical Man: John Broadus Watson and the Beginnings of Behaviorism* (New York: Guilford Press, 1989), 39–41, 99–111; David Cohen, *J. B. Watson, The Founder of Behaviourism: A Biography* (London: Routledge & Kegan Paul, 1979), 107–8.

33. John B. Watson, "Psychology as a Behaviorist Views It," *Psychological Review* 20 (1913): 158–77; idem, "An Attempted Formulation of the Scope of Behavior Psychology," *Psychological Review* 24 (September 1917): 329; note Watson's strictly physiological definition of attitude as explained in Donald Fleming, "Attitude: The History of a Concept," *Perspectives in American History* 1 (1967): 337–38.

34. See Marie Jahoda, "The Migration of Psychoanalysis: Its Impact on American Psychology," in *The Intellectual Migration: Europe and America, 1930–1960,* ed. Donald Fleming and Bernard Bailyn (Cambridge: Harvard University Press, Belknap Press, 1969), 425.

35. Philip J. Pauly, *Controlling Life: Jacques Loeb and the Engineering Ideal in Biology* (New York: Oxford University Press, 1987), 176.

36. See Ross, *G. Stanley Hall,* 420.

37. Some representative articles are V. V. Anderson, "A Psychiatric Guide for Employment," *Personnel Journal* 6 (1928): 417–41; James R. Angell, "Reasons and Plans for Research Relating to Industrial Personnel," *Journal of Personnel Research* 1 (1923): 1–6; E. J. Asher, "The Association Test as a Means of Determining the Relative Familiarity of Retail Stores," *Journal of Applied Psychology* 12 (1928): 437–46; John Wallace Baird, "The Legibility of a Telephone Directory," *Journal of Applied Psychology* 1 (1917): 30–37; Marion A. Bills, "Social Status of the Clerical Worker and His Permanence on the Job," *Journal of Applied Psychology* 9 (1925): 424–27; Alex. C. Crockett, "Testing Apprentices for the Burroughs Adding Machine Company," *Journal of Personnel Research* 5 (1927): 259–66; Samuel Gompers, "Coöperation of Workers in Study of Industrial Personnel Matters," *Journal of Personnel Research* 1 (1923): 53–55; A. J. Snow, "Labor Turnover and Mental Alertness Test Scores," *Journal of Applied Psychology* 7 (1923): 285–90; L. L. Thurstone, "Mental Tests for Prospective Telegraphers, A Study of the Diagnostic Value of Mental Tests for Predicting Ability to Learn Telegraphy," *Journal of Applied Psychology* 3 (1919): 110–17.

38. Kerry W. Buckley, "The Selling of a Psychologist: John Broadus Watson and the Application of Behavioral Techniques of Advertising," *Journal of the History of the Behavioral Sciences* 18 (July 1982): 207–21; Stephen Fox, *The Mirror Makers: A History of American Advertising and Its Creators* (New York: William Morrow & Co.,

1984), 85–86, insists that Watson's guidance at J. Walter Thompson was more symbolic than real; see also Peggy J. Kreshel, "John B. Watson at J. Walter Thompson: The Legitimation of 'Science' in Advertising," *Journal of Advertising* 19 (1990): 49–59.

39. J. Walter Thompson Company Archives. *General Platform on Johnson & Johnson Baby Powder* (1924); *Johnson & Johnson Advertisements; Report of Investigation for Market of Johnson & Johnson Baby Talcum* (October 1924); *J. Walter Thompson Company Newsletter* 43 (Sept. 4, 1924); 90 (July 23, 1925); 96 (Sept. 3, 1925); *Johnson & Johnson Account History* (1926); Duke University Special Collections Library, Durham, North Carolina.

40. *Johnson & Johnson Account History* (1926).

41. The following statement is rather typical of the pursuit of the average: "If there is in reality such a thing as an average American town, then every element which goes to make up the life of its inhabitants is of vital importance to all manufacturers, to all distributors of merchandise, to all advertising men, to all students of industrial and economic problems. For a national market is merely an enlargement of such an average community. If it is possible to find out what the inhabitants of the average American town eat, what they wear, how they spend their money, where they seek pleasure, how they study to advance themselves, then we are much nearer to . . . the answers to these questions when they are applied to a whole nation. It was early in 1925 that the Digest was prompted to consider this generalization, 'the average American town.' The problem was first to find a community which nearly approached this generalization and then to study it by every available process of analysis." *Zanesville and 36 Other American Communities: A Study of Markets and of the Telephone As a Market Index* (New York: Literary Digest, 1927), 14. The study of this Ohio town was performed in 1926 by R. O. Eastman & Co., a well-known market research firm.

42. Jean Matter Mandler and George Mandler, "The Diaspora of Experimental Psychology: The Gestaltists and Others," in *The Intellectual Migration,* 376.

43. Jürgen Habermas, *The Structural Transformation of the Public Sphere: An Inquiry into a Category of Bourgeois Society,* trans. Thomas Burger (Cambridge: MIT Press, 1991), 240; and Mona Ozouf, "Esprit public," in *Dictionnaire critique de la révolution française,* ed. François Furet and Mona Ozouf (Paris: Flammarion, 1988), 711–19.

44. James Bryce, *The American Commonwealth* (London: Macmillan & Co., 1889), 2:209–334.

45. Edward L. Bernays, *Crystallizing Public Opinion* (New York: Boni & Liveright, 1923), 68; see also William Leach, *Land of Desire: Merchants, Power, and the Rise of a New American Culture* (New York: Pantheon Books, 1993), 319–22.

46. For a concise treatment, see Susan Herbst, *Numbered Voices: How Opinion Polling Has Shaped American Politics* (Chicago: University of Chicago Press, 1993). On V. O. Key's paraphrasing of Lippmann's undifferentiated citizenry to describe the nineteenth century in his *Public Opinion and American Democracy* (New York: Alfred

A. Knopf, 1961), see Robert H. Wiebe, *Self-Rule: A Cultural History of American Culture* (Chicago: University of Chicago Press, 1995), 175. See also Moisi Ostrogorki, *La démocratie et les partis politiques* (1912; Paris: Librairie Arthème Fayard, 1993).

47. Floyd H. Allport, "Toward a Science of Public Opinion," *Public Opinion Quarterly* 1 (January 1937): 23; Harwood L. Childs, *An Introduction to Public Opinion* (New York: John Wiley & Sons, 1940), 48.

48. *Current Biography* (New York: W. W. Wilson Co., 1952), 200–202; *The New Yorker,* March 2, 1940, 20–22.

49. C. Harwell Wells, "The *Fortune* Survey and the Origins of the Scientific Opinion Poll" (unpublished paper, 1993); Wells elaborates in the last chapter of "Redrawing America's Boundaries: Market Research, 1900–1940" (Ph.D. diss., University of Virginia, 1998); see also Daniel Boorstin, *The Americans: The Democratic Experience,* 155–56.

50. George Gallup and Saul Forbes Rae, *The Pulse of Democracy: The Public-Opinion Poll and How It Works* (New York: Simon & Schuster, 1940), 6, 60; the "Average Opinion of Mankind" is the title of the last chapter.

51. Ibid., 289.

52. Theodor W. Adorno, "Freudian Theory and the Pattern of Fascist Propaganda (1951)," in *The Essential Frankfurt School Reader,* ed. Andrew Arato and Eike Gebhardt (New York: Urizen Books, 1978), 132; see also Max Horkheimer, "The End of Reason," in *The Essential Frankfurt School Reader,* 41, and Martin Jay, *The Dialectical Imagination: A History of the Frankfurt School and the Institute of Social Research, 1923–1950* (Boston: Little, Brown, 1973).

53. Hannah Arendt, *The Origins of Totalitarianism,* 2d enl. ed. (New York: Meridian Books, 1960), 315–16, 344–45; on Le Bon, see Serge Moscovici, *L'âge des foules,* rev. ed. (Paris: Éditions Complexe, 1991), 73–145.

54. Theodor W. Adorno, "Scientific Experiences of a European Scholar in America," trans. Donald Fleming, in *The Intellectual Migration,* 338–70.

55. Idem, "On the Fetish-Character in Music and the Regression of Listening (1938)," in *The Essential Frankfurt School Reader,* 276.

56. Kallen, "Behaviorism," in *Encyclopedia of the Social Sciences,* 2:495–98.

57. Herbert Marcuse, *One-Dimensional Man: Studies in the Ideology of Advanced Industrial Society* (Boston: Beacon Press, 1964).

58. As quoted in Jean M. Mandler and George Mandler, "The Diaspora of Experimental Psychology: The Gestaltists and Others," in *The Intellectual Migration,* 379; on Neumann, see Lewis A. Coser, *Refugee Scholars in America: Their Impact and Their Experiences* (New Haven: Yale University Press, 1984), 197–201.

59. Lionel Trilling, *The Liberal Imagination: Essays on Literature and Society* (New York: Viking, 1950), 237; see also James H. Jones, *Alfred C. Kinsey: A Public/Private Life* (New York: W. W. Norton, 1997).

60. Adorno, "Scientific Experiences," 368–69.

61. Carl Schmitt, *La notion de politique* (1927), trans. Marie-Louise Steinhauser, preface by Julien Freund (Paris: Calmann-Lévy, 1972), 131–53.

CHAPTER FOUR

1. Adam Smith, *An Inquiry into the Nature and the Causes of the Wealth of Nations* (London: Printed for W. Strahan & T. Cadell, 1776), book one, chap. viii, 99.

2. On this idea, see Olivier Zunz, "The Synthesis of Social Change: Reflections on American Social History," in *Reliving the Past: The Worlds of Social History,* ed. Olivier Zunz (Chapel Hill: University of North Carolina Press, 1985), 95; idem, "Recentrer l'histoire américaine," in *Chantiers d'histoire américaine,* ed. Jean Heffer and François Weil (Paris: Belin, 1994), 433–55; and as background for this chapter and the next one, idem, "Class," in *Encyclopedia of the United States in the Twentieth Century,* ed. Stanley I. Kutler (New York: Charles Scribner's Sons, 1996), 1:195–220.

3. Herein lies my disagreement with the second part of Robert H. Wiebe's book, *Self-Rule: A Cultural History of American Democracy* (Chicago: University of Chicago Press, 1995), 113–80, as I explain in my review, "History by Affirmation: The End of Democracy," *Reviews in American History* 24 (June 1996): 299–303.

4. Jürgen Kocka, "The Middle Classes in Europe," *Journal of Modern History* 67 (December 1995): 801.

5. As illustrated by the "kitchen debate" between Nixon and Khrushchev; see John Patrick Diggins, *The Proud Decades: America in War and in Peace, 1941–1960* (New York: W. W. Norton, 1988), 339.

6. As Alfred D. Chandler, Jr., has shown, in such fields as petroleum, rubber, machinery, food products, and transportation equipment, the 200 largest companies (measured in assets) already well entrenched in the American landscape by World War I were still among the giant companies in the 1970s; see his *The Visible Hand: The Managerial Revolution in American Business* (Cambridge: Harvard University Press, Belknap Press, 1977), 285–376, and idem, with the assistance of Takashi Hikino, *Scale and Scope: The Dynamics of Industrial Capitalism* (Cambridge: Harvard University Press, Belknap Press, 1990), 638–65; see also Thomas K. McCraw, *Prophets of Regulation: Charles Francis Adams, Louis D. Brandeis, James M. Landis, Alfred E. Kahn* (Cambridge: Harvard University Press, Belknap Press, 1984), 75.

7. C. Wright Mills, *White Collar: The American Middle Classes* (New York: Oxford University Press, 1951), ix–xiv, 63–76.

8. Olivier Zunz, *Making America Corporate, 1870–1920* (Chicago: University of Chicago Press, 1990), 126–27.

9. See, for instance, Alan Dawley, *Struggles for Justice: Social Responsibility and the Liberal State* (Cambridge: Harvard University Press, Belknap Press, 1991).

10. U.S. Department of Education, National Center for Education Statistics, *Digest*

NOTES TO PAGES 77–78

of Education Statistics (Washington, D.C.: GPO, 1988), 98; David B. Tyack, *The One Best System: A History of American Urban Education* (Cambridge: Harvard University Press, 1974), 57; see also Olivier Zunz, "Class," and Kenneth J. Lipartito and Paul J. Miranti, Jr., "The Professions," in *Encyclopedia of the United States in the Twentieth Century,* ed. Stanley I. Kutler, 1:201–b, 3:1415a–b; François Dubet, "Lycéens," in *Dictionnaire encyclopédique de l'éducation et de la formation,* ed. Claude Durand-Prinborgne, Jean Hassenforder, and François de Singly (Paris: Nathan, 1994), 635–38.

11. Reed Ueda, *Avenues to Adulthood: The Origins of the High School and Social Mobility in an American Suburb* (New York: Cambridge University Press, 1987), 186–219; see also idem, "Suburban Social Change and Educational Reform: The Case of Somerville, Massachusetts, 1912–1924," *Social Science History* 3 (October 1979): 167–203; and idem, "The High School and Social Mobility in a Streetcar Suburb: Somerville, Massachusetts, 1870–1910," *Journal of Interdisciplinary History* 14 (Spring 1984): 751–71.

12. Ueda, *Avenues to Adulthood,* 197–98; see also Joseph F. Kett, *Rites of Passage: Adolescence in America, 1790 to the Present* (New York: Basic Books, 1977), 237.

13. John Dewey, *The School and Society,* 1899, ed. Jo Ann Boydston, with preface by Joe R. Burnett (Carbondale: Southern Illinois University Press; London: Feffer & Simons, 1980), 38.

14. Their conclusions prompted important comparative studies of education and mobility in other industrialized nations and a still ongoing debate on the merits of the American case; for a summary, see Zunz, "Class," in *Encyclopedia of the United States in the Twentieth Century,* ed. Stanley I. Kutler, 1:199b, 206b, 207a; and Michael Lind, *The Next American Nation: The New Nationalism and the Fourth American Revolution* (New York: Free Press, 1995), 260, on the white supremacist dimension of the mobility argument.

15. Simon N. Patten, *The New Basis of Civilization* (New York: Macmillan, 1907), 69.

16. See Daniel M. Fox, *The Discovery of Abundance: Simon N. Patten and the Transformation of Social Theory* (Ithaca: Cornell University Press, 1967), 108–9; John R. Everett, *Religion in Economics: A Study of John Bates Clark, Richard T. Ely, and Simon N. Patten* (Morningside Heights: King's Crown Press, 1946), 122–24. Patten's voice was echoed by Father Ryan's in his Catholic University dissertation, *A Living Wage* (New York: Macmillan, 1906); see also Benjamin K. Hunnicutt, *Work without End: Abandoning Shorter Hours for the Right to Work* (Philadelphia: Temple University Press, 1988), 33–34, 88–98, 152, 313.

17. Walter Lippmann, *Drift and Mastery: An Attempt to Diagnose the Current Unrest,* rev. introduction and notes by William E. Leuchtenburg (1914; Madison: University of Wisconsin Press, 1985), 56. On the coming of mass consumption, see Daniel Boorstin's "consumption communities" in *The Americans: The Democratic Experience*

(New York: Vintage Books, 1974), 89–164; and Eric Lampard, "Structural Changes: Introductory Essay," in *Inventing Times Square: Commerce and Culture at the Crossroads of the World,* ed. William R. Taylor (New York: Russell Sage Foundation, 1991), 16–35.

18. Olivier Zunz, *The Changing Face of Inequality: Urbanization, Industrial Development, and Immigrants in Detroit, 1880–1920* (Chicago: University of Chicago Press, 1982), 218–40.

19. Ibid., 241–58.

20. On C. D. Wright, see Mary O. Furner, "Knowing Capitalism: Public Investigation and the Labor Question in the Long Progressive Era," in *The State and Economic Knowledge: The American and British Experiences,* ed. Mary O. Furner and Barry Supple (New York: Cambridge University Press; Washington, D.C.: Woodrow Wilson International Center for Scholars, 1990), 241–86; Margaret Frances Byington, *Homestead: The Households of a Mill Town,* issued as part of *The Pittsburgh Survey,* ed. Paul U. Kellogg (New York: Charities Publication Committee, 1910).

21. Zunz, *Changing Face of Inequality,* 234.

22. Idem, *Making America Corporate,* 132–48.

23. I am borrowing this translation from Goetz A. Briefs, *The Proletariat: A Challenge to Western Civilization* (New York: McGraw-Hill, 1937), 193; one will find the standard translation "all Socialist utopias came to nothing on roast beef and apple pie" in Werner Sombart, *Why Is There No Socialism in the United States?* trans. Patricia M. Hocking and C. T. Husbands, edited and introduced by C. T. Husbands, foreword by Michael Harrington (1906; White Plains: M. E. Sharpe, 1976), 106.

24. John Rogers Commons et al., *History of Labour in the United States,* 4 vols. (New York: Macmillan, 1918–1935); Selig Perlman, *A Theory of the Labor Movement* (New York: Macmillan, 1928), 154–55, 162–69, 182–99.

25. David A. Wells, *Recent Economic Changes and Their Effect on the Production and Distribution of Wealth and the Well-Being of Society* (New York: D. Appleton & Co., 1889), 26; Joseph Dorfman, *The Economic Mind in American Civilization,* vol. 3: *1865–1918* (New York: Viking, 1949), 131–36; Daniel T. Rodgers, *The Work Ethic in Industrial America, 1850–1920* (Chicago: University of Chicago Press, 1978), 117–22; Hunnicutt, *Work without End,* 42, 56–59, 90–91, 152. C. Harwell Wells elaborates on this point in "Redrawing America's Boundaries: Market Research, 1900–1940" (Ph.D. diss., University of Virginia, 1998).

26. Jack High, "Economic Thought," in *Encyclopedia of the United States in the Twentieth Century,* ed. Stanley I. Kutler, 3:1289–90; see also Alan R. Berolzheimer, "A Nation of Consumers: Mass Consumption, Middle-Class Standards of Living, and American National Identity, 1910–1950" (Ph.D. diss., University of Virginia, 1996), 78–92.

27. Ellis W. Hawley, "Economic Inquiry and the State in New Era America: Antistatist Corporatism and Positive Statism in Uneasy Coexistence," in *The State and*

Economic Knowledge, ed. Furner and Supple, 287–324; see also William Leach, *Land of Desire: Merchants, Power, and the Rise of A New American Culture* (New York: Pantheon Books, 1993), 352–78.

28. Josephine Young Case and Everett Needham Case, *Owen D. Young and American Enterprise: A Biography* (Boston: David R. Godine, 1982), 247, 252–53, 267, 270–71.

29. Meg Jacobs, "The Promise of Purchasing Power: Edward A. Filene and the Creation of an American Consumer Society" (Seminar paper, University of Virginia, 1994).

30. *Business Cycles and Unemployment: An Investigation under the Auspices of the National Bureau of Economic Research Made for a Committee of the President's Conference on Unemployment* (New York: McGraw-Hill, 1923), 144–45.

31. Henry S. Dennison, "Management," in *Recent Economic Changes in the United States: Report of the Committee on Recent Economic Changes of the President's Conference on Unemployment,* Herbert Hoover, Chairman (New York: McGraw-Hill, 1929), 2:524. Labor historians often dispute such optimistic assessments; see Frank Stricker, "Affluence for Whom?—Another Look at Prosperity and the Working Classes in the 1920s," in *Labor History Reader,* ed. Daniel J. Leab (Urbana: University of Illinois Press, 1985), 288–316.

32. Roy Dickinson, "An Old Industry to Be Advertised by its Labor Unions: Woodcarvers' Unions Plan to Revive an Ancient Art by Modern Methods," *Printers' Ink* 107 (May 29, 1919): 2–12; idem, "Ideas or Industrial Warfare?" *Printers' Ink* 116 (September 29, 1921): 33–43; idem, "Lower Prices and Better Selling as the Key to Normal Times," *Printers' Ink* 117 (October 6, 1921): 3–7, 145; idem, "Hooverizing the Department of Commerce: How This Government Department Has Been Reorganized to Meet the Actual Needs of American Business," *Printers' Ink* 118 (October 13, 1921): 28–36; idem, "Mars as a Sales Outlet: A One-Sided Discussion on Wages, Buying Power and Production in Relation to Advertising," *Printers' Ink* 119 (October 20, 1921): 128–42; idem, "Advertising Enables Manufacturer to Control His Production: No Longer at the Mercy of Jobbers, Brokers and Other Manufacturers if He Has a Standard Branded Line That Is Known to the Public," *Printers' Ink* 120 (October 27, 1921): 19–20; idem, "Getting the Sales Force and Factory Workers Acquainted: How Several Big Manufacturers Are Increasing Effort by a Two-Sided Appeal," *Printers' Ink* 122 (November 10, 1921): 57–60.

33. Idem, "Ideas or Industrial Warfare?" 33.

34. William T. Foster and Waddill Catchings, *Profits* (Boston: Houghton Mifflin Co., 1925), 234; see also William T. Foster, *Money* (Boston: Houghton Mifflin Co., 1923); and Leach, *Land of Desire,* 275–79. For a good introduction to Keynesianism, see James Tobin, "Consumption Function," in *International Encyclopedia of the Social Sciences,* ed. David L. Sills (New York: Macmillan & Free Press), 3:358–69.

35. *Recent Economic Changes in the United States,* 2:885; see also Hunnicutt, *Work without End,* 58.

36. Stanley Lebergott provides this high estimate in *The Americans: An Economic Record* (New York: W. W. Norton, 1984), 431–44, and *The American Economy: Income, Wealth, and Want* (Princeton: Princeton University Press, 1976), 290; according to Lebergott's computations, automobile ownership declined to 55 percent of families in 1935–36 before rising again to 58 percent in 1942; statistics for motor vehicles are available in *Historical Statistics of the United States: Colonial Times to 1970* (Washington, D.C.: GPO, 1976), 2:717, beginning only in 1948 with 54 percent of American families owning automobiles and 59 percent in 1950; for less rosy a picture of the twenties than Lebergott's, see Ronald C. Tobey, *Technology as Freedom: The New Deal and the Electrical Modernization of the American Home* (Berkeley: University of California Press, 1996), 28–39.

37. John Raskob, "Everyone Ought to Be Rich," *Ladies' Home Journal* 46 (August 1929): 9, 36.

38. See Kocka, "The Middle Classes in Europe," 804; see also idem, *White-Collar Workers in America, 1890–1940: A Social-Political History in International Perspective,* trans. Maura Kealey (Beverly Hills: Sage Publications, 1980), 16–33.

39. For general background on the history of the working class in America, see Joshua Freeman, Nelson Lichtenstein, Stephen Brier, *Who Built America? Working People and the Nation's Economy, Politics, Culture, and Society,* vol 2: *From the Gilded Age to the Present* (New York: Pantheon Books, 1991); Robert H. Zieger, *American Workers, American Union, 1920–1985,* 2d ed. (Baltimore: Johns Hopkins University Press, 1986), 3–61; and Olivier Zunz, "Class," in *Encyclopedia of the United States in the Twentieth Century,* ed. Stanley I. Kutler, 1:206.

40. Alan Brinkley, *Voices of Protest: Huey Long, Father Coughlin, and the Great Depression* (New York: Alfred A. Knopf, 1982), 199–200, 202.

41. Ibid., 145.

42. See James T. Patterson, *Grand Expectations: The United States, 1945–1974* (New York: Oxford University Press, 1996), 181.

43. On the Black bill, see Hunnicutt's *Work without End,* 3, 149–54, 157–59, 181–86, 240–49; Colin Gordon, *New Deals: Business, Labor, and Politics in America, 1920–1935* (New York: Cambridge University Press, 1994), 169; see also William E. Leuchtenburg, *Franklin D. Roosevelt and the New Deal, 1932–1940* (New York: Harper & Row, 1963), 56–57.

44. Hunnicutt, *Work without End,* 152.

45. On the proconsumers leanings of La Follette and Wagner, see Alan Brinkley, *The End of Reform: New Deal Liberalism in Recession and War* (New York: Alfred A. Knopf, 1995), 84; Hunnicutt, *Work without End,* 162–63.

46. Hunnicutt, *Work without End,* 172.

47. Gordon, *New Deals,* 183, 186–87; see also David R. Goldfield, "The South," in *Encyclopedia of the United States in the Twentieth Century,* ed. Stanley I. Kutler, 1: 68b–69b. For a view from a "center firm," see Case and Case, *Owen D. Young and American Enterprise,* 642–45.

48. Hunnicutt, *Work without End,* 195. Chairman of the Federal Reserve Board Marriner S. Eccles also believed that government spending would spur economic growth, but unlike Hopkins's emphasis on stimulating consumer demand with wages earned on public projects, Eccles viewed the government as a compensatory investing agent that would maintain the nation's price, profit, and credit system when banks and other financial institutions failed to invest in the economy; see William J. Barber, *Designs within Disorder: Franklin D. Roosevelt, the Economists, and the Shaping of American Economic Policy, 1933-1945* (New York: Cambridge University Press, 1996), 86–88.

49. Joseph B. Hubbard, ed., *Current Economic Policies: Selected Discussions* (New York: Henry Holt, 1934), 404–5; see also Gordon, *New Deals,* 169, 186.

50. *The National Recovery Administration: Report of the President's Committee of Industrial Analysis* (February 17, 1937), 2–3, 8.

51. Brinkley, *The End of Reform,* 46.

52. Robert M. Collins, *The Business Response to Keynes, 1929-1964* (New York: Columbia University Press, 1981), 62.

53. Brinkley, *The End of Reform,* 41.

54. Collins, *The Business Response to Keynes,* 63, 67, 69.

55. Brinkley, *The End of Reform,* 98.

56. Herbert Stein, *The Fiscal Revolution in America* (Chicago: University of Chicago Press, 1969), 109.

57. Ibid., 110–11; Collins, *The Business Response to Keynes,* 71. Brinkley attributes most of the argument to Leon Henderson; *The End of Reform,* 99.

58. Estimates for the New Deal years vary widely from a low of 3.4 percent in 1936 given by Larry C. Peppers, "Full Employment Surplus Analysis and Structural Change: The 1930s," *Explorations in Economic History* 10 (Winter 1973): 208, to a high of 5.4 percent in George T. Kurian, *Datapedia of the United States, 1790-2000: America Year By Year* (Lanham, MD: Bernan Press, 1994), 89, 441. For the Reagan years, see Richard H. K. Vietor, "Economic Performance" and Michael A. Bernstein, "Depressions and Recessions: The Business Cycle," in *Encyclopedia of the United States in the Twentieth Century,* ed. Stanley I. Kutler, 3:1177a–b, 1202b.

59. Collins, *The Business Response to Keynes,* 9, 10.

60. Barber, *Designs within Disorder,* 204.

61. Idem, "The Career of Alvin H. Hansen in the 1920s and 1930s: A Study in Intellectual Transformation," *History of Political Economy* 19 (Summer 1987): 204; their views, however, were too radical, and they had to settle for a compromise version of the full employment act.

62. As quoted in Steven Fraser's biography of Hillman, *Labor Will Rule: Sidney Hillman and the Rise of American Labor* (New York: Free Press, 1991), 260.

63. Ibid., 260; Brinkley, *The End of Reform,* 225.

64. Nelson Lichtenstein, *The Most Dangerous Man in Detroit: Walter Reuther and the Fate of American Labor* (New York: Basic Books, 1995), 175–93, 271–98.

65. David Morris Potter, *People of Plenty: Economic Abundance and the American Character* (Chicago: University of Chicago Press, 1954).

66. On the postwar social contract, see David L. Stebenne, "Introduction," Irwin M. Wall, "The French Social Contract: Conflict and Cooperation," Volker R. Berghahn, "The United States and the Shaping of West Germany's Social Compact," Andrew Gordon, "The Emergence of a Labor-Management Settlement in Japan, 1945–1960," David L. Stebenne, "The Postwar 'New Deal,'" and Charles S. Maier, "The Postwar Social Contract: Comment," *International Labor and Working-Class History* 50 (Fall 1996): 114–15, 116–24, 125–32, 133–39, 140–47, 148–56.

67. Marie Jahoda, "The Migration of Psychoanalysis: Its Impact on American Psychology," in *The Intellectual Migration: Europe and America, 1930–1960,* ed. Donald Fleming and Bernard Bailyn (Cambridge: Harvard University Press, Belknap Press, 1969), 432.

CHAPTER FIVE

1. As quoted in Merrill D. Peterson, *Lincoln in American Memory* (New York: Oxford University Press, 1994), 102. For variations, see *Recollected Words of Abraham Lincoln,* comp. and ed. Don E. Fehrenbacher and Virginia Fehrenbacher (Stanford: Stanford University Press, 1996), 122, 319, 502.

2. These were the new "politics of productivity," as Charles S. Maier has called them in "The Politics of Productivity: Foundations of American International Economic Policy after World War II," in *Between Power and Plenty: Foreign Economic Policies of the Advanced Industrial States,* ed. Peter J. Katzenstein (Madison: University of Wisconsin Press, 1978), 23–49; and "The Postwar Social Contract: Comment," *International Labor and Working-Class History* 50 (Fall 1996): 1148–56.

3. See Richard Hofstadter, *Social Darwinism in American Thought* (1955, rev. ed.; New York: G. Braziller, 1959). For an important corrective on the use of the term, see Robert C. Bannister, *Social Darwinism: Science and Myth in Anglo-American Social Thought* (Philadelphia: Temple University Press, 1979).

4. David Morris Potter, *People of Plenty: Economic Abundance and the American Character* (Chicago: University of Chicago Press, 1954), 102.

5. The idea of market stratification by price level came early to makers of technologically complex products; for instance, as early as 1910, Edison put on the market a line of phonographs with prices ranging for $200 to $12.50. But Edison and others did not specify the connection between price category and social class; see Susan Strasser, "Consumption," in *Encyclopedia of the United States in the Twentieth Century,* ed. Stanley I. Kutler (New York: Charles Scribner's Sons, 1996), 1021b–23b.

6. Richard S. Tedlow, *New and Improved: The Story of Mass Marketing in America* (New York: Basic Books, 1990), 150.

7. Alfred P. Sloan, Jr., *My Years with General Motors*, ed. John McDonald and Catherine Stevens (New York: Doubleday, 1964), 60, 61.

8. Tedlow, *New and Improved*, 159.

9. Idem, "Marketing," in *Encyclopedia of the United States*, ed. Stanley I. Kutler, 1058b; see also Daniel Boorstin, *The Americans: The Democratic Experience* (New York: Vintage Books, 1974), 551–55.

10. Sloan, *My Years*, 65.

11. Ibid., 137.

12. Lord and Thomas Agency, "Frigidaire, 1936, Phase 2 in a Problem of Mass Market Penetration," 1936, folder 79-10.1-95, Frigidaire Collection, GMI Alumni Foundation's Collection of Industrial History; I thank Shelley Nickles for this reference; Nickles elaborates on this point in "Object Lessons: Industrial Design, Household Appliances, and the American Middle Class in a Mass Consumer Society, 1920–1960" (Ph.D. diss., University of Virginia, 1998); see also Ronald C. Tobey, *Technology as Freedom: The New Deal and the Electrical Modernization of the American Home* (Berkeley: University of California Press, 1996).

13. Lord and Thomas Agency, "Frigidaire, 1936, Phase 2," folder 79-10.1-95; among the many titles on the therapeutic ethos of consumption, see Richard Wightman Fox and T. J. Jackson Lears, eds., *The Culture of Consumption: Critical Essays in American History, 1880–1980* (New York: Pantheon Books, 1983) and Lary May, ed., *Recasting America: Culture and Politics in the Age of the Cold War* (Chicago: University of Chicago Press, 1989).

14. On this concept, see Olivier Zunz, "The Synthesis of Social Change: Reflections on American Social History," in *Reliving the Past: The Worlds of Social History*, ed. Olivier Zunz (Chapel Hill: University of North Carolina Press, 1985), 95.

15. Richard Wightman Fox, "Epitaph for Middletown: Robert S. Lynd and the Analysis of Consumer Culture," in *Culture of Consumption*, ed. Fox and Lears, 101–41, 225–29; Robert Staughton Lynd and Helen Merrell Lynd, foreword by Clark Wissler, *Middletown: A Study in American Culture* (New York: Harcourt, Brace, 1929); Robert Staughton Lynd, "The People as Consumers," in *Recent Social Trends in the United States: Report of the President's Research Committee on Social Trends*, with a foreword by Herbert Hoover (New York: McGraw-Hill, 1933), 2:857–911; on the resistance to Lynd's speculative tone within the Hoover committee, see William A. Tobin, "Studying Society: The Making of Recent Social Trends in the United States, 1929–1933," *Theory and Society* 24 (August 1995): 537–65.

16. See Robert Bannister, *Sociology and Scientism: The American Quest for Objectivity* (Chapel Hill: University of North Carolina Press, 1987), 180; Chapin was a director of the SSRC from 1923 to 1928; see the entry on him in *American Men and Women of Science: Social and Behavioral Sciences*, 12th ed. (New York: Jaques Cattell Press, 1973), 1:373.

17. Bannister, *Sociology and Scientism*, 157; other efforts were underway in the 1920s. J. Walter Thompson's researchers working under Paul Cherington constructed

an ABCD home classification scheme connecting housing styles with social classes; see C. Harwell Wells, "Redrawing America's Boundaries: Market Research, 1900–1940" (Ph.D. diss., University of Virginia, 1998).

18. F. Stuart Chapin, "Socio-Economic Status: Some Preliminary Results of Measurement," *American Journal of Sociology*, 38 (1932): 581; for a useful analysis, see Alan R. Berolzheimer, "A Nation of Consumers: Mass Consumption, Middle-Class Standards of Living, and American National Identity, 1910–1950" (Ph.D. diss., University of Virginia, 1996), 323–36. Chapin's earnestness and lack of humor are ably rendered by Paul Fussell, *Class: A Guide through the American Status System* (New York: Summit Books, 1983), 87–96, 194–97.

19. See the entry on W. Lloyd Warner by Solon T. Kimball, *International Encyclopedia of the Social Sciences*, ed. David Sills (New York: Free Press, 1979), *Biographical Supplement*, 18:793; and Harold W. Pfautz and Otis D. Duncan, "A Critical Evaluation of Warner's Work in Community Stratification," *American Sociological Review* 15 (April 1950): 205–15.

20. Richard Gillespie, *Manufacturing Knowledge: A History of the Hawthorne Experiments* (New York: Cambridge University Press, 1991), 156.

21. On *Babbitt*, see Neil Harris, *Cultural Excursions: Marketing Appetites and Cultural Tastes in Modern America* (Chicago: University of Chicago Press, 1990), 193.

22. W. Lloyd Warner, *American Life: Dream and Reality* (Chicago: University of Chicago Press, 1953), 83; idem, with Marchia Meeker and Kenneth Eells, *Social Class in America; A Manual of Procedure for the Measurement of Social Status* (New York: Harper, 1960), 233, 239.

23. Warner, *American Life*, 22.

24. Henry A. Wallace, *The Century of the Common Man*, ed. Russell Lord (New York: Reynal & Hitchcock, 1943), 56–57.

25. All of these terms are defined in Warner, *American Life*, 74–77.

26. Vance Packard, *The Hidden Persuaders* (New York: Pocket Books, 1957), 98.

27. C. Wright Mills, review of *The Social Life of a Modern Community*, vol. 1, Yankee City Series, ed. by W. Lloyd Warner and Paul S. Lunt, *American Sociological Review* 7 (April 1942): 264–68. Penetrating criticism would also come in due course from social historian Stephan Thernstrom, who showed that there was no satisfactory way to estimate individual mobility patterns from Warner's scheme or to apprehend social change. Thernstrom also exposed Warner's naïve use of historical evidence and reliance more on hearsay than serious historical investigation in "Further Reflections on the Yankee City Series: The Pitfalls of Ahistorical Social Science," appendix to *Poverty and Progress: Social Mobility in a Nineteenth-Century City* (Cambridge: Harvard University Press, 1964), 225–39.

28. Ernest Dichter, *The Psychology of Everyday Living* (New York: Barnes & Noble, 1947), 212, 235–36; see also Daniel Horowitz, *Vance Packard and American Social Criticism* (Chapel Hill: University of North Carolina Press, 1994), 105–6.

29. Pierre Martineau, "Social Classes and Spending Behavior," *Journal of Market-*

ing 23 (October 1958): 125; idem, "It's Time to Research the Consumer," *Harvard Business Review,* 33 (July–August 1955): 45–54; see Dennis Grant Martin, "Consumer Symbolicum: The Advertising Legacy of Pierre Martineau" (Ph.D. diss., University of Illinois at Urbana-Champaign, 1985), 46.

30. Herbert Solow, "The Ripe Problems of United Fruit," *Fortune* 59 (March 1959): 97–100, 230, 232; see the entry on Burleigh Gardner in *American Men and Women of Science: Social and Behavioral Sciences,* 13th ed. (New York: Jaques Cattell Press, 1978), 420.

31. Paul F. Lazarsfeld, "An Episode in the History of Social Research: A Memoir," in *The Intellectual Migration: Europe and America, 1930–1960,* ed. Donald Fleming and Bernard Bailyn (Cambridge: Harvard University Press, Belknap Press, 1969): 272, 282–83, 300; idem, "The Psychological Aspects of Marketing Research," *Harvard Business Review* 13 (October 1934): 63, 64, 65–66. Lazarsfeld's work shows the difficulty of relying on the dichotomy Mark Smith establishes between "purposivists" and "objective service intellectuals" in *Social Science in the Crucible: The American Debate over Objectivity and Purpose, 1918–1941* (Durham: Duke University Press, 1994).

32. As recalled by Raymond Boudon in his introduction to Paul F. Lazarsfeld, *On Social Research and Its Language* (Chicago: University of Chicago Press, 1993), 8.

33. Werner Sombart wrote *Why Is There No Socialism in the United States?* in 1906 (edited and introduced by C. T. Husbands, foreword by Michael Harrington; White Plains: M. E. Sharpe, 1976).

34. Dichter, *Psychology of Everyday Living,* 113; Friedan's critique of motivational researchers is in *The Feminine Mystique* (New York: W. W. Norton, 1963), 208, 211, 226–29, 389.

35. See Daniel Horowitz's unpublished paper: "The Birth of a Salesman: Ernest Dichter and the Objects of Desire," n.d.

36. Paul Kleppner, "Critical Realignments and Electoral Systems," in *The Evolution of American Electoral Systems,* ed. Paul Kleppner et al. (Westport: Greenwood Press, 1981), 24; Michael E. McGerr, *The Decline of Popular Politics: The American North, 1865–1928* (New York: Oxford University Press, 1986), 5.

37. Wesley Mitchell, "The Backward Art of Spending Money," *American Economic Review* 2 (June 1912): 269–81.

38. Walter Lippmann, *Drift and Mastery: An Attempt to Diagnose the Current Unrest* (1914), rev. introduction and notes by William E. Leuchtenburg (Madison: University of Wisconsin Press, 1985), 54.

39. Kathryn Kish Sklar, *Florence Kelley and the Nation's Work: The Rise of Women's Political Culture, 1830–1900* (New Haven: Yale University Press, 1995), 309; Theda Skocpol, *Protecting Soldiers and Mothers: The Political Origins of Social Policy in the United States* (Cambridge: Harvard University Press, Belknap Press, 1992), 382–96; see also Allis Rosenberg Wolfe, "Women, Consumerism, and the National Consum-

ers' League in the Progressive Era, 1900–1923," *Labor History* 16 (Summer 1975): 378–92.

40. Rexmond C. Cochrane, *Measures for Progress: A History of the National Bureau of Standards* (Washington, D.C.: U.S. Department of Commerce, 1966), 302, 481–82.

41. See Norman Isaac Silber, *Test and Protest: The Influence of Consumers Union* (New York: Holmes & Meier, 1983), 4, 18. Membership figures are hard to come by; in early 1931, Schlink mentioned a figure of 15,000 subscribers but that was a fivefold increase from the preceding year; Frederick Schlink to Alice Edward, Executive Secretary of the American Home Economics Association, March 20, 1931, in box "consumer standardization," unmarked folder, AHEA archives, Alexandria, Va. I thank Maire Murphy for this reference. For other aspects of the consumer movement, see Rachel Bowlby, "Soft Sell: Marketing Rhetoric in Feminist Criticism," in *The Sex of Things: Gender and Consumption in Historical Perspective,* ed. Victoria de Grazia, with Ellen Furlough (Berkeley: University of California Press, 1996), 387, n. 3; Charles F. McGovern, "Sold American: Inventing the Consumer, 1890–1940" (Ph.D. diss., Harvard University, 1993), 181, 215, 226–53, 254–59, for a good analysis of Stuart Chase's and F. J. Schlink's, *Your Money's Worth: A Study in the Waste of the Consumer's Dollar* (New York: Macmillan, 1927) and the founding of Consumers' Research, Inc. See also Dana Frank, *Purchasing Power: Consumer Organizing, Gender, and the Seattle Labor Movement, 1919–1929* (New York: Cambridge University Press, 1994) for a case study of consumerism, labor activism, and gender relations within the working class; Richard L. D. Morse, ed., *The Consumer Movement: Lectures by Colston E. Warne* (Manhattan, Kansas: Family Economics Trust Press, 1993) for a discussion of the consumer movement by a founder of the Consumers Union; and Peter E. Samson, "The Emergence of a Consumer Interest in America, 1870–1930" (Ph.D. diss., University of Chicago, 1980) on the rise of consumer consciousness in the United States.

42. Although the trends Lizabeth Cohen describes in *Making a New Deal: Industrial Workers in Chicago, 1919–1939* (New York: Cambridge University Press, 1990), are correct, her tightly argued chronology is designed to make workers appear as if they were the main agents of New Deal reforms.

43. Reinhard Bendix and Seymour Martin Lipset, eds., *Class, Status, and Power: Social Stratification in Comparative Perspective* (New York: Free Press, 1953), especially the first edition, significantly revised in 1966.

44. Below them, Martineau placed 19.5 percent of the Chicago population in a "lower-lower" category of "unskilled laborers," "racial immigrants," and "people in nonrespectable occupations"; see his "Social Classes and Spending Behavior," 122–28, passim; idem, *Motivation in Advertising: Motives That Make People Buy* (New York: McGraw-Hill, 1957), 164.

45. Martineau, *Motivation in Advertising,* 164–65.

46. Martineau, "Social Classes and Spending Behavior," 126–29, passim.

47. W. Lloyd Warner, "A Methodological Note," in Horace R. Cayton and St. Clair Drake, *Black Metropolis: A Study of Negro Life in a Northern City,* with an introduction by William Julius Wilson (1945; Chicago: University of Chicago Press, 1993), 774–75.

48. Cayton and Drake, *Black Metropolis,* 430, 443.

49. Allison Davis, Burleigh Gardner, Mary Gardner, *Deep South: A Social Anthropological Study of Caste and Class* (Chicago: University of Chicago Press, 1941). Gardner's marketing firm, Social Research, Inc., evolved out of the University of Chicago Committee on Human Relations in Industry, which he formed just before World War II with Warner and Robert Havighurst, initially to help incorporate southern black migrants into local industry.

50. Edgar A. Steele, "Some Aspects of the Negro Market," *Journal of Marketing* 11 (April 1947): 399–401.

CHAPTER SIX

1. H. Richard Niebuhr, *The Kingdom of God in America* (New York: Willett, Clark & Co., 1937), x.

2. For general essays on cultural pluralism, see John Higham, "Ethnic Pluralism in Modern American Thought," in *Send These To Me: Immigrants in Urban America,* 2d ed. (Baltimore: Johns Hopkins University Press, 1984), 198–232; David A. Hollinger, "Ethnic Diversity, Cosmopolitanism, and the Emergence of the American Liberal Intelligentsia," in his *In the American Province: Studies in the History and Historiography of Ideas* (Bloomington: Indiana University Press, 1985), 56–73; Philip Gleason, "Identifying Identity: A Semantic History," *The Journal of American History* 69 (March 1983): 910–31; and *Speaking of Diversity: Language and Ethnicity in Twentieth-Century America* (Baltimore: Johns Hopkins University Press, 1992); Rudolph J. Vecoli, "Ethnicity and Immigration," in the *Encyclopedia of the United States in the Twentieth Century,* ed. Stanley Kutler (New York: Charles Scribner's Sons, 1996), I:161–94; Werner Sollors, ed., *Theories of Ethnicity: A Classical Reader* (New York: New York University Press, 1996); and idem, ed., *The Invention of Ethnicity* (New York: Oxford University Press, 1989); on political pluralism, see David B. Truman, *Governmental Process: Political Interests and Public Opinion,* 2d ed. (1951, 1971; reprint, Berkeley: Institute of Governmental Studies, University of California, 1993); and Paul F. Bourke, "The Pluralist Reading of James Madison's Tenth Federalist," *Perspectives in American History* 9 (1975): 271–79; on the connection between cultural and political pluralism, see my own essay, "The Genesis of American Pluralism," *The Tocqueville Review/La Revue Tocqueville* 9 (1987–88): 201–20, first published in French as "Genèse du pluralisme américain," *Annales: Économies, Sociétés, Civilisations* (Mars–Avril 1987): 429–44.

3. Even though the term is often used in that latter acceptation, as in David A.

Gerber, *The Making of an American Pluralism: Buffalo, New York, 1825–1860* (Urbana: University of Illinois Press, 1989), 119–20.

4. On the importance of nineteenth-century localism, see Robert H. Wiebe, *Self-Rule: A Cultural History of American Democracy* (Chicago: University of Chicago Press, 1995), 1–111.

5. John C. Calhoun, *A Disquisition on Government and a Discourse on the Constitution and Government of the United States,* ed. Richard K. Cralle, (Charleston, N.C.: Press of Walker & James, 1851), published posthumously.

6. See Alexis de Tocqueville, *Democracy in America,* vol. 1, 1835, vol. 2, 1840, trans. Henry Reeve, revised by Francis Bowen and further revised by Phillips Bradley, with an introduction by Daniel J. Boorstin (New York: Vintage Books, 1990), especially 1:94, 153, 163, 165, 198, 213, 243, 246–48, 260, 267, 300, 329–30; 2:106–20, 2:297–302; as Yehoshua Arieli explains in *Individualism and Nationalism in American Ideology* (Baltimore: Penguin Books, 1966), 206: "the term 'individualism' was coined by the Saint-Simoniens to characterize the condition of men in nineteenth-century society—their uprootedness, their lack of ideals and common beliefs, their fragmentation, and their ruthless competitive and exploitative attitudes which evolved from this legitimized anarchy"; socialism promised the opposite; see also Alan Shain, *The Myth of American Individualism: The Protestant Origins of American Political Thought* (Princeton: Princeton University Press, 1994), 84–115; for a contemporary American formulation of individualism, see Ralph Waldo Emerson, *Self-Reliance* (1841, 1847), *Essays and Lectures,* Library of America (New York: Viking, 1983), 282; to compare Tocqueville and Emerson, see Robert N. Bellah, "Are Americans Still Citizens?" *The Tocqueville Review/La Revue Tocqueville,* 7 (1985/86): 89–96.

7. Richard L. McCormick, "Ethno-Cultural Interpretations of American Voting Behavior," *Political Science Quarterly* 89 (June 1974): 351–77.

8. William James, *The Varieties of Religious Experience: A Study in Human Nature,* being the Gifford Lectures on Natural Religion delivered at Edinburgh in 1901–1902, *Writings, 1902–1910,* Library of America (New York: Viking, 1987), 196.

9. Harold Bloom, *The American Religion: The Emergence of the Post-Christian Nation* (New York: Simon & Schuster, 1992), 192–233.

10. See Richard Wightman Fox, *Reinhold Niebuhr: A Biography* (New York: Pantheon Books, 1985); idem, "H. Richard Niebuhr's Divided Kingdom," *American Quarterly* 42 (March 1990): 93–101, and idem, "Protestantism," in the *Encyclopedia of the United States in the Twentieth Century,* ed. Stanley I. Kutler, 4:1491–1509.

11. Tocqueville, *Democracy in America,* 1:43, 177, 300, 304; 2:125–27, 134–45. Philip Schaff, who reported on the American religious character to his native Germany in the 1850s made observations similar to Tocqueville's. As Perry Miller points out, Schaff saw in America "a sort of extended Switzerland," where "theology is the daughter of the church and must not rebel against the mother"; see Philip Schaff, *America: A Sketch of Its Political, Social, and Religious Character,* ed. Perry Miller (Cambridge: Harvard University Press, Belknap Press, 1961), xii, xxix. See also Daniel Walker

Howe, "Protestantism, Voluntarism, and Personal Identity in Antebellum America," in *New Directions in American Religious History*, ed. Harry S. Stout and D. G. Hart (New York: Oxford University Press, 1997), 206–35.

12. H. Richard Niebuhr, *The Social Sources of Denominationalism* (New York: Henry Holt, 1929), 29; see also Nathan O. Hatch, *The Democratization of American Christianity* (New Haven: Yale University Press, 1989).

13. Niebuhr, *Social Sources*, 13, 63, 65; Richard Hofstadter, *Anti-Intellectualism in American Life* (New York: Alfred A. Knopf, 1963), 90–104; George M. Marsden, *Fundamentalism and American Culture: The Shaping of Twentieth Century Evangelicalism, 1870–1925* (New York: Oxford University Press, 1980), 72–74.

14. Niebuhr, *Social Sources*, 12, 13, 204, 205, 226; local histories confirm many of these points; see, for instance, Arthur E. Puotinen, "Ameliorative Factors in the Suomi Synod–Socialist Movement Conflict," in *The Faith of the Finns: Historical Perspectives on the Finnish Lutheran Church in America*, ed. Ralph F. Falkaner (East Lansing: Michigan State University Press, 1972), 227–49.

15. Niebuhr, *Social Sources*, 205.

16. David Martin, *A General Theory of Secularization* (New York: Harper & Row, 1979), 30.

17. R. Laurence Moore, *Religious Outsiders and the Making of Americans* (New York: Oxford University Press, 1986), xi.

18. Martin, *General Theory*, 29.

19. Henry F. May, *Ideas, Faiths, and Feelings: Essays on American Intellectual and Religious History, 1952–1982* (New York: Oxford University Press, 1983), 171–72.

20. Reginald Horsman, *Race and Manifest Destiny: The Origins of American Racial Anglo-Saxonism* (Cambridge: Harvard University Press, 1981), 5, 6.

21. On mutual avoidance, see John Higham, "Integrating America: The Problem of Assimilation," in *Send These To Me*, 185.

22. Kathleen Neils Conzen, "German Americans and the Invention of Ethnicity," in *America and the Germans: An Assessment of a Three-Hundred-Year History*, ed. F. Trommler and J. McVeigh (Philadelphia: University of Pennsylvania Press, 1985), 1: 141–47.

23. Ibid., 139; see also Gerber, *Making of an American Pluralism*, 198–99, 225–26.

24. We see this in the rich intellectual life of New York's Lower East Side Russian-Jewish community at the turn of the century, especially in the writings of Abraham Cahan, another apostle of the pluralist vision born of the urban ethnic experience; see Moses Rischin, ed., *Grandma Never Lived in America: The New Journalism of Abraham Cahan* (Bloomington: Indiana University Press, 1985). And on community building, see Arthur A. Goren, *New York Jews and the Quest for Community: The Kehillah Experiment, 1908–1922* (New York: Columbia University Press, 1970), 1–24.

25. Jon Gjerde, *The Minds of the West: Ethnocultural Evolution in the Rural Middle West, 1830–1917* (Chapel Hill: University of North Carolina Press, 1997).

26. William James, *The Will to Believe and Other Essays in Popular Philosophy* (1897), *Writings, 1878–1899,* Library of America (New York: Viking, 1992), 447–48. See also Gerald E. Myers, *William James: His Life and Thought* (New Haven: Yale University Press, 1986), 307–43, and Paul Jerome Croce, *Science and Religion in the Era of William James,* vol. 1, *Eclipse of Certainty, 1820–1880* (Chapel Hill: University of North Carolina Press, 1995), especially 225–31.

27. James, *Varieties of Religous Experience,* 104.

28. Alan Ryan, *John Dewey and the High Tide of American Liberalism* (New York: W. W. Norton, 1995), 193.

29. John Dewey, "Pluralism," in *Dictionary of Philosophy and Psychology,* ed. James Mark Baldwin (New York: Macmillan, 1901), 2:306; the most comprehensive guide to Dewey's work is Robert B. Westbrook, *John Dewey and American Democracy* (Ithaca: Cornell University Press, 1991).

30. John Dewey, *The School and Society,* 1899, ed. Jo Ann Boydston, with preface by Joe R. Burnett (Carbondale: Southern Illinois University Press; London: Feffer & Simons, 1980), 31, 38, 73; idem, *Democracy and Education: An Introduction to the Philosophy of Education* (New York: Macmillan, 1916); for "Deweyism" at work in the school of the single-tax community of Fairhope, Alabama, see Paul M. Gaston's chapter on Marietta Johnson, *Women of Fair Hope* (Athens: University of Georgia Press, 1984), 66–117, 128–33.

31. Paul F. Bourke, "The Pluralist Reading of James Madison's Tenth Federalist," *Perspectives in American History* 9 (1975): 271–95.

32. Arthur F. Bentley, *The Process of Government,* ed. Peter H. Odegard (1908; Cambridge: Harvard University Press, Belknap Press, 1967), 211. For a summary of Bentley's ideas, see Dorothy Ross, *The Origins of American Social Science* (New York: Cambridge University Press, 1991), 330–39.

33. For the Progressive generation, empowering groups was, as historian Philip J. Ethington put it well in *The Public City: The Political Construction of Urban Life in San Francisco, 1850–1900* (New York: Cambridge University Press, 1994), 283, "a lot easier than attempting to play Saint Peter and separate the elect from the corrupt."

34. Walter Lippmann, *Drift and Mastery: An Attempt to Diagnose the Current Unrest,* rev. introduction and notes by William E. Leuchtenburg (1914; Madison: University of Wisconsin Press, 1985), 59–60.

35. William Barton explained his first 1782 design as follows: "The thirteen pieces, barways, which fill up the Field of the Arms, may represent the several States; and the same Number of Stars upon a blue Canton, disposed in a Circle, represent a new Constellation, which alludes to the new Empire, formed in the World by the Confederation of those States— Their Disposition, in the form of a Circle, denotes the Perpetuity of it's Continuance, the Ring being the Symbol of Eternity," as reproduced in Richard S. Patterson and Richardson Dougall, *The Eagle and the Shield: A History of the Great Seal of the United States* (Washington, D.C.: GPO, 1976), 61.

36. Charles Beard, *An Economic Interpretation of the Constitution of the United*

States, 1913, with a new introduction by Forrest McDonald (New York: Free Press, 1986), 14–15; James Madison, alias Publius, "The Federalist X," November 22, 1787, in *The Debate on the Constitution: Federalist and Antifederalist Speeches, Articles and Letters During the Struggle Over Ratification,* ed. Bernard Bailyn, Library of America (New York: Viking, 1993), 1:404–11.

37. Richard Hofstadter, *The Progressive Historians: Turner, Beard, Parrington* (New York: Alfred A. Knopf, 1968), 208. Daniel T. Rodgers points out in *Contested Truths: Keywords in American Politics Since Independence* (New York: Basic Books, 1987), 185, that Beard knew Marx primarily through E. R. A. Seligman.

38. On Laski, see Rodgers, *Contested Truths,* 196–97; Bourke, "Pluralist Reading of James Madison's Tenth Federalist," 272–74.

39. Laski to Holmes, August 1, 1916, *Holmes-Laski Letters: The Correspondence of Mr. Justice Holmes and Harold J. Laski, 1916–1935,* ed. Mark DeWolfe Howe, with a foreword by Felix Frankfurter (Cambridge: Harvard University Press, 1953), 1:9. The following year, Laski explained what he meant: "If Wisconsin wants an income tax it can obtain one by winning the assent of its citizens. If Manchester wants a ship canal it must persuade parliament that its needs are more important than the jealousies of Liverpool," in *Studies in the Problem of Sovereignty* (New Haven: Yale University Press, 1917), 271.

40. Kallen's essay is reprinted in Sollors, ed., *Theories of Ethnicity;* idem, *Culture and Democracy in the United States* (New York: Boni & Liveright, 1924); see also Gleason, *Speaking of Diversity,* 25, 26.

41. Hollinger, *In the American Province,* 58–61.

42. Russell A. Kazal provides a good summary of the debates in "Revisiting Assimilation: The Rise, Fall, and Reappraisal of a Concept in American Ethnic History," *American Historical Review* 100 (April 1995): 437–71.

43. Richard Hofstadter, *The Age of Reform: From Bryan to F.D.R.* (New York: Alfred A. Knopf, 1955), 161; Thomas K. McCraw, *Prophets of Regulation* (Cambridge: Harvard University Press, Belknap Press, 1984), 101–8; Alpheus T. Mason, *Brandeis: A Free Man's Life* (New York: Viking, 1946), 627, 635–36.

44. Leonard Baker, *Brandeis and Frankfurter: A Dual Biography* (New York: Harper & Row, 1984), especially 159–81; see also John L. Thomas, "Louis Brandeis' Utopia," *Reviews in American History* 13 (March 1985): 94–106. Responding to the brief portrait of Brandeis I had sketched in my essay on "The Genesis of American Pluralism," mentioned above, sociologist David Riesman, who had been Brandeis's law clerk at the Supreme Court in the 1935–36 term has this much to add: Brandeis "was against big cities . . . and his greatest animosity concerned Detroit. He did not like the idea of workmen smoking cigarettes, and he was certainly not sympathetic to big unions, any more than to big anything. We never discussed his Zionism, because I was 'universalist' and anti-Zionist, but my sense of it was that he saw Israel in an agrarian mode, redeeming the Jews from urbanism and bigness. He identified much

more with Louisville than with Boston, even though he had been a 'swell' in Boston."
D.R. to O.Z., 13 August 1990.

45. Martin E. Marty, *Modern American Religion: The Irony of It All, 1893–1919*
(Chicago: University of Chicago Press, 1986), 1:153.

46. Grant Wacker, "The Protestant Awakening to World Religions," in *Between
the Times: The Travail of the Protestant Establishment in America, 1900–1960,* ed.
William R. Hutchison (New York: Cambridge University Press, 1989), 257–59.

47. John Higham, *Strangers in the Land: Patterns of American Nativism* (New
Brunswick: Rutgers University Press, 1955), 87.

48. The idea of adjustment to real social and cultural situations was key to the
success of the Social Gospel; on social Christianity and social science, see Josiah Strong,
The New Era, or The Coming Kingdom (New York: Baker & Taylor, 1893),121, 237;
Simon N. Patten, *The Social Basis of Religion* (New York: Macmillan, 1911), 195,
204, 227–47; Harry F. Ward, ed., *Social Creed of the Churches* (New York: Eaton &
Mains, 1912), 3, 9, 71; John Marshall Barker, *The Social Gospel and the New Era* (New
York: Macmillan, 1919), v. On the failure of home missions to convert immigrants, see
Twentieth Annual Report, Woman's Home Mission Society of the Virginia Conference,
Methodist Episcopal Church, South, Norfolk, Virginia, May 18–20, 1910 (Rich-
mond: S. B. Adkins, 1910), 6, 37–39; Laura G. Craig, *America, God's Melting Pot;
A Parable-Study* (New York: Fleming H. Revell Co., 1913), 14, 15, 21; Samuel Leslie
Morris, *The Task that Challenges: Home Mission Text Book* (Richmond: Presbyterian
Committee of Publication, 1917), 59–70; Coe Hayne, *For a New America* (New York:
Council of Women for Home Missions and Missionary Education Movement of the
United States and Canada, 1923), 143–55, 164; William P. Shriver, *What Next in
Home Missions* (New York: Council of Women for Home Missions and Missionary
Education Movement, 1928), 195–97; Hermann N. Morse, ed., *Home Missions, To-
day and Tomorrow: A Review and Forecast* (New York: Home Missions Council,
1934), 125–49, 265–66; see also Theodore Abel, *Protestant Home Missions to Catholic
Immigrants* (New York: Institute of Social and Religious Research, 1933); on liberal
Protestants' increasing acceptance of commercial leisure, see Richard Wightman Fox,
"The Discipline of Amusement," in *Inventing Times Square: Commerce and Culture at
the Crossroads of the World,* ed. William R. Taylor (New York: Russell Sage Foundation,
1991), 95–96; for an excellent review of recent scholarship, see Jon Butler, "Protestant
Success in the New American City, 1870–1920," in *New Directions in American Religious History,* ed. Stout and Hart, 296–33.

49. E. Digby Baltzell, *The Protestant Establishment: Aristocracy and Caste in
America* (New York: Random House, 1964), 209–18.

50. Emory Stevens Bucke, ed., *History of American Methodism* (New York: Ab-
ingdon Press, 1964), 2:593–99, 3:381, 395.

51. Kenneth T. Jackson, *The Ku Klux Klan in the City, 1915–1930* (New York:
Oxford University Press, 1967), xi–xv, 3–9, 18, 235, 240–46, 251–55.

52. Quoted in John T. McGreevy, "Thinking on One's Own: Catholicism in the American Intellectual Imagination, 1928–1960," *Journal of American History* 84 (June 1997): 104; see also Oscar Handlin, *Al Smith and His America* (Boston: Little, Brown & Co., 1958), 4, 117–20, 131–35, and Allan J. Lichtman, *Prejudice and the Old Politics: The Presidential Election of 1928* (Chapel Hill: University of North Carolina Press, 1979), 230–46.

53. See Herbert Hoover, *American Individualism,* 1922, and *The Challenge to Liberty,* 1934 (West Branch, Iowa: Herbert Hoover Presidential Library Association, 1989), 42, 181.

54. H. Richard Niebuhr, *The Kingdom of God in America* (New York: Willett, Clark & Co., 1937), vi–vii, x–xii.

55. Ibid., 193.

56. On secularization, see Harvey Cox, *The Secular City: Secularization and Urbanization in Theological Perspective,* rev. ed. (New York: Macmillan, 1966), especially 108–29, 193–94; Henry F. May, *Ideas, Faiths, and Feelings,* 135; R. Laurence Moore, "Secularization: Religion and the Social Sciences," in *Between the Times,* ed. Hutchison, 233–52; George M. Marsden, *The Soul of the American University: From Protestant Establishment to Established Nonbelief* (New York: Oxford University Press, 1994), 6–7, 265–66, 332–34; and Max Weber's 1906 essay, "The Protestant Sects and the Spirit of Capitalism" in *From Max Weber: Essays in Sociology,* trans. and ed. H. H. Gerth and C. Wright Mills (New York: Oxford University Press, 1946), 302–22.

57. James, *Varieties of Religious Experience,* 461.

58. May sees in these two facts evidence that the breakdown of the national Protestant religion was an American variant of a worldwide secularization process; see his *Ideas, Faiths, and Feelings,* 180.

59. James T. Patterson, *Grand Expectations: The United States, 1945–1974* (New York: Oxford University Press, 1996), 17.

60. Robert N. Bellah, *The Broken Covenant: American Civil Religion in Time of Trial,* 1975, rev. ed. (Chicago: University of Chicago Press, 1992), 168, 172, 178.

61. See Will Herberg, *Protestant, Catholic, Jew: An Essay in American Religious Sociology* (Garden City: Doubleday, 1955), 45–47, 56 n. 11, 56 n. 12, 69, 129, 166, 172, 186, 227, 253, 273; Ruby Jo Reeves Kennedy, "Single or Triple Melting-Pot: Intermarriage Trends in New Haven, 1870–1940," *American Journal of Sociology* 49 (January 1944): 331–39, and "Single or Triple Melting-Pot: Intermarriage in New Haven, 1870–1950," *American Journal of Sociology* 58 (July 1952): 56–59.

62. Paul Blanshard, *American Freedom and Catholic Power* (Boston: Beacon Press, 1949), 5; idem, *Communism, Democracy, and Catholic Power* (Boston: Beacon Press, 1951), 3–5; on Blanshard, see Patterson, *Grand Expectations,* 17, 18 and McGreevy, "Thinking on One's Own," 97–100, 104–6, 124, 127.

63. Martin E. Marty, *Modern American Religion: Under God, Indivisible, 1941–1960* (Chicago: University of Chicago Press, 1996), 3:294–312, 354–75.

64. Edwin S. Gaustad, "The Pulpit and the Pews," and David W. Wills, "An Endur-

ing Distance: Black Americans and the Establishment," in *Between the Times*, ed. Hutchison, 37–38, 172; Bucke, ed., *History of American Methodism*, 3:427–41, 481–90, 553–54.

65. Torn as they were among their feelings of sin of segregation, duty of racial integration, respect for voluntary separation on the part of blacks, and simultaneous outright exclusion of them as John T. McGreevy shows in *Parish Boundaries: The Catholic Encounter with Race in the Twentieth-Century Urban North* (Chicago: University of Chicago Press, 1996), 31–32, 50–51.

66. Lippmann, *Drift and Mastery*, 115.

67. Theodore J. Lowi, *The End of Liberalism: Ideology, Policy, and the Crisis of Public Authority* (New York: W. W. Norton, 1969), 58–59.

68. On the shift from Wilson's "Christian nation" to Eisenhower's "religious nation," see Marty, *Modern American Religion*, 3:296.

69. When addressing a meeting of the directors of the Freedom Foundation at the Waldorf-Astoria in New York City, Eisenhower said "government makes no sense unless it is founded on deeply felt religious faith—and I don't care what it is," *New York Times*, 23 December 1952, 16. For another Eisenhower statement on religion conveying much of the same meaning, see Marty, *Modern American Religion*, 3:300.

CHAPTER SEVEN

1. Jean-Jacques Rousseau, *Discourse on the Origins and the Foundations of Inequality among Men*, 1755, in *Jean-Jacques Rousseau: The First and Second Discourses*, ed. Roger D. Masters, trans. Roger D. Masters and Judith R. Masters (New York: St. Martin's Press, 1964), 103.

2. See Robert B. Westbrook, *John Dewey and American Democracy* (Ithaca: Cornell University Press, 1991), 205; John Dewey, "America in the World," *Nation* 106 (1918): 287, reprinted in *The Middle Works of John Dewey, 1899–1924: Essays on China, Japan, and the War, 1918–1919*, ed. Jo Ann Boydston (Carbondale: Southern Illinois University, 1976–83), 11:70–72.

3. On machine politics, see Ira Katznelson, *City Trenches: Urban Politics and the Patterning of Class in the United States* (New York: Pantheon Books, 1981), 19, 67–71. Alexander Keyssar will discuss ways of limiting participation of those likely to vote socialist in his forthcoming *History of the Right to Vote in the United States*.

4. Leon Fink, "Labor, Liberty, and the Law: Trade Unionism and the Problem of the American Constitutional Order," *Journal of American History* 74 (December 1987): 906, 915; Christopher L. Tomlins, *The State and the Unions: Labor Relations, Law, and the Organized Labor Movement in America, 1880–1960* (New York: Cambridge University Press, 1985), 44; see also Morton J. Horwitz, *The Transformation of American Law, 1780–1860* (1977; reprint, Cambridge: Harvard University Press, 1981), 186–88.

5. Fink, "Labor, Liberty, and the Law," 913.

6. Richard J. Oestreicher, *Solidarity and Fragmentation: Working People and Class Consciousness in Detroit, 1875–1900* (Urbana: University of Illinois Press, 1986), 112.

7. Herbert G. Gutman, *Work, Culture, and Society in Industrializing America: Essays in American Working-Class and Social History* (New York: Alfred A. Knopf, 1976), 293–343.

8. Henry Carter Adams, *Two Essays: Relation of the State to Industrial Action*, 1887, and *Economics and Jurisprudence*, 1896, ed. Joseph Dorfman (reprint, New York: A. M. Kelley, 1969), 89–90, 160; see also Dorothy Ross, "Socialism and American Liberalism: Academic Social Thought in the 1880s," *Perspectives in American History* 11 (1977–78): 14–50, 53–56, 62–72, 76–79.

9. Theda Skocpol, *Protecting Soldiers and Mothers: The Political Origins of Social Policy in the United States* (Cambridge: Harvard University Press, Belknap Press, 1992), 293–302. According to Morton Keller, *Regulating a New Society: Public Policy and Social Change in America, 1900–1933* (Cambridge: Harvard University Press, 1994), 201, workmen's compensation programs covered "about a quarter of the industrial workforce."

10. David A. Hollinger argues in "The 'Tough-Minded' Justice Holmes, Jewish Intellectuals, and the Making of an American Icon," in *The Legacy of Oliver Wendell Holmes*, ed. Robert W. Gordon (Stanford: Stanford University Press, 1992), 216–28, 307–13, that a group of pluralists-progressives adopted Holmes and refashioned him to their purpose; G. Edward White adds that Holmes was a free spirit and an agnostic, not a libertarian; he believed that if capital was allowed to be big, then labor could be big as well; see White's discussion of *Vegelahn* v. *Guntner* in *Justice Oliver Wendell Holmes: Law and the Inner Self* (New York: Oxford University Press, 1993), 287–89. Holmes's dissent in *Lochner* v. *New York* is in *The Essential Holmes: Selections from the Letters, Speeches, Judicial Opinions, and Other Writings of Oliver Wendell Holmes, Jr.*, ed. Richard A. Posner (Chicago: University of Chicago Press, 1992), 305–7.

11. Charles Sanders Peirce, "Evolutionary Love," 1893, in *Darwinism and the American Intellectual: An Anthology*, ed. Raymond Jackson Wilson, 2d ed. (Chicago: Dorsey Press, 1989), 146.

12. Ethnic and working-class consciousness did not reinforce each other as easily as Gutman suggested in *Work, Culture, and Society*, 3–78, or Lizabeth Cohen in *Making a New Deal: Industrial Workers in Chicago, 1919–1939* (New York: Cambridge University Press, 1990), 319, 362–63.

13. John Higham, *Send These To Me: Immigrants in Urban America*, rev. ed. (Baltimore: Johns Hopkins University Press, 1984), 3–70.

14. Olivier Zunz, *The Changing Face of Inequality: Urbanization, Industrial Development, and Immigrants in Detroit, 1880–1920* (Chicago: University of Chicago Press, 1982), 285–398. John Bodnar, *Workers' World: Kinship, Community, and Protest in an Industrial Society, 1900–1940* (Baltimore: Johns Hopkins University Press, 1982), 184–85, captures well working-class conservatism.

15. On the large structural transformations, see Olivier Zunz, "Class," in *Encyclopedia of the United States in the Twentieth Century,* ed. Stanley I. Kutler (New York: Charles Scribner's Sons, 1996), 1:195–220.

16. David Levering Lewis, *W. E. B. Du Bois: Biography of a Race, 1868–1919* (New York: Henry Holt, 1993), 281.

17. Eric Foner, *Reconstruction: America's Unfinished Revolution, 1863–1877* (New York: Harper & Row, 1988), 255.

18. John Dittmer, "The Education of Henry McNeal Turner," in *Black Leaders of the Nineteenth Century,* ed. Leon Litwack and August Meier (Urbana: University of Illinois Press, 1988), 265.

19. Foner, *Reconstruction,* 579–80, 587.

20. *Plessy* v. *Ferguson,* 163 US 537 (1896) at 551; C. Vann Woodward, *The Strange Career of Jim Crow* (New York: Oxford University Press, 1955), 104, 105; William Graham Sumner, *Folkways: A Study of the Sociological Importance of Manners, Customs, Mores and Morals* (Boston: Ginn & Co., 1907), 82–84, 381–82.

21. W. E. B. Du Bois, *The Souls of Black Folk* (1903), *Writings,* Library of America (New York: Viking, 1986), 390.

22. G. Edward White, *The American Judicial Tradition: Profiles of Leading American Judges* (New York: Oxford University Press, 1976), 140.

23. *Civil Rights Cases,* 109 US 3 (1883) at 61.

24. *Plessy* v. *Ferguson,* 163 US 537 (1896) at 559.

25. As quoted in White, *The American Judicial Tradition,* 143. In the South, some women reformers were more responsive to Harlan's call than their male counterparts; see Glenda Elizabeth Gilmore, *Gender and Jim Crow: Women and the Politics of White Supremacy in North Carolina, 1896–1920* (Chapel Hill: University of North Carolina Press, 1996).

26. Robert Ezra Park, *Human Communities: The City and Human Ecology* (New York: Free Press, 1952), 14, 18, 78–79, 100, 151, 170, 172, 196, 198–99; Higham, *Send These to Me,* 216–19; Martin Bulmer, *The Chicago School of Sociology: Institutionalization, Diversity, and the Rise of Sociological Research* (Chicago: University of Chicago Press, 1984), 118–20.

27. On the 1917 Supreme Court ruling abolishing public zoning for racial purposes and the resulting increase in the use of private restrictive covenants, see Thomas Lee Philpott, *The Slum and the Ghetto: Neighborhood Deterioration and Middle-Class Reform, Chicago, 1880–1930* (New York: Oxford University Press, 1978), 189–200. For a good sociological profile of white rioters, see Roberta Senechal, *The Sociogenesis of a Race Riot: Springfield, Illinois, in 1908* (Urbana: University of Illinois Press, 1990).

28. Alain Locke, *The New Negro,* 1925 (New York: Atheneum, 1980), 3–25, 301–40; on black professionals, see Kenneth L. Kusmer, *A Ghetto Takes Shape: Black Cleveland, 1870–1930* (Urbana: University of Illinois Press, 1976), 81–84, 103, 235–36, 243–47.

29. Kathryn Kish Sklar, "The Historical Foundations of Women's Power in the

Creation of the American Welfare State, 1830–1930," in *Mothers of a New World: Maternalist Politics and the Origins of the Welfare States,* ed. Seth Koven and Sonya Michel (New York: Routledge, 1993), 51–53, 60–75; Paula Baker, "The Domestication of Politics: Women and American Political Society, 1780–1920," *American Historical Review* 89 (June 1984): 620–22, 635–47; Seth Koven and Sonya Michel, "Womanly Duties: Maternalist Politics and the Origins of Welfare States in France, Germany, Great Britain, and the United States, 1880–1920," *American Historical Review* 95 (October 1990): 1076–1108, and Theda Skocpol, *Protecting Soldiers and Mothers.*

30. Ellen Carol DuBois, "Outgrowing the Compact of the Fathers: Equal Rights, Woman Suffrage, and the United States Constitution, 1820–1878," *Journal of American History* 74 (December 1987): 846.

31. Ibid., 849.

32. Women also helped spread a changing conception of such weaker members of society as the institutionalized population of insane asylums, the mentally sick, the deaf and mute, and abandoned orphans for which reformers like Dorothy Dix had campaigned for decades.

33. Skocpol, *Protecting Soldiers and Mothers,* 370–71.

34. *Muller* v. *Oregon,* 208 US 412 (1908) at 422.

35. Lester Ward, "Mind as a Social Factor," 1913, in *Darwinism and the American Intellectual,* ed. Wilson, 128–29; see also John C. Burnham, *Lester Frank Ward in American Thought* (Washington, D. C.: Public Affairs Press, 1956).

36. Linda Gordon, *Pitied but Not Entitled: Single Mothers and the History of Welfare, 1890–1935* (New York: Free Press, 1994), 49.

37. *Adkins* v. *Children's Hospital,* 261 US 525 (1923) at 553; *The Essential Holmes,* ed. Posner, 308; see also Nancy Cott, *The Grounding of Modern Feminism* (New Haven: Yale University Press, 1987), 117–42.

38. Edward D. Berkowitz, "Social Welfare," in *Encyclopedia of the United States in the Twentieth Century,* ed. Kutler, 1:471–90.

39. On the concept of "reconstructions" in American history and C. Vann Woodward's role in defining the "Second Reconstruction," see John Higham, "Coda: Three Reconstructions," in *Civil Rights and Social Wrongs: Black-White Relations Since World War II,* ed. John Higham (University Park: Pennsylvania State University Press, 1997), 179–89, 207–8.

40. Keller, *Regulating a New Society,* 305–6.

41. Rosalind Rosenberg, *Divided Lives: American Women in the Twentieth Century* (New York: Hill & Wang, 1992), 105.

42. Gordon, *Pitied but Not Entitled,* 293.

43. David B. Truman, *The Governmental Process: Public Interests and Public Opinion,* 2d ed. (1951, 1971; reprint, Berkeley: Institute of Governmental Studies, University of California, 1993), 67.

44. I return to these issues in the next chapter.

45. Gordon, *Pitied but Not Entitled*, 293–94.

46. Elaine Tyler May, *Homeward Bound: American Families in the Cold War Era* (New York: Basic Books, 1988), 162–64.

47. Zunz, *Changing Face of Inequality*, 318–25.

48. August Meier and Elliott Rudwick, *Black Detroit and the Rise of the UAW* (New York: Oxford University Press, 1979), 34.

49. A number of labor leaders were liberals on issues of race, as Nelson Lichtenstein shows in *The Most Dangerous Man in Detroit: Walter Reuther and the Fate of American Labor* (New York: Basic Books, 1995), 371–95.

50. See Herbert Hill, *Black Labor and the American Legal System* (Washington, D.C.: Bureau of National Affairs, 1977), 262–63, idem, "The Problem of Race in American Labor History," *Reviews in American History* 24 (June 1996): 189–208.

51. Gunnar Myrdal, *An American Dilemma: The Negro Problem and Modern Democracy* (New York: Harper & Bros., 1944).

52. Thurgood Marshall in *University of California Regents* v. *Bakke*, 438 US 265 (1978) at 400.

53. Daryl Scott, *Contempt and Pity: Social Policy and the Image of the Damaged Black Psyche, 1880–1996* (Chapel Hill: University of North Carolina Press, 1997), 119–36; see also Richard Kluger's superb narrative, *Simple Justice: The History of the Brown v. Board of Education and Black America's Struggle for Equality* (New York: Alfred A. Knopf, 1975), 316–45.

54. For a brief discussion of this well-known episode of the civil rights movement and Casey Hayden's memo on "Sex and Caste," see James T. Patterson, *Grand Expectations: The United States, 1945–1974* (New York: Oxford University Press, 1996), 645.

55. Hugh Davis Graham, *The Civil Rights Era: Origins and Development of a National Policy, 1960–1972* (New York: Oxford University Press, 1990), 12, 134–36, 206–7; see also Bruce J. Dierenfield, *Keeper of the Rules: Congressman Howard W. Smith of Virginia* (Charlottesville: University Press of Virginia, 1987), 191–98, 201, 213, 234; Carl Brauer, "Women Activists, Southern Conservatives, and the Prohibition of Sex Discrimination in Title VII of the 1964 Civil Rights Act," *Journal of Southern History* 49 (February 1983): 42; Leila J. Rupp and Verta Taylor, *Survival in the Doldrums: The American Women's Rights Movement, 1945 to the 1960s* (New York: Oxford University Press, 1987), 176–77; and Cynthia Harrison, *On Account of Sex: The Politics of Women's Issues, 1945–1968* (Berkeley: University of California Press, 1988), 177–78.

56. The Bakke case signals the beginning of the backlash against affirmative action; see Nathan Glazer, *Affirmative Discrimination* (New York: Basic Books, 1975), 168–95.

57. C. Vann Woodward, *Thinking Back: The Perils of Writing History* (Baton Rouge: Louisiana State University, 1986), 92.

58. *University of California Regents* v. *Bakke* at 402.

59. *Civil Rights Cases*, 109 US 3 (1883) at 46.

60. Graham, *The Civil Rights Era*, 97–98, 188, 196–97, 212, 226–31, 250, 284–87, 296, 324–25, 387–89, 391, 410, 459, 460.

61. David A. Hollinger, *Post-Ethnic America: Beyond Multiculturalism* (New York: Basic Books, 1995), 19–50.

62. For an instructive debate on multiculturalism, see Gary Kulik, "Editor's Introduction," John Higham, "Multiculturalism and Universalism: A History and Critique," Gerald Early, "American Education and the Postmodernist Impulse," Gary Gerstle, "The Limits of American Universalism," Nancy A. Hewitt, "A Response to John Higham," Vicki L. Ruiz, "'It's the People Who Drive the Book': A View from the West," and Higham, "Rejoinder," *American Quarterly* 45 (June 1993): vii–viii, 195–256.

CHAPTER EIGHT

1. Homer Bigart, "Japan Signs, Second World War Is Ended," New York *Herald Tribune*, September 2, 1945, in *Reporting World War II. Part II: American Journalism, 1944–1946*, Library of America (New York: Viking, 1995), 773.

2. Jeffry M. Diefendorf, Axel Frohn, Hermann-Josef Rupieper, eds., *American Policy and the Reconstruction of West Germany, 1945–1955* (Washington, D.C.: German Historical Institute and New York: Cambridge University Press, 1993); Carolyn Eisenberg, *Drawing the Line: The American Decision to Divide Germany, 1944–1949* (New York: Cambridge University Press, 1996); Melvyn P. Leffler, "The Struggle for Germany and the Origins of the Cold War," Alois Mertes Memorial Lecture, Occasional Paper no. 16 (Washington, D.C.: German Historical Institute, 1996); and especially Charles S. Maier, *In Search of Stability: Explorations in Historical Political Economy* (New York: Cambridge University Press, 1987).

3. Michael J. Hogan, *The Marshall Plan: America, Britain, and the Reconstruction of Western Europe, 1947–1952* (New York: Cambridge University Press, 1987), 27; the reference to the British Treasury official is on 427.

4. Although realizing the importance of the Marshall Plan for Western Europe, pro-American, influential French political scientist (and regular columnist in *Le Figaro*) Raymond Aron wrote: "En trois ans, le plan Marshall se rendit lui-même inutile" [it took only three years for the Marshall plan to become, on its own terms, unnecessary]; *Mémoires. Cinquante ans de vie politique* (Paris: Julliard, 1983), 361, 390.

5. Melvyn P. Leffler, "Truman's Decision to Drop the Atomic Bomb," *International House of Japan Bulletin* 15 (Summer 1995): 1–7; Sakamoto Yoshikazu, "The International Context of the Occupation of Japan," in *Democratizing Japan: The Allied Occupation*, ed. Robert Ward and Sakamoto Yoshikazu (Honolulu: University of Hawaii Press, 1987), 42–43, 48–75.

6. Herbert D. Croly, *The Promise of American Life* (1909; New Brunswick: Transaction Publishers, 1993), 22.

7. Carol Gluck, "The Past in the Present," in *Postwar Japan as History*, ed. Andrew Gordon (Berkeley: University of California Press, 1993), 64–95.

8. Toku Baelz, *Awakening Japan: The Diary of a German Doctor: Erwin Baelz*, introduction by George Macklin Wilson (Bloomington: Indiana University Press, 1974), x, 72.

9. Yukichi Fukuzawa, *An Encouragement of Learning*, trans. by David Dilworth and Umeyo Hirano (Tokyo: Sophia University, 1969), xi, 1.

10. Fred G. Notehelfer, "Rural Japan and the Outside World in Meiji Japan," *Tocqueville Review/La Revue Tocqueville* 16, 2 (1995): 23–39.

11. Samuel Smiles, *Self-Help; with Illustrations of Conduct and Perseverance*, with an introduction by Asa Briggs (London: J. Murray, 1958); Earl H. Kinmonth, *The Self-Made Man in Meiji Japanese Thought: From Samurai to Salary Man* (Berkeley: University of California Press, 1981), 20, 27.

12. Byron K. Marshall, *Capitalism and Nationalism in Prewar Japan: The Ideology of the Business Elite, 1868–1941* (Stanford: Stanford University Press, 1967), 57.

13. Sheldon Garon, *The State and Labor in Modern Japan* (Berkeley: University of California Press, 1987), 7–8, 39–119, 165–68, 170–72.

14. Kenneth B. Pyle, "Advantages of Followership: German Economics and Japanese Bureaucrats, 1890–1925," *Journal of Japanese Studies* 1 (Autumn 1974): 129.

15. Robert B. Westbrook, *John Dewey and American Democracy* (Ithaca: Cornell University Press, 1991), 241–42.

16. Beard was a bit pessimistic since universal suffrage for men was passed in 1925, only two years after the earthquake. Charles A. Beard, "Municipal Research in Japan: A Report to American Research Workers," *National Municipal Review* 12 (September 1923): 520–23; idem, "Japan's Statesman of Research," *Review of Reviews* 68 (September 1923): 296–98; idem, "Rebuilding in Japan," *Review of Reviews* 68 (October 1923): 373–82; idem, "American Influence on Municipal Government in the Orient," *National Municipal Review* 14 (January 1925): 7–11; idem, "War with Japan: What Shall We Get out of It?" *Nation* 120 (March 25, 1925): 311–13; idem, "Memorandum Relative to the Reconstruction of Tokyo, Presented to Viscount S. Gotō by Charles A. Beard," *Far Eastern Review* 21 (June–July 1925): 252–56; Beard and K. Sawada, "Reconstruction in Tokyo," *Review of Reviews* 71 (March 1925): 268–70. See also Yasua Endo "Charles A. and Mary Beard in Japan in the 1920s," in *The Reconstruction of the Image of Contemporary America in Politics, Culture, and History*, ed. Nagayo Homma (Tokyo: University of Tokyo Press, 1990), 141–57 (in Japanese); Shun-Ichi J. Watanabe, "Metropolitanism as a Way of Life: The Case of Tokyo, 1868–1930," in *Metropolis, 1890–1940*, ed. Anthony Sutcliffe (London: Mansell, 1984), 403–29.

17. Michael A. Barnhardt, *Japan Prepares for Total War: The Search for Economic Security, 1919–1941* (Ithaca: Cornell University Press, 1987), 91–104, 108–9; Marshall, *Capitalism and Nationalism in Prewar Japan*, 3, 30–41, 50, 77–92, 96–97,

102–3, 108, 113–14, 119; Arthur E. Tiedemann, "Big Business and Politics in Prewar Japan," in *Dilemmas of Growth in Prewar Japan,* ed. James William Morley (Princeton: Princeton University Press, 1971), 267–316.

18. Speaking of the defeated country as a "political, economic and spiritual vacuum," Douglas MacArthur felt that "Japan had become the world's great laboratory for an experiment in the liberation of a people"; see his *Reminiscences* (New York: McGraw-Hill, 1964), 282.

19. Ruth Benedict, *The Chrysanthemum and the Sword: Patterns of Japanese Culture* (Boston: Houghton Mifflin, 1946); Margaret M. Caffrey, *Ruth Benedict: Stranger in This Land* (Austin: University of Texas Press, 1989), 318–26.

20. Alexis de Tocqueville, *Democracy in America*, vol. 1, 1835, vol. 2, 1840, trans. Henry Reeve, revised by Francis Bowen and further revised by Phillips Bradley, with an introduction by Daniel J. Boorstin (New York: Vintage Books, 1990), 2:98–99; Benedict, *The Chrysanthemum and the Sword*, 73, 96.

21. Ibid., 95–96.

22. Louis Hartz, *The Liberal Tradition in America: An Interpretation of American Political Thought Since the Revolution* (New York: Harcourt, Brace, 1955), 3–5; see Dorothy Ross's analysis in "The Liberal Tradition Revisited and the Republican Tradition Addressed," *New Directions in American Intellectual History,* ed. John Higham and Paul K. Conkin (Baltimore: Johns Hopkins University Press, 1979), 116–20.

23. Hidemasa Morikawa, *Zaibatsu: The Rise and Fall of Family Enterprise Groups in Japan,* foreword by Alfred D. Chandler, Jr. (Tokyo: University of Tokyo Press, 1992), 17.

24. Howard B. Schonberger, *Aftermath of War: Americans and the Remaking of Japan, 1945–1952* (Kent: Kent State University Press, 1989), 36; Marlene J. Mayo, "American Economic Planning for Occupied Japan: The Issue of Zaibatsu Dissolution, 1942–1945," in *The Occupation of Japan: Economic Policy and Reform,* ed. Lawrence H. Redford (Norfolk: MacArthur Memorial, 1980), 205–28; idem, "American Wartime Planning for Occupied Japan: The Role of Experts," in *Americans as Proconsuls: United States Military Government in Germany and Japan, 1944–1952,* ed. Robert Wolfe (Carbondale: Southern Illinois University Press, 1984), 21, 29–34, 36, 38, 40–42, 46–51.

25. See Thomas A. Bisson, *Zaibatsu Dissolution in Japan* (Westport: Greenwood Press, 1954) for this text, 3.

26. Michael Schaller, *The American Occupation of Japan: The Origins of the Cold War in Asia* (New York: Oxford University Press, 1985), 20–51, 65–72; idem, *Douglas MacArthur: The Far East General* (New York: Oxford University Press, 1989), 135–57.

27. Schaller, *The American Occupation of Japan,* 109–10, 114–15; Theodore Cohen, *Remaking Japan: The American Occupation as New Deal,* ed. Herbert Passin (New York: Free Press, 1987), 137–40, 150–55, 168–70, 371–73.

28. Gary H. Tsuchimochi, *Education Reform in Postwar Japan: The 1946 U.S. Edu-

cation Mission, foreword by Carol Gluck (Tokyo: University of Tokyo Press, 1993), 108-69.

29. Akira Amakawa, "Japanese Reactions for Political Reform under the Allied Occupation," in *The Occupation of Japan, 1945–52,* ed. Ian Nish (London: London School of Economics, 1991), 23–40.

30. Kyoko Inoue, *MacArthur's Japanese Constitution: A Linguistic and Cultural Study of Its Making* (Chicago: University of Chicago Press, 1991), 16; see also Mayo "American Wartime Planning for Occupied Japan," 20, 45–51; Robert Ward, "Presurrender Planning: Treatment of the Emperor and Constitutional Changes," and Theodore McNelly, "'Induced Revolution': The Policy and Process of Constitutional Reform in Occupied Japan," in *Democratizing Japan,* ed. Ward and Sakamoto, 1–41, 76–106.

31. Beate Sirota Gordon, *The Only Woman in the Room* (New York: Kōdansha America, 1998) [first published as *1945 nen no Kurisumasu (Christmas in 1945)* (Tokyo: Kashiwa Shobo, 1995)]; Susan Pharr, "The Politics of Women's Rights," in *Democratizing Japan,* ed. Ward and Sakamoto, 221–52; see also Gail Lee Bernstein, *Recreating Japanese Women, 1600–1945* (Berkeley: University of California Press, 1991), 175–216, 239–66.

32. Interview with Professor Fujio Ikado, Tokyo, June 1996.

33. Interview with Professor Eiji Takemae, Tokyo, June 1996.

34. Tony Smith, *America's Mission: The United States and the Worldwide Struggle for Democracy in the Twentieth Century* (Princeton: Princeton University Press, 1994), 52–59, 62–63, 74–75.

35. MacArthur, *Reminiscences,* 313.

36. Ronald P. Dore, *Land Reform in Japan* (Oxford: Oxford University Press, 1959), 175; Richard J. Smethurst, *Agricultural Development and Tenancy Disputes in Japan, 1870–1940* (Princeton: Princeton University Press, 1986), 293–95, 360, 369.

37. D. Clayton James, *Triumph and Disaster, 1945–1964: The Years of MacArthur* (Boston: Houghton Mifflin Co., 1985), 3:92.

38. Dore, *Land Reform,* 54; John W. Dower, *Empire and Aftermath: Yoshida Shigeru and the Japanese Experience, 1878–1954* (Cambridge: Harvard University Press, 1979), 329–32.

39. MacArthur, *Reminiscences,* 314.

40. Croly, *Promise of American Life,* 214.

41. See Cohen, *Remaking Japan,* 34; Ariga Michiko, "Deconcentration during the Allied Occupation of Japan," in *The Occupation of Japan: Economic Policy and Reform,* ed. Redford, 204–62.

42. Shigeru Yoshida, *The Yoshida Memoirs: The Story of Japan in Crisis* trans. Kenichi Yoshida (Boston: Houghton Mifflin Co., 1962), 150; Takafusa Nakamura, *The Postwar Japanese Economy: Its Development and Structure, 1937–1994,* 2d ed. (Tokyo: University of Tokyo Press, 1995), 25–26.

43. Ibid., 25.

44. Bisson, *Zaibatsu Dissolution,* 73–77, 91–93; Eleanor M. Hadley, *Antitrust in Japan* (Princeton: Princeton University Press, 1970), 67–70, 73, 86, 125–46.

45. See the critical review of Cohen's *Remaking Japan* by Eleanor M. Hadley, *Journal of Japanese Studies* 14 (Summer 1988): 480–85.

46. Marius B. Jansen, "Intellectuals, Social Change, and Foreign Policy in Interwar Japan," *Tocqueville Review/La Revue Tocqueville* 16, 2 (1995): 59–78.

47. Interview with Professor Takafusa Nakamura, Tokyo, June 1996.

48. See Cohen, *Remaking Japan,* 196.

49. Ibid., 200.

50. Ibid., 188, 193–96, 204–11.

51. As William James called the American Philosophical Association; see Daniel J. Wilson, *Science, Community, and the Transformation of American Philosophy, 1860–1930* (Chicago: University of Chicago Press, 1990), 134.

52. Schonberger, *Aftermath of War,* 117; estimates vary slightly depending on sources, see Mikio Sumiya, "Contemporary Arrangements: An Overview," in *Workers and Employers in Japan: The Japanese Employment Relations System,* ed. Kazuo Okochi, Bernard Karsh, Solomon B. Levine (Tokyo: Tokyo University Press, 1974), 69.

53. Ibid., 62, and interview with Professor Masanori Nakamura, Tokyo, June 1996.

54. Schonberger, "American Labor's Cold War in Occupied Japan," *Diplomatic History* 3 (Summer 1979): 249–72; idem, *Aftermath of War,* 131, 330, 370–71.

55. Ibid., 11–39, 161–97; Sakamoto, "The International Context of the Occupation of Japan," in *Democratizing Japan,* ed. Ward and Sakamoto, 43.

56. Yoshida said "Recovery from this historic 'stumble' will require years to complete, but it is the task before my country now," *Yoshida Memoirs,* 7.

57. James Lee Kauffman, "A Lawyer's Report on Japan Attacks Plan to Run Occupation," *Newsweek,* December 1, 1947, 36–38.

58. George F. Kennan, *Memoirs, 1925–1950* (Boston: Little, Brown, 1967), 375–96; Wilson D. Miscamble, *George F. Kennan and the Making of American Foreign Policy, 1947–1950* (Princeton: Princeton University Press, 1992), 252–58, 264–73.

59. As described in chaps. 4 and 7.

60. Chalmers Johnson, *MITI and the Japanese Miracle: The Growth of Industrial Policy, 1925–1975* (Stanford: Stanford University Press, 1982), 111–14; Hidemasa Morikawa, "The Organizational Structure of Mitsubishi and Mitsui Zaibatsu, 1868–1922: A Comparative Study," *Business History Review* 44 (Spring 1970): 62–83; idem, *Zaibatsu,* 46–47, 54–55, 98–99, 218–19, 247.

61. John G. Roberts, *Mitsui: Three Centuries of Japanese Business* (New York: Weatherhill, 1973, 1989), 227, 282–86, 292, 302–3, 309–10, 315–19, 321, 330, 352–55, 401, 408; Johnson, *MITI and the Japanese Miracle,* 112.

62. Ibid., 157; Johannes Hirschmeier and Tsunehiko Yui, *The Development of Japanese Business,* 2d ed. (London: George Allen & Unwin, 1981), 236–63; Roberts, *Mitsui,* 320–36, 348–59; on the concept of interdependence, see W. Mark Fruin, *The*

Japanese Enterprise System: Competitive Strategies and Cooperative Structures (Oxford: Clarendon Press, 1992), 16–56.

63. See Bai Gao, "Arisawa Hiromi and His Theory for a Managed Economy," *Journal of Japanese Studies* 20 (Winter 1994): 115–53.

64. For instance, Nakamura, *The Postwar Japanese Economy*, 43.

65. Ibid., 37–43.

66. Bruce Cumings, "Japan's Position in the World System," and Charles Yuji Horioka, "Consuming and Saving," in *Postwar Japan as History*, ed. Gordon, 34–63, 284–85.

67. Frank Costigliola, *Awkward Dominion: American Political, Economic, and Cultural Relations with Europe, 1919–1933* (Ithaca: Cornell University Press, 1984), 141, 157–64; Thomas P. Hughes, *American Genesis: A Century of Invention and Technological Enthusiasm, 1870–1970* (New York: Viking, 1989), 8, 249–94.

68. Croly, *Promise of American Life*, 3–26; Walt W. Rostow, with Richard W. Hatch, *An American Policy in Asia* (Cambridge: Massachusetts Institute of Technology, 1955), viii, 43–46; Rostow, *The Stages of Economic Growth: A Non-Communist Manifesto* (Cambridge: Cambridge University Press, 1960), ix. 7–9, 31–35, 158; Cyril E. Black, *Comparative Modernization: A Reader* (New York: Free Press, 1976), 1–104, 117–30; Raymond Grew, "Modernization and Its Discontents," *American Behavioral Scientist* 21 (November–December 1977): 289–312; John Whitney Hall, "Changing Conceptions of the Modernization of Japan," in *Changing Japanese Attitudes Toward Modernization*, ed. Marius Jansen (Princeton: Princeton University Press, 1965), 7–41.

69. Croly, *Promise of American Life*, 5.

70. Christopher Lasch, "Progress," in *A Companion to American Thought*, ed. Richard Wightman Fox and James T. Kloppenberg (Cambridge, Mass.: Blackwell, 1995), 546–48.

71. See Reischauer as quoted by John W. Dower, "E. H. Norman, Japan and the Uses of History," introduction to *Origins of the Modern Japanese State: Selected Writings of E. H. Norman*, ed. John Dower (New York: Pantheon Books, 1975), 44.

72. Thomas K. McCraw, "From Partners to Competitors: An Overview of the Period since World War II," in *America vs. Japan*, ed. Thomas K. McCraw (Boston: Harvard Business School Press, 1986), 1–33, 373–84. The Japanese household's savings rate was 20 percent of disposable income in 1978; it was still the highest in the world at 14.8 percent in 1988 vs. 6.6 percent in the United States; *Japan Times*, January 18, 1990, T7. In 1990, Nippon Housing Loan Company, a leading mortgage firm began offering 100 year mortgages to spread the purchase of a home over three generations, *Financial Times*, January 31, 1990, 1.

73. Simon Christopher Partner, "Manufacturing Desire: The Japanese Electrical Goods Industry in the 1950s" (Ph.D. diss., Columbia University, 1997), 322–23.

74. Dower, "E. H. Norman," 48.

75. Ibid., 34.

76. Andrew Gordon, "La 'disparition' du mouvement ouvrier au Japon après 1945," *Le Mouvement Social,* no. 173 (Octobre–Décembre 1995): 35–67; idem, *The Evolution of Labor Relations in Japan Heavy Industry, 1853–1955,* Harvard East Asian Monographs 117 (Cambridge: Council on East Asian Studies and Harvard University Press, 1985), 342–48; see also Robert E. Cole and Ken'ichi Tominaga, "Japan's Changing Occupational Structure and its Significance," in *Japanese Industrialization and Its Social Consequences,* ed. Hugh Patrick (Berkeley: University of California Press, 1976), 53–96; Tadashi Fukutake, *The Japanese Social Structure: Its Evolution in the Modern Century,* trans. and with a foreword by Ronald Dore, 2d ed. (Tokyo: University of Tokyo Press, 1989), 107–22.

77. Sydney Crawcour, "The Japanese Employment System," *Journal of Japanese Studies* 4 (1978): 225–45.

78. Hiroshi Ishida, *Social Mobility in Contemporary Japan: Educational Credentials, Class and the Labor Market in a Cross-National Perspective,* with a foreword by John H. Goldthorpe (Stanford: Stanford University Press, 1993), 202; Kuzushi Ohkawa, "Personal Consumption in Dualistic Growth," in *Economic Growth: The Japanese Experience Since the Meiji Era,* ed. Kuzushi Ohkawa and Lawrence Klein (Tokyo: International Conference on Economic Growth, 1966), 655–77.

79. J. Victor Koschmann, "Intellectuals and Politics," in *Postwar Japan as History,* ed. Gordon, 404.

80. Ronald Dore, "La particularité du Japon," in *Les capitalismes en Europe,* ed. Colin Crouch and Wolfgang Streeck (Paris: Éditions La Découverte, 1996), 27–45.

81. What would constitute an appropriate consumption level for the Japanese is a recurrent topic in the Japanese Economic Planning Agency's annual "White Paper on the Life of the Nation," (Japan: Foreign Press Center). For a good analysis of the gender gap in Japan, see Robert J. Smith, "Gender Inequality in Contemporary Japan," *Journal of Japanese Studies* 13 (1987): 1–25.

CHAPTER NINE

1. As quoted by G. Edward White, *Justice Oliver Wendell Holmes: Law and the Inner Self* (New York: Oxford University Press, 1993), 383.

2. See Alva Johnston's three-part article, "Profiles: The National Idea Man," *New Yorker,* February 10, 1945, 28–35, February 17, 26–34, February 24, 30–39; and Walter A. Jackson, *Gunnar Myrdal and America's Conscience: Social Engineering and Racial Liberalism, 1938–1987* (Chapel Hill: University of North Carolina Press, 1990), 31.

3. Earl Lewis, "Race," in *Encyclopedia of the United States in the Twentieth Century,* ed. Stanley I. Kutler (New York: Charles Scribner's Sons, 1996), 1:131.

4. Joseph A. Schumpeter, *The Economics and Sociology of Capitalism,* ed. Richard Swedberg (Princeton: Princeton University Press, 1991), 298, 300, 305.

5. Akira Iriye, *The Globalizing of America, 1913–1945,* volume 3 of *The Cambridge History of American Foreign Relations* (New York: Cambridge University Press, 1993), 141.

6. Joan Hoff Wilson, *Herbert Hoover: Forgotten Progressive* (Boston: Little, Brown, 1975), 232, 259–60.

7. Ron Robin, *The Barbed-Wire College: Reeducating German POWs in the United States during World War II* (Princeton: Princeton University Press, 1995), 6, 69, 146.

8. Wendell L. Willkie, *One World* (New York: Simon & Schuster, 1943), 159, 161.

9. Pap Ndiaye, "Du nylon et des bombes. Du Pont de Nemours, l'État américain et le nucléaire, 1930–1960," *Annales: Histoire, Sciences Sociales* 50 (Janvier–Février 1995): 53–73; Stuart W. Leslie, *The Cold War and American Science: The Military-Industrial-Academic Complex at MIT and Stanford* (New York: Columbia University Press, 1993).

10. As quoted by Peter Galison, "The Many Faces of Science," in *Big Science: The Growth of Large-Scale Research,* ed. Peter Galison and Bruce Hevly (Stanford: Stanford University Press, 1992), 15; see James Hershberg, *James B. Conant: Harvard to Hiroshima and the Making of the Nuclear Age* (New York: Alfred A. Knopf, 1993).

11. See Nicholas Lemann's two essays, "The Structure of Success in America," *Atlantic Monthly,* August 1995, 41–60; and "The Great Sorting," *Atlantic Monthly,* September 1995, 84–100.

12. Vannevar Bush, *Science: The Endless Frontier: A Report to the President, July 1945* (Washington, D.C.: GPO, 1945); on Bush, see Donald E. Stokes, *Pasteur's Quadrant: Basic Science and Technological Innovation* (Washington, D. C.: Brookings Institution Press, 1997), 2–5; on the respective influence of military and civil sectors on American higher education, see Roger L. Geiger, *Research and Relevant Knowledge: American Research Universities since World War II* (New York: Oxford University Press, 1993).

13. Walt W. Rostow, *The Stages of Economic Growth: A Non-Communist Manifesto* (Cambridge: Cambridge University Press, 1960), 73–92.

14. Walter Heller, *New Dimensions of Political Economy* (Cambridge: Harvard University Press, 1966), 12.

15. John Courtney Murray, S.J., *We Hold These Truths: Catholic Reflections on the American Proposition* (New York: Sheed & Ward, 1960), 16.

16. There are many variants of consensus history. Daniel Boorstin has most consistently relied on the idea of persistent American traits in the first two volumes of his trilogy (on the colonial experience and the national experience of Americans); see John Higham, "The Cult of the 'American Consensus': Homogenizing Our History," *Commentary* 27 (February 1959): 95–99 and John F. Diggins, "Consciousness and Teleology in American History: The Burden of Daniel J. Boorstin," *American Historical Review* 76 (February 1971): 99–118; Boorstin displayed significantly more ambivalence in his last volume, *The Americans: The Democratic Experience* (New York: Random House, 1973), which covers the period under discussion in this book.

INDEX

DeForest, Robert, 33
Delano, Frederic, 88
Deming, W. Edwards, 177
Devine, Edward T., 44
Dewey, John, 98; on education, 77, 142; on inquiry, 20-23, 201n.45; on Japan, 163; on pluralism, 116, 125–26, 138, 142; on the service intellectual, 42; on social science, 39, 50, 56. *See also* Pluralism
Dichter, Ernest, 103, 106
Dickinson, John, 87
Dickinson, Roy, 83
Dodge, Joseph, 176
Dore, Ronald, 170
Douglass, Frederick, 145, 152
Dower, John, 180
Drake, St. Clair, 110–11
Draper, William, 174
Du Bois, W. E. B., 143, 187
Du Pont de Nemours, E. I., & Co., 4, 9, 12, 85, 95
Durant, William T., 95
Durkheim, Emile, 33, 38

Eccles, Marriner S., 220n.48
Edison, Thomas, 9
Edwards, Corwin, 171, 177
EEOC, 152, 154
Einstein, Albert, 20–21
Eisenhower, Dwight D., 134, 233n.69
Eliot, Charles, 8, 15
Ely, Richard, 27–29, 32, 34
Emerson, Ralph Waldo, 119; and *Self Reliance*, 167

Federal Council of Churches, 131, 134
Fessenden, Reginald, 10
Filene, Edward, 82, 88, 103
Fisher, Irving, 81
Fitzgerald, Deborah, 13
Flinn, Alfred D., 10, 59
Ford, Henry, 75, 81, 94–95
Fordism, 177
Forest, Lee de, 10, 21
Forrestal, James, 174
Foster, William Trufant, 83

Frankel, Lee, 34
Frazier, Franklin E., 110
Friedan, Betty, 106, 154
Fukuzawa, Yukichi, 162
Furet, François, xvi

Galbraith, John K., 91
Gallup, George, 63–64
Galton, Francis, 48-50, 52
Gardner, Burleigh, 103–4, 108, 111
Gates, Frederick, 31
Gaustad, Edwin, 134
GE, 4, 9, 11, 15, 81–82, 88
Geertz, Clifford, xv
General Electric Corporation. *See* GE
General Motors Corporation. *See* GM
Gerschenkron, Alexander, 197n.11
Gilman, Daniel Coit, 14
Glass, Carter G., 184
GM, 88, 150; and consumption ladder, 94–97; Research Corporation, 4; and "Treaty of Detroit," 90. *See also* Labor movement; Marketing; Sloan, Alfred P.
Goddard, Henry H., 51, 54
Goebbels, Joseph, 65
Goldmark, Josephine, 146
Gordon, Linda, 147–48
Gotō, Shimpei, 41, 163
Gould, Steven J., 55
Great Depression, 85–86, 133, 162, 184; social scientists' response to, 43–44; and welfare legislation, 148. *See also* New Deal
Green, William, 86

Hale, George Ellery, 16, 52
Hall, G. Stanley, 58
Hall, John, 179
Hansen, Alvin, 89
Harlan, John Marshall, 143, 154, 187
Harper, William Rainey, 31
Harriman, W. Averell, 88
Hart, Hastings H., 35–36
Hartz, Louis, xiv, 165
Haskell, Thomas, 197n.14
Hayes, Rutherford, 143
Heller, Walter, 187